Praise for Work Naked

"Three centuries after we first started going to centralized workplaces, someone has finally broken through the weight of tradition and given us a guide to the next generation of work and workplaces. *Work Naked* is your escape route from the world of cubicles, time clocks, and all the other vestiges of the Stone Age of the workplace."
—Gil Gordon, telecommuting consultant and author, *Turn It Off: How to Unplug From the Anytime-Anywhere Office Without Disconnecting Your Career*

"This book is truly essential reading for anyone who is seriously committed to creating work options that really meet the needs of professional men and women."
—Laraine T. Zappert, clinical professor of psychiatry and behavioral sciences at Stanford University School of Medicine and author, *Getting It Right: How Working Mothers Successfully Take Up the Challenge of Life, Family, and Career*

"Cynthia Froggatt strips away the seven (actually eight) veils that have prevented us from seeing what the future office will be like. What matters isn't territory any more. We can all change our lives far more profoundly if we dare seize control of our time. This new dimension of freedom will reshape not just our workstyles but the entire landscape of the new century."
—Francis Duffy, founder DEGW and author, *The New Office*

"In this enormously useful book, Cynthia Froggatt explains with frankness why managers need to improve the way they treat employees. She writes the simple truth that the best managers treat employees with dignity and trust, giving them the necessary freedom to balance overwhelming life and work issues."
—Marilyn Zelinsky, senior editor, *Home Office Magazine*, and author, *New Workplaces for New Workstyles* and *Practical Home Office Solutions*

"With compelling stories about high performing free agents and corporate employees, *Work Naked* breaks confining stereotypes about how and where people work. An experienced workplace consultant, Froggatt provides practical guidelines to corporate managers about how to support value-adding work anytime, anyplace."
—Michael Joroff, senior lecturer, Massachusetts Institute of Technology, and workplace consultant, author, lecturer, and researcher

"A highly useful exploration of the joys and gains of broadening the range of styles, places, and time structures which we define as 'real work.' It is filled with useful data tied to stimulating case examples."
—Fritz Steele, consultant on organizational and environmental change, Portsmouth Consulting Group

"In a highly readable style combining survey data with case study examples and simple checklists and diagnostic tools, Froggatt presents a strong case for working virtually. For managers thinking about how to introduce and implement some form of virtual work, *Work Naked* is likely to become an indispensable primer."
—Franklin Becker, professor and chair, Department of Design & Environmental Analysis, and director of the International Workplace Studies Program, Cornell University

"This enlightening book will sharpen a corporate leader's ability to become a master on the 'infrastructure gameboard.' Froggatt's practical case studies enable readers to understand how, by providing the correctly balanced infrastructure of physical and virtual workspaces for employees, they can promote the development of the kind of revolutionary innovations which fuel today's fiercely competitive businesscape and lead to increased shareholder value."
—Nancy Johnson Sanquist, director of strategic real estate initiatives for Peregrine Systems and fellow of the International Facility Management Association (IFMA)

"*Work Naked* is not simply an alternative to the traditional workplace or workstyle. It is evidence of the liberation of workers from hierarchical burdens, frustration due to mistrust, overwork, stress, fixed work hours, idea-hoarding, and unpleasant work environments. Froggatt shows us a map to the knowledge society that will replace industrial society in the 21st century."
—Mototsugu Nakatsu, president, Nakatsu CRE/FM Consulting Inc, Tokyo, Japan

"If you want your company to be more successful and the place people want to work, you must read this book. Cynthia Froggatt, an experienced workplace consultant, tells us how to enable people to do their best work."
—Peter Lawrence, chairman and founder, Corporate Design Foundation

Work
Naked

Work *Naked*

Eight Essential Principles
for Peak Performance
in the Virtual Workplace

CYNTHIA C. FROGGATT

JOSSEY-BASS
A Wiley Company
San Francisco

Published by

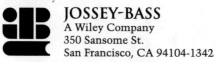

JOSSEY-BASS
A Wiley Company
350 Sansome St.
San Francisco, CA 94104-1342

www.josseybass.com

Jossey-Bass books and products are available through most bookstores. To contact Jossey-Bass directly, call (888) 378-2537, fax to (800) 605-2665, or visit our website at www.josseybass.com.

Substantial discounts on bulk quantities of Jossey-Bass books are available to corporations, professional associations, and other organizations. For details and discount information, contact the special sales department at Jossey-Bass.

We at Jossey-Bass strive to use the most environmentally sensitive paper stocks available to us. Our publications are printed on acid-free recycled stock whenever possible, and our paper always meets or exceeds minimum GPO and EPA requirements.

Interior design by Claudia Smelser.
Illustrations by Kevin Pope.

Library of Congress Cataloging-in-Publication Data

Froggatt, Cynthia C.
    Work naked: eight essential principles for peak performance in the virtual workplace/by Cynthia C. Froggatt—1st ed.
        p. cm—(The Jossey-Bass business & management series)
    Includes bibliographical references and index.
    ISBN 0-7879-5390-3 (alk. paper)
    1. Employee empowerment. 2. Industrial relations. 3. Labor productivity.
4. Knowledge management. I. Title. II. Series.
    HD50.5 .F76 2001
    658.3—dc21   2001000184

FIRST EDITION
HB Printing   10 9 8 7 6 5 4 3 2 1

The Jossey-Bass
Business & Management Series

To *Henry,*
Madeline,
Nicholas, and
Samuel

who took the initiative in December 1998
to ask that this book be dedicated
"to the Guss kids who love being naked!"

Contents

Preface

The central message of this book is simple: there is untapped potential within the workforce that can be revealed by trusting and supporting employees to work where and when they are most effective. To take full advantage of that freedom to choose where and when to work, employees need to be unencumbered by outdated corporate rules and trappings. This book is for leaders and managers who are interested in shedding those traditional mindsets and unleashing hidden potential—within individuals and organizations.

Some may ask, "How much more productive can we possibly get?" My answer is *significantly more productive:* in ways you've never considered before. How are we constraining individual and organizational potential today?

- By wasting time commuting at peak traffic hours and making workers conform to a 9-to-5 routine.
- By thinking we can manage workers most effectively by seeing them in the office every day.
- By embroiling employees in bureaucracy and office politics.
- By spending too much time in lengthy corporate meetings.
- By housing employees in one-size-fits-all cubicles that are not tailored to their unique workstyles.

- By providing environments where it is difficult to concentrate and easy to be interrupted.

- By devoting resources to lavish corner offices and executive dining rooms rather than equipping employees for optimal mobility and connectivity.

- By not using our technology tools to their best advantage.

- By not trusting employees to make smart choices about the best place and time for their work.

In my consulting work, I have come across many situations where supporting remote and mobile workstyles would solve significant business problems. Unfortunately, there is often resistance to initiating these new ways of working. The hurdles to overcome are rarely technological; they are usually cultural. This kind of change involves challenging long-held beliefs about the best ways to perform work and manage people. The process of letting go, of giving up control, is not an easy one. It is essential, though, for survival in the knowledge economy.

Some companies have attempted to implement mobile or remote work strategies without dealing with the unstated cultural issues. Frustration, low productivity, and even failure are the typical results. Whether you are trying to implement new ways of working from the start, refining an existing program, or reviving a failed effort, this book will be useful. It is structured to help you identify and overcome the pitfalls that are difficult to foresee.

This book is not just about telework or telecommuting or virtual office or integrated workplace strategies or alternative officing. It is not just about letting people work from home. It is about giving individuals control over their workstyles. It is about liberating workers from the layers and layers of outdated corporate norms and mind-sets that assume management knows the best routine for workers to follow. It is about management's letting go so as to uncover higher levels of performance and satisfaction.

This book is not full of policies and contracts and agreements and forms. It is full of success stories and profound statistics that answer the question, "Why should mobility and flexibility not only be tolerated but wholeheartedly embraced?" There are many lessons to be learned from the full range of workers who already have the freedom and autonomy to shape their own workstyles. Some of the stories come from corporate employees who are considered telecommuters, virtual office workers, or road warriors. Other lessons come from leaders and members of large and small virtual organizations. There is also a lot to be learned from free agents, contract workers, and leaders of home-based businesses. You'll hear from the people who led their company's effort to go virtual or allow employees to work from home and learn how they overcame resistance. The examples include companies that encourage mobility so that people can support customers better as well as companies that allow flexibility so that employees can handle work and personal responsibilities. The payoffs are both tangible, such as reduced costs of turnover, and intangible, such as happier employees and families.

This book has been written for business leaders and managers who are looking for ways to achieve one or more of the following goals:

- Pursue new growth opportunities.
- Attract, retain, and develop high-quality talent.
- Maximize creativity and innovation.
- Respond faster to market changes and customer demands.
- Expand into new locations (nationally or internationally).
- Reduce costs and overhead.
- Encourage more open communication and knowledge sharing.
- Improve employee morale and commitment.

- Increase customer satisfaction.
- Optimize quality of products and services.
- Facilitate more powerful use of technology.

It is for leaders who want their companies to be considered an "employer of choice" and an admirable competitor. It is for managers who have struggled to implement new ways of working in their departments or companies with limited success. It is for corporate decision makers who can't understand why people aren't using the existing alternative work arrangements. It is for leaders of virtual teams or organizations who think they could be working better. It is for graduating college students and younger members of the workforce who want a different workstyle and lifestyle from that of their baby-boomer parents. It is for all workers who would like to change the way they work—for whatever reason.

The Introduction and the first chapter explain the origin of "Work Naked" and the value of remote and mobile work strategies. The next eight chapters focus on the layers of obstacles to be shed in the course of implementing each of the eight Work Naked principles:

- Initiative
- Trust
- Joy
- Individuality
- Equality
- Dialogue
- Connectivity
- Workplace Options

The last chapter restates and summarizes the eight principles, then presents a list of resources for further study and action. Start by reading the introductory material to get a good understanding of why these eight principles are important. Then read the chapters in any order you desire. Try reading the ones that intrigue you the most or scare you the least. Go with your gut feeling—it will probably lead you to the chapters that are most important for your company. At some point, it would be useful to have read all the chapters. The principles work together as a system rather than forming a sequence. All eight principles need to be revealed before you can realize the full benefits of freeing your employees to work where and when they are most effective.

New York, New York   *Cynthia C. Froggatt*
March 2001

Acknowledgments

Writing this book has been a joyful experience that would not have been possible without the involvement of the people recognized here. I extend my enthusiastic and heartfelt thanks to . . .

- Kathe Sweeney, editor at Jossey-Bass, who helped me move from book proposal to final manuscript with her smart feedback and excitement for the subject. And to her colleagues at Jossey-Bass and Wiley, Todd Berman, Katie Crouch, Cheryl Greenway, Ellen Silberman, Tess Woods, Mary Garrett, Hilary Powers, Paula Goldstein, Mary Zook, Sheri Gilbert, Karen Warner, Adrienne Biggs, Bernadette Walter, P. J. Campbell, Matthew Garcia, and the sales force, who helped make this into a readable, marketable book.

- Rita Rosenkranz, literary agent, who saw a valuable book hidden inside a very rough proposal, worked with me to make it into a good proposal, and found the ideal publisher for the book.

- Marilyn Zelinsky Syarto, who was instrumental in helping me translate the idea into a book proposal.

- Scott Shuster, who first suggested the idea of writing a book after corresponding with me about the *Wall Street Journal* article.

- Sue Shellenbarger, whose decision to print excerpts of my letter in her *Wall Street Journal* column brought "work naked" to light.

- My parents, Elizabeth and John Froggatt, who have lovingly demonstrated that there are rules to follow and rules to break.

- Timothy J. Keating, a talented photographer and teacher, who makes me laugh and truly understands the meaning of "work naked." Thank you, love.

- Annie Lionni, who believed in me and in this book even when I didn't. And to Annie, her husband Peter Guss, and their children, Madeline, Samuel, Nicholas, and Henry for providing a nurturing, creative environment in New York and Montauk where this book came to life.

- Terry Keenan, who has been my friend and special adviser on statistics and research methods ever since we roomed together in Sage Hall at Cornell University. And to Terry and her husband, Carlos Indacochea, who over the years have warmly hosted me in their homes in Ithaca, New York; Lima, Peru; and Falls Church, Virginia.

- Jean-Pierre Bonin and Michael Santaferrara, who are the best neighbors a single girl who works from home could ever ask for.

- Trudy McCrea, who kept the principles positive and has been a good business adviser and friend since we studied together at Penn State.

- Mary Overly Davis, whose positive outlook and keen sense of organization I strive to emulate every day.

- Jerry Davis, who convinced me to work at HOK Consulting—where I had the opportunity to advise AT&T on their telework program.

- Marty Pospeshil, who was a great client at AT&T.

- Helen Rauch Hughes, a trusted adviser, who has been a great cheerleader for the book.

- Nancy Sanquist and Jim Johnson, who make conferences fun and have provided important encouragement along the way.

- Barbara Brennan, Lisa Cole, Kent Holliday, John Steigerwald, Michele Snyder, Deborah Tillman Stone, and Mark Stone, who have never tired of discussing this book with me, have passed on good ideas about profiles and trends, and have been great friends.

- Members of *Fast Company*'s Company of Friends, Cornell's Facilities Planning and Management E-Mail Network, and the President's Council of Cornell Women, who supported my efforts, offered advice, and provided important links to case studies.

- Nancy Winston and Stephen Balsam, who kept my attention focused on the book.

- Walt Spevak, Kathy Clinton, and Zadie Dressler, who were instrumental in developing and distributing the Autodesk questionnaire—and the 515 Autodesk employees who completed the survey.

- Nancy and Bart Mills, Jane Brody, Bill Weiss, Chris Newell, Diane Hall, Will Pape, Shelly Porges, and Karen Walker, who graciously agreed to be interviewed in the early days of the book proposal.

- Adam Rothberg, who offered early, positive feedback on the book proposal.

- The four anonymous reviewers for their helpful comments and suggested changes.

- All those who were interviewed and are quoted in the book. Thank you for your time and attention and your quick response during the permissions process.

- Everyone who was interviewed and not quoted or was helpful in finding interviewees. Even though you are not named in the text of the book, your contribution shaped my thoughts and the contents: Marty Anderson, Lorraine Aronowitz, Laurie Bachmann, Christine Barber, Ayelet Baron, Jim Bedrick, Michael Bell, Bill Betts, Livit Callentine, Ron Carleton, Ellie Kosson Carleton, Cherryl Carlson, Phidias Cinaglia, Rachel Cohen, David Coleman, Cathrine Cotman, Pavel Curtis, Stacy Davis, Hank DeCillia, Ralph Denton, Michael Donovan, Rebecca Drill, Evelyn Eskin, Anne Ferguson, Neon Fet, Charles Fishman, Lis Fleming, Dan Froggatt, John Girard, David Goldsmith, Jennifer Goodwyn, Mara Green, Susan Halik, Les Hamashima, Alan Hedge, Michael Joroff, Tracy Ellen Kamens, Lisa Kanarek, Karen Kemerling, Sara Kim, Peter Kimmel, Dean Koyanagi, Gloria Lang, Jason Largever, Susan Lau, Pippo Lionni, Lucie Macelova, Paula Malakoff, John Maloney, Gail Martin, Mike McGlynn, Eileen McMorrow, David Molpus, Tina Nader, Rob Obenreder, Noe Palacios, Mary Speed Perri, John Perri, Nancy Persily, Elaine Petrowski, Lilly Platt, Steve PonTell, Susan Ramsey, Wendy Richman, Ken Robertson, Laurie Robinson, Kathryn Romley, Karol Rose, Heath Row, David Rupert, Marie Schulz, David Short, Paula Sidle, William Sims, Jared Skolnick, Burke Stinson, Tabatha Sturm, Catherine Peters Svoboda, John Tackett, Peter Valentine, Deb VanderMolen, Lynda Ward, Thaisa Way, Kathy Wolf, and Renee Zuckerbrot.

- The endorsers who carefully read the manuscript and provided enthusiastic quotes. Your support means a lot to me.

- Finally, I am eternally grateful to Emiliano Castro, whose life and untimely death in 1994 helped me realize the true value of having the freedom to work naked.

Thank you. Thank you all.

Work
Naked

The Origin of "Work Naked"

To fully appreciate the value of the concepts presented in this book, you should understand the history behind the phrase "Work Naked."

On August 20, 1997, Sue Shellenbarger's "Work & Family" column in the *Wall Street Journal* took on the advertisers: "Madison Avenue May Need to Alter Image of '90s Telecommuter." The television ads depicting telecommuters as bunny-slipper–clad, pajama-wearing women who decline to shower on work-at-home days are inaccurate and unfair, according to Shellenbarger. Yes, as she pointed out, the majority of telecommuters are male and as her small sample indicated, most shower and dress for work (even though no one may see them). Her column ended with the following note, "Full disclosure: I'm a telecommuter. I shower every morning. I only work in my jammies before dawn."[1] While I am a regular reader of Sue's column and typically agree with her point of view, this time I disagreed. In fact, her column touched a nerve; I couldn't stop thinking about it all day. I felt the issue was a much larger one and quickly dashed off the following response:

Dear Sue:

I thoroughly enjoyed your column "Madison Avenue May Need to Alter Image of '90s Telecommuter" in today's WSJ. I would broaden the notion to say that U.S. organizations, and possibly society in general, must alter their image of the WORKER and WORK (I'm not sure we can blame Madison Avenue for this one). Only then, will remote work or telework truly flourish. Let me explain.

Regardless of what you are wearing (pajamas, bunny slippers, or nothing), are you working if no one can SEE you?

We've never fully made the transition from manual labor to knowledge-based working. It is very easy to see when a farmer or factory-worker, construction worker, etc. is working because they are expending physical energy on visible tasks. In fact, it could be argued that the harder one is working, the more they sweat (so there is a visible hierarchy of effort). This doesn't translate well to white-collar work. So we have created a complex system of visual cues to signify that (or give the impression that) someone is working. "The office" is a stage where people "perform their work" for others to SEE. Wearing a business suit, sitting behind a desk, talking on the phone, being in a meeting, operating a computer, bumping into the CEO in the parking lot at 9:00 pm, among other activities send a message that the performer is hard at work. Technology has bumped it up a notch— sending e-mail, faxes, voicemails (especially at odd hours)—gives the impression of productivity. And, frankly, all these activities might result in very high quality work. But then again, the movement toward casual dress codes is proof that our brains operate just as well when we are wearing jeans as when we are wearing a Tahari suit.

Pajama-wearing need not convey a negative image.

Scott Adams, as a ten-year-old, identified his desire for a life-long career that would allow him to work in his pajamas. As he explained in a recent presentation at the alt.office conference, *cartoonist* seemed to be the only achievable option, having rejected the three other choices he felt permitted pajama-work: pope, Supreme Court justice, and Hugh Hefner's job as head of the Playboy empire. We all know that after a detour into corporate life, he successfully realized his goal. Imagine a world devoid of Dilbert had that ten-year-old set the lofty goal "to wear a suit and tie and sit in a big office" for his working years.

I understand your concern about the TV ads depicting an inaccurate image of telecommuters, but on the positive side, the ads do at least challenge the myth that you can only be productive in the "appropriate business trappings." In all the ads I've seen, the teleworker is shown to be a high performer. We struggle so much with measuring performance quality that we often resort to relying on the LOOK of work — "face-time" — rather than the results.

Knowledge work is not something to be observed with the eye.

I confess, I was one of those annoying students in college and grad school who didn't appear to colleagues to be working very hard. I sat in the back of the class, rarely went to professors' office hours, did not put in much face-time at the library, read the assignments the night before the exam, sat down to type a major paper 6 hours before it was due, and was rewarded with A's and B's. Fortunately, I was graded on the basis of quality of result, not some outdated notion of how hard work should LOOK. The fact is, I was "working" when people thought I was playing or at least not paying attention. I could hear as much from the back of the class as those in the front. I was THINKING about the term paper when I was walking, cycling, showering, etc. But others couldn't SEE me thinking. They could see someone typing, reading, talking to a professor after class, or sitting in the library, but these activities don't necessarily translate into a quality product reflecting innovative thinking.

We grapple with similar issues in the workplace. *Remote work of any kind challenges the practice of visual monitoring of work, raising anxieties in managers and nonmanagers alike.* It is comforting to think that getting up, showering, dressing, going to the office, and chatting with colleagues over coffee will be interpreted as "strong commitment to work" before you've even turned the computer on. *Abandoning the old "face-time" measurement is difficult, but successful teleworkers are leading the way.*

I think the advertisers should be congratulated for getting people talking about telecommuting and depicting it as a productive, flexible, fun way to work.

As for my personal telecommuting style, I dispense with the pajamas and bunny slippers, opting instead to work naked for the first hour of phone calling and e-mailing, then shower. Do I miss nylon stockings and the rush-rush of the office? NO. Do I feel better about my performance? Absolutely! Do I think having the freedom to work where, when, and how you choose might work for others? Definitely. Change is always an opportunity for learning.

Sue Shellenbarger printed the italicized excerpts of my fax in a September 24, 1997, letters column titled "These Telecommuters Just Barely Maintain Their Office Decorum."[2] Two other readers, it seems, wrote to Sue with stories about nakedness in the home office. The column was very funny and somewhat out of character for the conservative *Wall Street Journal.*

On the morning it appeared in the *Wall Street Journal,* I sent an e-mail message to everyone in my on-line address book. The subject line read "work naked," and the message encouraged recipients to look for my "insightful and REVEALING commentary on telework" in that day's paper. The response was overwhelming!

The majority of respondents applauded my honesty, agreed that being liberated from the trappings (and politics) of most corporate environments improved creativity, and then shared their own quirky workstyle secrets. There were some negative or less-than-enthusiastic replies, though. The ones that angered me the most involved some sort of "sex sells" remark. "No, honesty sells," I replied defensively. Then I explained more about my living and working situation and why I started this practice of working without clothing early in the morning. I live alone and work from a small Manhattan apartment. I'm very productive late in the evening (from 10 P.M. to midnight), need seven to eight hours of sleep a night, and take pride in being available to clients when they need me. (These three factors are sometimes at odds with each other.) One client was a morning person who arrived at the office before 7 A.M. and liked to start his day by coordinating with me on the progress of a particular project. Knowing that "morning people" think of late-risers as lazy, I would sleep with a notebook and the cordless phone next to my bed so I could take his call on the first ring! It didn't matter that I wasn't dressed in business clothes and sitting at a desk in an office. After finishing the call, I'd check e-mail and return some voicemail before going for a bike ride in Central Park or taking a shower. And, on many days, I just wouldn't get around to dressing for a while. So, it wasn't a conscious choice to work naked, but it turned out to be very convenient.

Of course, I enjoyed reading the comments from the people who said, "Yes! I do the same thing." They sent rather long, detailed descriptions of their work habits and the benefits they derive from working in a nontraditional way. One e-mail message painted a very clear picture of a bathing-suit–clad worker lounging on a boat with laptop, cell phone, and pet dog within easy reach. Another colleague explained that she takes difficult client calls from home, dressed only in her underwear, so she's more relaxed for a tough negotiation. It was reassuring to me that most of these people who shared their "secret work contexts" were not entrepreneurs running their own businesses from home, they were corporate workers who were trusted and equipped to make smart choices about the most effective work environment for the situation.

Some wrote to tell me why I shouldn't work naked ("you could catch a cold") or why they wouldn't work naked ("the neighbors might talk"). To the latter I replied, "Hey, you know, whatever works for you! Saying everyone should work naked would be as crazy as, for instance, saying everyone should work in a business suit (oooops, we've done that, haven't we?)." I was most disheartened by e-mail from people who saw the value of having more freedom to make workstyle choices, but felt trapped in companies where it wouldn't be allowed. Worse yet, they were timid about finding a different employer that would allow that kind of freedom.

At first, I wanted to dismiss the less-than-enthusiastic responses—just delete them from my inbox. Then I realized that there was a lot to be learned by pursuing the personal feelings and corporate policies behind the negative reactions. If the positive experiences of individuals and corporations that I had collected could be transferred to the more negative or resistant types, some significant obstacles to performance could be removed. The obstacles are usually mind-sets and traditional corporate norms that we need to challenge ourselves to reexamine. Consider the following questions to start the rethinking process. Strip away the suit and tie, corner office, and reserved parking space; would your employees be more productive or less productive? Now, let go of face-time with the boss, office gossip, constant interruptions from coworkers, and 9-to-5 working hours; would your employees be more creative or less creative? If your employees had the freedom to choose where and when to work, would they be more effective or less effective? Envision your organization naked (in the figurative sense), unencumbered by all the traditional corporate rules and trappings; would your employees feel liberated or exposed? Please join me in pursuing the "work naked" metaphor to learn how your organization can get the most out of remote and mobile work strategies.

Why Work Naked?

The Eight Work Naked Principles

Should your employees have the freedom to work naked?
Yes, now is the time to free employees to work where and when
they are most effective.

Let's face facts. Corporate America has been downsized, rightsized,
flattened, outsourced, reengineered, empowered, delayered, di-
vested, tri-vested, co-located, decentralized, merged, and purged.
Still, companies continue to search for ways to sustain their competitive advantage. It's time to reinvent your company by shedding
the layers of outdated rules and trappings of the old economy that
keep workers tethered to their desks. If you want your customers
to embrace new ways of doing business (e-commerce), you've
got to encourage your employees to experience new ways of working (remote and mobile work strategies). When people have the

mobility and connectivity to work from remote locations (whether that is a client site, hotel, or home), individual and organizational performance improves.

Who are these remote and mobile workers? How do companies benefit from letting people work this way? The following four stories describe how people are working differently, why they have chosen a nontraditional workstyle, and the advantages for the worker and the company.

Marshall Simmonds had no interest in relocating from the resort town of Bend, Oregon, when New York City–based About.com recruited him to be its search engine specialist. Simmonds, a twenty-eight-year-old fan of running, hiking, and snowshoeing, spends about a third of his time in About.com's offices in New York City or at conferences and the remaining two-thirds working from his home. He's responsible for helping more than eight hundred globally dispersed About.com subject guides optimize their Web pages to appear well on search engines and he does much of that work by e-mail. When he is in Oregon, his workday often starts early in the morning and extends until late at night, but in between he takes breaks for recreational activities with friends. What are the advantages? Simmonds gets to do exciting work and lead a healthy lifestyle; About.com gets access to his talent without relocating him to New York City.

Cynthia Doyle, vice president of human resources at Chase Manhattan Bank, works five days a week from her home on the coast of Massachusetts between Boston and Cape Cod. Once a month she travels to New York City to meet with colleagues she used to work with every day. In 1995, when Doyle's husband was transferred to Boston, she and her manager agreed that she would work in New York two days and from home for three days a week until she finished her project. At the end of that assignment, Chase didn't want to lose a valuable employee who had been with the company for ten years, so Doyle became one of its first full-time telecommuters. Cynthia enjoys this workstyle because she avoids wasting time commuting and gets to take her twin sons to pre-school in the morning and be around the house when her thirteen-year-old daughter comes home from school in the afternoon.

Donald Richards, area vice president for e-commerce sales at NCR, oversees the work of eighteen employees, but only goes to his Atlanta office a hundred hours a year. He is part of NCR's Virtual Workplace Program, which equipped the sales force to work from anywhere and saved the company millions of dollars in real estate costs. Richards coordinates with his team members by phone each Monday from his home office and then travels to customer meetings for most of the week. He loves having the flexibility to structure his schedule to work when he is most productive, stay out of traffic jams, and clear time to spend with his children when they are home from college.

Jane Brody, personal health columnist for the *New York Times*, commuted to the office five days a week for the first twenty years of her tenure with the paper. When she started writing books on health and nutrition in addition to her weekly column, Jane and her editor agreed that it was a better use of her time to do some of her work from home. She avoided an hour-long subway commute each way and could work at her "peak times" rather than during the traditional office hours. Working at home in sweatpants and a T-shirt was, as Jane says, "much more conducive to deep creative thinking than dressing up and going to the office where there were constant interruptions." Her twin sons were in college by then so she had no problem getting the privacy she needed in her home office. Eventually, she developed a routine of working from home four days a week and commuting to the office one day a week to attend a staff meeting, pick up mail, and interact with colleagues. She has maintained that same schedule even though she took early retirement in 1998 and now works as a contract writer for the *Times*. Because both Brody and her management were comfortable with this remote work arrangement, the employment transition has been a smooth one.

In each case, there were different reasons for adopting remote or mobile workstyles. In all four cases, rethinking where and when work is performed has enabled individuals to integrate their work and their personal life. This level of autonomy has benefits for a single, twenty-something dot-commer, an early retiree with grown children, and all workers in between. Today's remote and mobile workers do not fit into a clearly defined mold. The Telework America Survey 2000 (conducted by the International Telework Association and Council) gives us a sense of the characteristics of teleworkers. Defined as full-time workers who perform some work from home or a telework center during normal business hours, the representative sample of teleworkers was 65 percent male, 35 percent female with an average age of forty. Two-thirds lived with a spouse or significant other; one-third lived with children under six years of age. A full 82 percent reported that they had some college education and the median annual income was roughly $50,000. The average one-way commute to work for the teleworkers was 19.7 miles and they primarily lived in urban areas as opposed to small towns or rural areas. The majority of the teleworkers (54 percent) were full-time employees, 13 percent were contract workers, 24 percent were self-employed, and 9 percent operated home businesses. In total, half the teleworkers worked for companies employing more than 1,500 people.[1] Remote and mobile work strategies are being used by a wide range of workers in both small and large companies.

What Is at Stake for Business Leaders?

Companies today face many challenges to their profitability and competitive advantage. Most business leaders agree that employees are the most valuable corporate asset—and many are finding that it is getting more and more difficult to recruit these valuable assets. In McKinsey's study, "The War for Talent," 75 percent of corporate officers surveyed said they could not attract and retain the high-quality talent they needed to pursue all growth opportunities.[2] When Hewitt Associates asked a hundred leaders of traditional companies about obstacles to evolving into e-businesses and competing against dot-coms and start-ups, 41 percent cited difficulty hiring talented employees.[3] According to a June 2000 survey of the Society of Human Resource Managers (SHRM), the average voluntary turnover rate for all member companies was 17 percent and for companies with more than five thousand employees it was 25 percent.[4] That means that along with trying to hire additional employees to handle growth, large companies need to hire replacements for one out of every four employees annually. The struggle to fill job openings and the high cost of replacing employees will continue to have a significant effect on the performance of traditional and nontraditional businesses. Staffing issues will dominate the corporate agenda in the knowledge economy.

At the same time that the demand for talented employees has been outstripping the supply, workers have been asking for more freedom and autonomy to adapt their work schedules to accommodate nonwork concerns. In a 1999 Work Trends survey, researchers found that 95 percent of working adults were concerned about spending more time with their immediate family and 87 percent were concerned about getting enough sleep. Furthermore, 88 percent complained about feeling stress from work demands and 92 percent said they were concerned about having flexibility in their schedules to take care of family needs. Almost half of all workers (46 percent), would like to have the opportunity to work from home some of the time.[5]

How many employees are given the freedom to work outside the corporate office during normal business hours? Nilles reports in the Telework America Survey 2000 that there were 16.5 million full-time workers in the United States who performed work from home or a telework center during normal business hours on a regular basis. While the number of teleworkers increased steadily throughout the 1990s, this study found that another 19.4 million U.S. workers would like to perform some of their work from home and had jobs that would permit this kind of arrangement. Only one-third of the non-teleworkers felt their employers would be supportive of remote or mobile work strategies.[6] These findings suggest that organizations still have a lot to gain by encouraging new ways of working.

The profiles of Marshall Simmonds, Cynthia Doyle, Don Richards, and Jane Brody illustrated how remote and mobile workstyles can solve a company's need for access to high-quality talent and support an employee's need for better work-life integration. Research reinforces this conclusion—both sides win if these new ways of working are implemented effectively. In Pratt's 1999 study of teleworkers, she found that most were more satisfied with their jobs and more productive as a result of being able to do some work from home; they also took fewer sick days and were more likely to stay with their current employers.[7] The other surveys and case studies described throughout this book demonstrate that workers who have more autonomy over their place and time of work report the following types of benefits:

- More strategic use of work time. (For some this means more time with clients.)
- Less time spent commuting or fewer hours driving during high traffic times.
- Fewer disruptions and enhanced ability to concentrate.
- Flexibility to work at peak performance times.
- Improved self-management skills.
- Enhanced creativity from fewer constraints and more variety in activities.
- Lower stress levels and higher morale.
- Decreased absenteeism. (There's no work time lost when a child is sick.)

- Improved collaboration skills. (This means better use of colleagues' time.)
- Focus on results rather than office politics.

The impact of improved individual performance on overall corporate performance can be significant. These effects include improved customer service, increased sales and revenue, reduced turnover and its associated costs, access to a larger talent pool, and in some cases, reduced overhead and real estate costs. These new work strategies can also help a company achieve its goal of being a good neighbor by reducing traffic, energy usage, and pollution.

What's Standing in the Way of Remote and Mobile Work Strategies?

It sounds like a simple proposition: free your employees to work where and when they are most effective. Some people think that technological, legal, security, and tax concerns are the biggest hurdles to overcome when implementing new work strategies; I think they are wrong. It is important to have the right policies, procedures, and equipment in place, but corporate norms and unwritten rules thwart many change efforts even when the infrastructure for remote and mobile work has been established. For instance, when workers are given the freedom to decide where to work, some employees choose to spend a great deal or all of their work hours at the traditional workplace. That should be totally acceptable when that work routine is genuinely well-suited for them. Problems arise, though, if workers continue to "go to the office" just because they believe raises and promotions will be affected by how much time the boss sees them spending there or other reasons that do not relate to performance.

Each company has its own definition of an "effective worker." Some cultures reward the early riser who gets in before the boss while others look favorably on workers who stay late and go to the office on weekends. Unfortunately, these beliefs are based on appearances rather than measurable results and are just a few of the outdated mind-sets that hinder the acceptance of new workstyles. Review the *Work Naked Checklist: Obstacles to Peak Performance in the Virtual Workplace* (pages 15–16) to explore which stated and unstated norms in your company may be constraining performance.

After completing the checklist, total the number of "True" responses you checked on the twenty-five-item list and compare that total to this key:

- *True = 0, False = 25.* If none of these statements seems remotely familiar, your organization already provides an excellent context for remote and mobile work. Congratulations!

- *True = less than 5.* If you found less than five of the statements to be true, there are relatively few obstacles to virtual work in your organization. In fact, your company probably already has a number of people working in nontraditional ways and has made a sincere effort to be an "employer of choice."

- *True = 5 to 15.* For those who checked between five and fifteen items, there is some work to be done. Your company has probably taken some steps to move away from a traditional, formal corporate culture. Perhaps you've already made the transition to casual business attire, started flattening the hierarchy, and implemented a results-based performance measurement system. Still, your company is probably not yet willing to give employees the freedom to make decisions about where and when to work and these attitudes will need to change.

- *True = more than 15.* If more than fifteen of these statements describe the values and norms (whether stated or unstated)

Work Naked Checklist: Obstacles to Peak Performance in the Virtual Workplace

True or False: Which statements reflect the beliefs or norms (both stated and unstated) of your company? (Check all that are true.)

❑   **1.** If work isn't your top priority, you will not be a top performer.

❑   **2.** The more time you spend at the office, the better your chances for promotion.

❑   **3.** If you look busy, even frantic, you must be very productive.

❑   **4.** Wearing a beeper and carrying a cell phone are sure signs that you have a *really* important job and you are a *really* important person.

❑   **5.** Face-to-face interaction is the only real way to build and maintain relationships.

❑   **6.** The quality of communication is directly proportional to the amount of time a team spends together.

❑   **7.** Frenetic travel schedules, lack of sleep, ulcers, and constant complaints about workload are traits of dedicated, valuable workers.

❑   **8.** Dressing in business attire gives you a serious attitude about work and shows your sense of discipline.

❑   **9.** Calling the office on your cell phone from the beach when you are on vacation means you are a devoted, indispensable worker.

❑   **10.** Calling the office on your cell phone from your backyard garden when you are working from home for the day means you must be goofing off.

❑   **11.** Getting to work early in the morning shows you are a very hard worker.

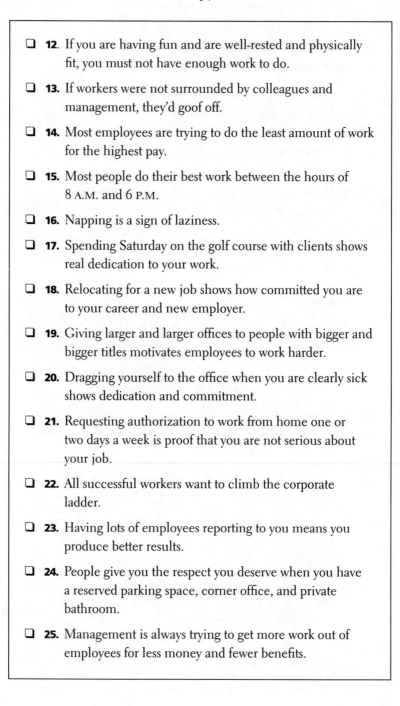

❏ **12**. If you are having fun and are well-rested and physically fit, you must not have enough work to do.

❏ **13**. If workers were not surrounded by colleagues and management, they'd goof off.

❏ **14.** Most employees are trying to do the least amount of work for the highest pay.

❏ **15.** Most people do their best work between the hours of 8 A.M. and 6 P.M.

❏ **16.** Napping is a sign of laziness.

❏ **17.** Spending Saturday on the golf course with clients shows real dedication to your work.

❏ **18.** Relocating for a new job shows how committed you are to your career and new employer.

❏ **19.** Giving larger and larger offices to people with bigger and bigger titles motivates employees to work harder.

❏ **20.** Dragging yourself to the office when you are clearly sick shows dedication and commitment.

❏ **21.** Requesting authorization to work from home one or two days a week is proof that you are not serious about your job.

❏ **22.** All successful workers want to climb the corporate ladder.

❏ **23.** Having lots of employees reporting to you means you produce better results.

❏ **24.** People give you the respect you deserve when you have a reserved parking space, corner office, and private bathroom.

❏ **25.** Management is always trying to get more work out of employees for less money and fewer benefits.

in your organization, there are fairly substantial obstacles to successfully freeing employees to work where and when they are most effective.

The good news if you're in the over-fifteen group is that your company has the most to gain from overcoming these challenges. Yours is probably a traditional, hierarchical organization where image is emphasized. The overriding philosophy is that the best way to run a profitable business is to have all employees report to a corporate workplace for a prescribed number of hours a day and that longer work hours lead to higher productivity. It is most likely that your industry or geographic region has not yet been affected by talent shortages, changing customer relationships, and other trends that have provoked great upheaval in other organizations. You have a chance to stay ahead of these changes by implementing these new work strategies before your business is affected by the trends that make them imperative.

Redefining Corporate Culture in the Virtual Workplace

Remote and mobile workers can't thrive in a traditional corporate culture where outdated norms and trappings keep them tethered to their desks. They need an environment where old mind-sets have been peeled away and the following eight principles are embraced:

- *Initiative:* To encourage this we need to shed the layers of fear of change, the status quo, and "But we've always done it this way; why change now?"
- *Trust:* To achieve this we need to shed the layers of outdated performance measures and satisfactorily answer the questions,

"How will I know they are working?" and "How will I know I am being productive?"

- *Joy:* To promote this we need to shed the layers of workaholism and images of work as stressful drudgery; we need to reinforce the philosophy that relaxed, healthy workers who enjoy their work and personal life provide better client service and are more productive.

- *Individuality:* To emphasize this we need to shed the layers of fixed work hours, conformity, and one-routine-fits-all thinking, and then help employees understand their individual contribution and discover which workstyles suit them best.

- *Equality:* To build this we need to shed the layers of corporate trappings and status symbols that reinforce old hierarchies, encourage territoriality, and waste corporate resources.

- *Dialogue:* To encourage this we need to shed the layers of office politics and idea hoarding in favor of open communication and knowledge sharing.

- *Connectivity:* To generate this we need to shed reliance on face-to-face interaction and educate employees about how to use current technology to support relationships appropriately and develop a new sense of community.

- *Workplace Options:* To develop these we need to shed the layers of long commutes, cubicle-land, and the limiting home office versus corporate office choice; then think creatively about how to reuse and redesign existing places.

The good news is that all eight of these principles exist underneath the layers of outdated mind-sets and trappings; they don't have to be built anew, they simply have to be uncovered and nurtured. Companies that have made the effort to shed these excess layers have discovered that there are more benefits than they originally expected. For example, when traditional organizations decide to implement new work strategies, managers often devote a lot of energy to developing a checklist that will help workers determine whether they'd be good candidates for remote and mobile work. The list usually begins with, "Are you a self-starter? Yes or No." Well, how many people would honestly answer, "No, I need a kick in the pants from someone else to get down to work"? The tool may not be that helpful to employees, but these checklists can be very valuable when managers realize that the qualities of a good remote or mobile worker are the qualities of a good worker. (Can any manager really afford to hire someone who's going to need close monitoring to ensure they are producing?) Similarly, the individuals and organizations profiled in the following chapters demonstrate that the principles of companies that leverage remote and mobile work are the principles of successful, agile businesses. These companies are better positioned to sustain their competitive advantage in the future than their more traditional counterparts.

Initiative

Shedding the Layers of

Complacency,

Fear of Change, and

Resistance to New Ways of Working

Everyone dies (*eventually*).
Everything changes (*continually*).

My intention is not to scare you. It is to put forth two certain, in-evitable truths: death and change. (I take exception to the old adage about death and taxes: some people find ways to avoid paying taxes.) Fear often grows out of uncertainty. Therefore, if change is seen as a certainty, it is less likely to provoke fear. If we can learn to wel-come change, indeed *instigate* change, then we can take full ad-vantage of the opportunities it presents. Without constant change, a system is likely to die—especially in business.

The Importance of Initiative

Would you describe your current workplace as "toxic" or one where "employees are valued"? That was the question posed by an informal survey on *Fast Company*'s Web site in early 1999.[1] The response was disappointing: just over 50 percent of the respondents characterized their work environment as negative. The comments readers posted on the Web site described work scenarios where they were stressed out, overwhelmed with responsibilities, and generally not treated as intelligent, capable adults. I posted this question, "Why do people stay trapped in these situations?" Some said they would have to relocate to change employers and didn't want to move. Some thought the level of "toxicity" was the same in their entire industry and they were not ready to change careers yet. Some felt they were too old to change jobs, and others just didn't think there were other options. In most cases, they had done very little to change bad situations.

Do you think 50 percent of your employees would describe themselves as being trapped in a toxic environment? Consider the effect this could be having on morale, productivity, and profitability. Unhappy workers who do not try to change negative situations are unlikely to be top performers. The perception that there is no way to improve circumstances or that it is just too much trouble to attempt a change is the greatest obstacle to taking initiative. Unwillingness to even consider new approaches to how work is performed presents the most significant hurdle to successful implementation of remote and mobile work strategies. The first step for you as a corporate leader is to explore your own feelings about initiating change. Then you can set about encouraging employees to overcome their acceptance of the status quo and fear of the unknown.

Becoming More Comfortable with Change

To take full advantage of virtual work strategies, you and your employees need to be very comfortable with change in general. First, eliminate the phrase *change management* from your vocabulary because it is a misnomer. Change can't be managed; it can be initiated or encouraged but not controlled or managed. People should strive to be change leaders, change catalysts, or change agents — not change managers. If more workers considered themselves change agents, organizations would be agile enough to keep up with the constantly evolving business environment.

"Too much change" is a common complaint among employees; I hear people say, "I can't wait until these changes end and things get back to normal." Change is viewed as a burden and a temporary disruption, not as a reality or an opportunity. There is no magic tool that will let you or your employees control the pace of change or turn it on and turn it off as desired. It is relatively impossible to control events or other people, but we can control our attitudes and reactions to what happens around us. This is where real progress can be made.

We each make a choice to see events in a positive way or a negative way. One characteristic that distinguishes leaders of change from victims of change is their perspective. Even the worst failure can also be viewed as a learning experience. It's a good idea to explore your own point of view before considering what it takes to lead change. Since technological advances have been responsible for many of the recent changes in everyone's work and personal lives, I'd ask you to think about all the major developments in technology that have occurred in your lifetime. List them out. Highlight the ones that have affected you directly. I've developed what I call my "personal technology timeline" to put these changes into perspective.

Personal Technology Timeline

I was born in 1960. In 1976, as a high school junior, I learned how to use a slide rule in my chemistry class. The following year, we were permitted to use calculators in physics (but only after the school board debated whether use of calculators might favor wealthier students since they were so expensive at the time). As a college freshman, I used a keypunch, stack of cards, and large mainframe computer to run simple statistical programs. By the end of college, I had access to a computer terminal that could "dial in" to a mainframe, but I still had to walk across campus to pick up a printout. In 2001, I depend on a laptop, laser printer, and the Internet to do my work.

Could I do without any of these technological improvements? Probably, but I wouldn't want to go back to the days of slide rules and typewriters. I welcome every new technology tool even though it usually disrupts the way I have been working. Sure it takes awhile to learn about new hardware or upgrade software, but it usually pays off pretty quickly.

Once you've listed out the major developments that have affected you personally, think about whether you would give up any of those tools. During conference presentations, after I share my lifetime history of technology, I ask audience members to tell me their most and least favorite technological advances. Laptop computers and voicemail are typically the most favored tools. Beepers and e-mail are often cited as the most hated advances. Usually, cellular phones make it onto both the loved and hated lists. Further discussion makes it clear that being accessible all the time, getting a hundred e-mail messages a day, and facing the expectation of quick responses can result in high stress and feeling overwhelmed. Laptops, voicemail, and sometimes cell phones, on the other hand, generally give people a sense of freedom and control. In all cases, it is not technology that causes joy or stress, it is how people use it (or misuse or overuse it). We may not be able to stop technological developments, but we can certainly influence the way technology is used.

Let's take a closer look at cellular phones. Most people love them when they need to call for car repair from the side of a deserted highway, for instance. I hate them when a colleague spends half of a business lunch talking on a cell phone instead of talking to me. I hate them when they ring during a presentation. But I don't curse the cellular phone industry. I realize that cell phones are controlled by their owners and it is the way some people use this tool that annoys me. I'm sure you can think of more examples like this one. Consider these stories when you diagram your Personal Technology Timeline. By the end of that exercise, you should achieve the following goals:

- Recognize the many changes that have occurred and have been beneficial during your lifetime.
- Realize that you have adapted successfully to many changes in the past.
- Understand that rethinking the way tools are used can reduce the stress associated with loss of control.

Initiating Change

Throughout the change process, leaders must be mindful of a basic fact of corporate life: people follow the leader very well. That is, employees follow management's actions, not their words. Change agents must set an example for workers to follow.

When Deb McKenzie was asked to lead the implementation of the Flexible Work Environment initiative at LEXIS-NEXIS in 1995, she had to admit that she didn't really believe it would be good for their salespeople to work from home when they weren't calling on customers. She realized that she had to change her own attitude before leading this initiative. McKenzie's first step was to educate herself about new ways of working by gathering data online, talking to consultants and leaders of similar programs, and benchmarking. She discovered that LEXIS-NEXIS had about twenty salespeople who had been working from home for several years. After talking with them about strengths and weaknesses of this arrangement and learning that they had all made the top sales group, she moved herself home to experience the benefits first-hand. This gave her the credibility and enthusiasm she needed to convince others to rethink the way they worked.

Like McKenzie at LEXIS-NEXIS, you should learn from others' experiences before embarking on your own program to change the way people work. Start by looking for good examples within your own company. In most organizations, the sales and marketing people have had long experience with remote management. Search for department managers who have outsourced work to freelancers or contractors that do not work on site. Find out if special arrangements have been made for certain employees to work from home following the birth of a child, while recovering from a health problem, when a spouse has been relocated, or while dealing with some other personal situation. When you find relevant cases, talk to the workers and the managers about the advantages and disadvantages of these arrangements. Ask for advice on how to resolve problems that may have occurred. Then learn about other organizations' experiences. Seek out successful virtual office and telework examples that have been in existence for at least two years (you'll find many in this book). Make sure these programs have been studied closely before you try to replicate them.

After addressing your own concerns about new ways of working, learn how employees feel about what is working well and what needs to be improved in your department or company. This feedback will help determine whether it would be valuable for your company to give workers the freedom to work where and when they are most effective. Ask employees these two simple questions: *What enables your performance?* and *What limits your performance?* Your job is to listen to the input and encourage everyone to participate by giving them several ways to respond to the questions. Focus groups (small discussions of ten to fifteen employees) are useful because they give participants a chance to hear and build on others' answers to the questions. Written submissions, through e-mail for example, may be a more comfortable way for others to express their point of view. There should also be at least one way to respond anonymously such as by posting comments on a Web site or using a suggestion box.

These two questions are focused not on gathering solutions but on defining the problems that exist. The discussions you have with employees should highlight positive and negative features of the current work environment. If some things are working well, you may not want to change them. Certainly, the biggest opportunities for improvement involve the factors that are limiting high performance. Employees frequently say their productivity would improve if they could, for example, spend more time with clients, concentrate for an extended period of time, have better access to information, waste less time in meetings, or get decisions made faster.

At this early stage in the change process, it's useful to discourage discussions of how to solve the problems. Ask probing questions about the underlying problems and current situation. *How much time are you spending with clients now? What kinds of things disrupt your ability to concentrate? What information would you like to see? How much time are you spending in meetings and why do you think it is wasteful? How long do certain decisions take? What would be more acceptable? What is the decision-making process?* After all employees have had the chance to be part of the discussion, a summary of the key findings should be distributed to everyone who participated. This helps ensure their involvement in the future.

Overcoming Resistance to New Ways of Working

In most organizations, some of the issues raised by employees about what limits or enables their performance could be addressed by letting people have more control over where and when they work. For example, if someone expressed a desire to work where there are fewer distractions and interruptions, this could certainly be achieved by allowing them to choose an appropriate setting where they can concentrate. Having more freedom to shape their own workstyle would have two important outcomes for workers: their quality of work life would improve, and they would have to accept responsibility for making choices that enhance performance rather than inhibit it. This level of autonomy and accountability may be unfamiliar to employees and may, in some cases, be unwelcome. As a change leader, you need to be aware that implementation of mobile and remote work strategies may raise anxiety levels and resistance by both managers and employees.

Let's look at some of the typical concerns that arise when a traditional organization considers implementing telecommuting, virtual office strategies, or other telework programs that give employees the ability to work remotely. The following are just some of the responses you might hear when you ask managers, *What are your biggest fears about letting workers decide where and when to work?*

- They would never come into the office—I would never see them again.
- They wouldn't do any work.
- I'd get fired because my subordinates were not doing their work.
- Teamwork would suffer—employees wouldn't talk to each other.
- Corporate culture would get lost; there wouldn't be any shared values.
- I wouldn't be able to give employees direction or monitor their progress.
- I'd miss socializing with my employees.
- I wouldn't know how to evaluate their performance and give raises.

- Clients would think we were unprofessional.
- I'd have to spend a lot of money to equip my employees to work from somewhere else.
- We'll start getting a lot of workers' compensation claims because of accidents in the home office.
- I couldn't get my job done if I didn't have instant access to my employees all day long.

Managers are not the only people who have misgivings about remote and mobile work strategies. For employees, the freedom to make workstyle decisions comes with a lot of responsibility. These are some typical responses you may hear when you ask workers, *What are your biggest fears about being given the freedom to choose where and when you work?*

- I wouldn't get the tools I need to do my work.
- I'd feel lonely and isolated.
- They would take my office away; I worked hard to get a corner office.
- I won't get promoted if I'm not seen at the office.
- I need an administrative assistant to do all my typing; I couldn't get my job done without one.
- There are too many distractions for me at home; I wouldn't get anything done.
- How would I know what to work on each day?
- I'm not sure I could motivate myself to work without my boss and coworkers around.
- My boss would expect me to work all the time.
- I must be with my teammates to get my job done.
- My boss wouldn't be able to see how hard I work.
- My spouse would make me mow the lawn and do other chores during work hours.

- My neighbors would think I had lost my job if they saw me around during the day.

These are all valid concerns. Many of these issues, though, are based on misperceptions or premature assumptions about what the new workstyle program might entail. In total, between the two questions, I've listed twenty-five typical responses. The five underlying themes represented by these twenty-five answers can be summarized as follows:

1. All work would be done remotely and in isolation.
2. The primary work site would be at home.
3. Freedom would be used to shirk responsibilities or cheat the company.
4. It would be impossible to direct and evaluate performance.
5. The company could not or would not provide the training, tools, or support services necessary to get the job done.

The first two themes are based on the erroneous assumption that employees who can choose their workplace would work from home five days a week and never again meet with colleagues. This can be overcome quickly and easily through education. For the most part, virtual office workers, teleworkers, and others who are free to choose where they work spend some portion of the week at the office and some time working from a client site, home, or another remote location. As responsible workers, they make sure they have enough interaction with managers, colleagues, clients, and others to ensure their success. Even in the limited cases where employees work from home on a full-time basis, they typically meet face-to-face with their manager or colleagues once a month. Understanding how other companies have structured mobility programs typically dispels resistance caused by these misperceptions.

There are examples of successful programs later in this chapter and throughout the rest of the book. These are the kinds of case studies that should be communicated to employees during the implementation process.

If managers are concerned that some workers may abuse this freedom by goofing off or making false workers' compensation claims (the third of the underlying themes), these potential "system cheaters" are probably engaging in this same type of behavior now while they are *in* the office. This is a problem that exists today and should be confronted before giving those employees the opportunity to decide where and when they work. A small minority of "system cheaters" should not put an end to an initiative that could benefit the majority of workers.

The fourth underlying theme takes shape in questions like "How will I evaluate performance if I don't see my staff every day?" and "How will I know what to work on?" To overcome these fears, we have to first examine how productivity is currently monitored. If results-based performance measures have not yet been implemented in your organization, it must make that transition before a remote work program can succeed. Many organizations have dealt with this issue in the process of changing the way people work. This issue is addressed in greater detail in the chapter on Principle #2: Trust.

Finally, managers and employees must be confident that the new workstyle initiative will be supported with appropriate resources in order to dispel the fears behind the fifth underlying theme. Worries that employees will not be properly equipped or supported to work in a mobile way are usually rooted in similar past experiences. For instance, perhaps when new software was installed, people did not get proper training. Or when new hardware was distributed, it was not backed up with qualified help desk personnel. When employees have been disappointed more than once, they are very wary of leaping into a new program. These fears can be dispelled by developing a program that provides the training, equipment, technical support, and management commitment that employees need to be comfortable and productive. Involving employees in shaping the solutions helps build the required confidence.

A Simple Exercise to Educate and Involve Employees

In general, much of the resistance to new ways of working is based on a false sense that it comes down to an either-or choice between all work being performed on site and all work being performed at a remote site. Barry Johnson has developed a tool called *polarity management* to help people see all sides of an issue and overcome this type of problem.[2] Start with a blank chart that depicts two choices, in this case "on-site work" versus "remote work."

POSITIVES		POSITIVES
On-Site Work		Remote Work
NEGATIVES		NEGATIVES

Blank Polarity Management Chart

Encourage staff to help fill out the chart in focus groups or other small meetings. One by one, complete each quadrant—starting with the positive features of doing all work on site (which is probably an accurate description of the existing situation). Here's what the chart might look like when discussions are finished.

POSITIVES	POSITIVES
+ Team cohesiveness	+ Proximity to clients
+ Management oversight and direction	+ More time for personal priorities and family
+ Informal communication	+ More productive time
+ Access to shared equipment and support services	+ Ability to work at peak times
On-Site Work	**Remote Work**
− Disruptions	− Isolation
− Long commute	− Less contact with colleagues
− Not enough interaction with clients	− "Out of sight, out of mind"
− Work-life balance problems	− Loss of shared values
NEGATIVES	NEGATIVES

Completed Polarity Management Chart

It is important to complete and discuss the chart with diverse groups of employees. You'll notice that some participants will be more passionate about one or two of the quadrants and less involved in the discussions about the others. This is one of the important features of Johnson's polarity management exercise. As he explains, the "crusaders" (we'll call them change agents) come to these meetings with a good understanding of the negative aspects of the existing situation and the positive aspects of the proposed alternative. They are blind, though, to the other half of the chart: the positive features of the current system and the possible negative outcomes of the new strategy. Likewise, the people Johnson calls "tradition-bearers" (we'll stick with that name) can see only the positives of the current situation and the pitfalls of the proposed change. This exercise helps both groups, the change agents and the tradition-bearers, see all sides of the problem.

The completed charts also form the basis for the problem solution stage. Participants should now understand that this is not an either-or choice. The goal is to work on a solution that combines the best of both on-site work and remote work—to focus on the top half of the chart. Leaders need to get both change agents and tradition-bearers to participate in shaping the solution: one group provides enthusiasm and new ideas; the other brings caution and a keen eye for possible glitches.

Consider Whether Participation Should Be Voluntary or Mandatory

One of the most critical decisions to make when developing and implementing a remote and mobile work strategy is whether participation should be required or optional. Mandatory programs are driven by business process improvement; they are typically designed to improve customer service and capitalize on real estate reductions. Voluntary programs are usually a response to employees' needs for more flexibility where the goals are improving work-life balance and becoming an "employer of choice." To understand the differences between these approaches, it is helpful to look closely at two very successful programs: NCR's Virtual Workplace Program and Nortel Networks' telework strategy. The two programs have several important features in common:

- Management had clear goal in mind.
- Management made a compelling case for change.

- Resources were committed to the program.
- Measures of success were closely monitored.
- Initial goals were achieved.

There is a significant difference, though. Participation in NCR's program was mandatory, whereas at Nortel people volunteered to change the way they worked. This one factor had a tremendous impact on the types of people involved, expenditures for equipment, and the overall structure of the programs.

NCR's Virtual Workplace Program

At NCR, three thousand employees of the U.S. marketing division participate in the Virtual Workplace Program started in 1995 (that represents approximately 25 percent of the U.S. workforce, 10 percent of the worldwide staff). Dan Accrocco, one of NCR's project leaders, conservatively estimates that the company has realized a 15–20 percent improvement in productivity and net annualized real estate cost savings of $12–$13 million as a result of implementing this mobile and remote work strategy. The participants in the Virtual Workplace Program are responsible for sales and professional services and work primarily from a client site, field office, or from home. These workers don't have their own dedicated office space at NCR anymore. When they go into an NCR field office (once a week on average), a workstation is available, but desk-sharing ratios range between 7:1 and 10:1.

Why was this change initiated? When the virtual office program was started, NCR had fallen on tough times financially. NCR had to do something drastic that would allow it to cut costs by eliminating expensive and often underutilized office space while finding a way for employees to spend more time with their customers selling more product. The goal was a lofty one: to return NCR to profitability. Instead of just closing offices and sending people home as some other companies had done, NCR engaged in a comprehensive, integrated approach to improving sales productivity. Its managers and staff took time to reengineer work processes and tools, rethink which work was performed by administrative support and which tasks the salesperson should focus on, and talk candidly with people about what was needed to improve their performance.

Because this was a business-driven initiative, employees were not *asked* to volunteer for the Virtual Workplace Program, they were *required* to participate. According to Accrocco, "If the choice had been offered, many would not have volunteered to equip their home, give up their own office, and work in a different way." This was a dramatic new way of working for NCR's employees with obvious business advantages. When fully equipped to work from home, associates could avoid driving all the way back to the field office. Relationships with customers improved because more time was spent in face-to-face conversations with them. The new portable hardware and software allowed NCR staff to download information the client needed while they were right there at the client site. It took some workers three or more months to make the adjustment and begin realizing that this new way of working also offered them schedule flexibility that enabled quality time with family, stress relief, freedom from commuting, and enhanced productivity.

The transition was eased, in part, because the deployed program was one that had been designed with the input of the sales and professional services staff. It was equally important that the initiative was well-supported in terms of senior management commitment and funding:

- Representatives of Real Estate, Information Technology, Human Resources, and the U.S. Marketing Business Process Team were dedicated to the implementation effort—it was their full-time job, not just an extra duty.

- All participants were fully equipped to work mobile and from home (at an average cost per person of $5,000) — they received a laptop, extra phone lines, an allowance for furniture, a printer, and a special telephone.

- Training was provided for management and nonmanagement staff.

- Special help desks and additional technology support were made available.

- The program was closely monitored and refined from its initial roll-out onward.

Did NCR achieve its goals? Yes, 1996 was a turnaround year for the company and NCR continues to meet its performance objectives. Was there resistance, fear, and apprehension? Yes, and it was dispelled through training and education programs as well as an appeals process that employees could use to opt out of the Virtual Workplace Program. Keep in mind, certain employees were required to participate, but they were not forced to work from home. They could choose between at least three workplace options: client site, home, and shared workstation in a field office (a dedicated, on-site workstation is the only option that has been removed). This gives them the freedom to create a work environment that suits them best.

Based on the success of the strategy, participation in the Virtual Workplace Program became a condition of employment for people in sales and professional services jobs. There have been several reorganizations since the initial implementation and each new leader has supported the program. There is clear commitment from management that as staff additions happen, investments are made in new technology, not bricks and mortar. Accrocco has stayed involved in evaluating the program and benchmarking with peer organizations that have implemented similar programs. He has also been expanding the program to NCR's European and Asian offices.

Ongoing success, he believes, depends on continued cooperation among the business units, Real Estate, Human Resources, and Information Technology, and on "commitment to providing excellent twenty-four-hour support; people should not feel abandoned out there."

Typically, if a company like NCR mandates employee participation, it also mandates management support and provides the appropriate structure, training, equipment, network, maintenance, and funding. Unfortunately, voluntary programs often suffer from voluntary, unreliable commitment from management (resulting in resistance, lack of funding, and inconsistent implementation). An important advantage of a mandatory program is that people are pushed to try out the new way of working. Most participants gradually realize the benefits and adapt to the change. Through her research on telework, Sumita Raghuram of Fordham University has found that "organizations (and people) that use voluntary teleworking are more likely to give it up after a short trial period (too much hassle) than those who commit themselves to go through it completely (we're all in it together). Feelings of isolation (perception of career damage) are more likely under voluntary programs."[3] Raghuram points out that many voluntary programs do not adequately address needs of newcomers. Most mandatory programs have "buddy systems" or other arrangements for linking new hires with coworkers who are already working remotely (and therefore not as available for on-site informal interaction and learning).

Many companies have voluntary telecommuting programs that have been just one component of a flexible work arrangement policy (including compressed workweeks, flextime, job sharing, and other options) and have been "on the books" for several years. Although available to the staff, remote work options are rarely promoted or supported in a significant way. Often, only the most assertive or needy employees request authorization to work from home one or more days per week. Nortel Networks has taken a very different approach to its voluntary telework program.

Nortel Networks Telework Solutions

Back in the early 1990s, remote and mobile work trends were being tracked closely by Nortel's marketing staff because of the potential new markets for telecommunications products and services. When their research showed the significant advantages of these new ways of working, Nortel's executives wondered if these strategies would be good for their own employees. When they considered the positive impact telework could have on employee satisfaction and productivity, management committed to actively promoting it internally.

Tony Smith, then telework program leader at Nortel, says mandatory participation in the work-from-home initiative "would not have fit with the goals of the program" and was not considered by the strategy development team when they started in mid-1994. Voluntary participation offers better buy-in, he believes, and estimates that only about 20 percent of Nortel's 60,000 employees could work from home given the jobs they currently perform. There are now more than 7,500 employees working from home three or more days per week, which represents approximately 12 percent of the world-wide staff.

By all measures, Nortel is meeting its original goal of improving employee satisfaction and productivity. Surveys of teleworkers, their managers, and non-teleworking coworkers have found the following:

- Ninety percent of teleworkers reported increased satisfaction with their work.
- Eighty-eight percent reported increased productivity.
- Individual productivity improved by 10–22 percent on average (according to self-report and manager evaluation).
- Ability to work as a team was better in 40 percent of the cases.

In the Nortel annual employee survey conducted by Gallup, teleworkers scored 11 percent higher on employee satisfaction measures than the overall Nortel population did. In addition, teleworkers scored 16 percent higher on intention to stay with the company, 19 percent higher on feeling valued, and 10 percent higher on willingness to recommend Nortel as an employer. The people who have chosen to participate in the telework program come from a range of Nortel's business units and represent a wide variety of managerial and nonmanagerial job functions—sales, marketing, information systems, product management, corporate staff, customer service, human resources, finance, technology.

Smith credits the following factors for the success of the program:

- A fifty-three-person, cross-functional team is dedicated to the promotion and administration of the telecommuting and remote access programs.

- Promotional programs include regularly scheduled educational programs and full-scale "home office" demonstrations (with ISDN lines) that employees can test out on their way to the cafeteria at ten of their major sites.

- Leaders are good role models—several vice presidents are active teleworkers.

- Senior executives have challenged their business units to meet particular targets for involvement in telework.

Incidentally, the policy does not dictate the equipment that must be provided for the employee's home or that the employee must give up space at the office. Nortel is committed to providing teleworkers the tools they need to perform their jobs and has published guidelines for equipment and furniture that should be provided. The goal is to fully equip the employee in one place, not at both home and the office. Half of the teleworkers have given up their workspace on site and work from home three or more days per week. These workers are eligible to receive furniture for their home offices.

Smith sees clear advantages to empowering the managers to develop solutions that work best for their employees and type of work. He advises that the shift to telework is a "culture change—people won't throw their career on something that is not tested, proven, and integrated slowly." Through training, Nortel managers receive guidance on how to manage differently and employees are reassured that out of sight does not mean out of mind when it comes to raises and promotions. On an ongoing basis, a network of managers who work from home or manage teleworkers have volunteered to talk with other managers who are considering this new way of working.

Clearly, both NCR and Nortel Networks and their employees have realized benefits of remote and mobile work strategies. Which approach is better for your company, mandatory or voluntary participation? Let's explore the advantages and disadvantages of the two approaches.

For strategies with mandatory involvement, these are the advantages:

- Achieve business goals (for example, improve client relationships, increase sales).
- Reduce real estate costs (usually).
- Maintain consistent approach due to the necessary full implementation and administration system.
- Focus on effective performance rather than attendance.
- Include everyone—no one feels left out.
- Provide better equipment and furniture.
- Improve emergency preparedness.
- Reduce middle management resistance.

The disadvantages of mandatory programs are as follows:

- Evoke participant resistance (only a possibility, but could be strong if it occurs).

- Risk having some employees resign rather than participate.
- Incur high costs to equip and support workers.
- Invade home and family life.
- Risk negative effect on productivity.
- Place too much emphasis on cost savings.
- Require development or better use of results-based performance measurement techniques.
- Make some employees fear that they are one step closer to being outsourced.

Voluntary initiatives usually offer the following advantages:

- Increase morale and empowerment.
- Improve productivity.
- Improve chances for success—choice leads to better attitude.
- Produce automatic buy-in: no resistance from volunteers.
- Reduce implementation cost relative to mandatory program.
- Improve quality of life for employees.
- Improve attraction and retention of staff.
- Allow screening of volunteers.
- Permits use on a temporary basis by employees.

The disadvantages of voluntary programs are as follows:

- Risk nonparticipant resentment.
- Can't guarantee full operational benefits or real estate savings.
- Do not allow for control over participation rate.
- Risk lack of middle management endorsement.

- Permit confusion over equipment and furniture investments to be made by the company.

- Expose managers to need to confront volunteers who would not be good candidates (do not meet selection criteria).

One approach is not necessarily better than the other. Your decision about whether to mandate participation or let employees decide for themselves should be based on the corporate culture and business goals of your organization. Some companies use both approaches, but for different purposes. For example, the sales and marketing departments may be required to work remotely while other employees are given the choice to participate. Also, the reality is that every program has aspects that are required as opposed to optional. Consider this: if participation is mandated, what choices will employees be able to make about workplaces or work hours? If participation is optional, will volunteers be required to make their own business case for being allowed to work from home or another location? Will they be required to supply their own equipment or give up their dedicated workspace?

In either case, whether employees choose to participate or are required to do so, leaders need to make a compelling case for employees to go along. Employees need to understand *why* a change is happening. They should be reassured that this change is in response to external conditions or internal constraints, not a revelation that "we've been doing the wrong thing all these years." Don't be afraid to share information with the staff. If the change is expected to improve customer satisfaction, share the customer survey findings. If you hope to beat out competition for new talent, explain turnover rates and industry trends to the staff. If cost reduction is a goal, share financial data with employees. Be clear about the outcomes you are looking for in terms of the business goals and the level of participation. Once the program is under way, monitor its effects and refine it as needed.

Make It Easy for People to Take Initiative— Conduct a Pilot Test

People rarely volunteer for radical change when the risks are too high. This applies both to managers and to employees—who may worry that they are being used as guinea pigs and are not sure of the repercussions if they fail at this new way of working. One way of minimizing the risks is to conduct a pilot test of the proposed program. The Administrative Appeals Office (AAO) of the Immigration and Naturalization Service (INS) conducted a pilot program that serves as a good role model.

In April 1998, Terrance M. O'Reilly, director of the Administrative Appeals Office, and Mary Mulrean, deputy director of the Administrative Appeals Office, initiated a six-month Flexiplace pilot program. Flexiplace is a federal government initiative (led by the General Services Administration) designed to give employees more choices in terms of where they work. Of the forty-five staffers in the AAO, twenty volunteered to work from home four days a week. Anyone who wanted to participate was allowed to be in the pilot. All forty-five officers (attorneys and nonattorneys who adjudicate applications and petitions) took part in preimplementation and postimplementation surveys so that the full impact of this new way of working could be analyzed.

Because this office has a very sophisticated electronic tracking system for assignment and completion of cases, the performance improvement of nearly 40 percent more cases handled was indisputable. Mulrean reports that the surprising result was that the number of cases handled increased for both flexiplacers and those who worked in the office five days a week (although productivity did not increase at the same rate for the in-office group). There was a recognizable increase in the quality of the work as well. Fewer decisions were sent back for revisions or other problems. Both groups attributed some of the productivity gains to fewer interruptions and an improved ability to concentrate. E-mail correspondence took care of many conversations that used to take place in the office. Those who worked from home saved two to three hours a day in commuting time to downtown Washington, D.C., and had more flexibility to, for instance, drop a child off at day care later or go to a doctor's appointment at lunch time. Based on the documented success, the pilot was deemed a success and has become integrated into the way the group does its work.

Because this pilot was started by the leaders and involved all the employees in some way (whether they worked from home or not, everyone was surveyed and monitored), the chances for success were much higher. The measured outcomes were more likely to be followed closely by the entire group, not just those who were working from home. In this case, they could see that when some employees change the way they work, everyone's work changes. Typically, there are fewer distractions and an enhanced ability to concentrate for those who continue to work from the traditional workplace because there are fewer people there and fewer meetings.

Positive experiences with a new way of working encourage others to take initiative. Successful pilot testers are inclined to become enthusiastic change agents who talk to all their colleagues and friends about how much they like the program.

Chapter Summary: Initiative

Fear of change is the first obstacle to overcome when considering remote and mobile work strategies. This chapter has described techniques for uncovering the sense of initiative and passion for change that may be stifled by outdated and unstated attitudes. Leaders and employees have valuable roles to play in revealing initiative.

WHAT CHANGE AGENTS NEED TO TAKE RESPONSIBILITY FOR:

- Understand the value of remote and mobile work strategies.
- Listen to employees' ideas and concerns about changing the way they work.

- Find out if examples of remote work already exist in your company and explore the strengths and weaknesses of those arrangements.

- Learn about successful practices that have been tested and implemented by other organizations.

- Whether involvement is mandatory or optional, structure the program to optimize participation and success.

- Build a compelling case for change.

- Support new work initiatives with appropriate staffing and financial resources.

- Be a good role model.

- Keep employees involved in the change process.

WHAT ALL EMPLOYEES SHOULD ACCEPT RESPONSIBILITY FOR:

- Make leaders aware of your fears and concerns about new ways of working.

- Listen to management's reasons for changing where and when work is performed.

- Be willing to develop a more positive attitude about change.

- Participate in planning new work strategies.

- Volunteer to test out new options.

- Offer positive and negative feedback to improve the way work is performed.

Trust

Shedding the Layers of

Management Control,

Outdated Performance Measures,

and Mistrust

Picture this: a man lying in a hammock reading a magazine—a woman riding a bike in a park—a man sitting in a cubicle staring at a computer screen—a woman and a man dressed in business suits talking over lunch in a busy restaurant.
Which people are working?

Which ones are not only working, but actually being productive? The answer is frustrating: we don't know. We can't know. Based on the information given, which is only visual, these questions can't be answered.

The temptation might be to characterize the first two situations as leisure activities and the second two as work activities. But what if the man in the hammock was an editor reading a competitor's magazine? What if the one using a computer was shopping for a friend's birthday present on the Internet? Knowledge work is performed in our heads; we carry it around with us and think about it even when we're not in the office. Many of the technology tools and physical trappings that sometimes accompany work are misleading. But if we can't rely on our eyes, what can we use to evaluate whether someone is working and being effective?

The most common reaction from management to proposals for remote and mobile work strategies is, "How will I know they are working?" Many managers still believe that when employees come to the office every day and look like they are working, they must be productive. This is a dangerous misperception. It causes managers and employees alike to value face-time (being visible at the office) too highly; this keeps people tethered to the corporate office unnecessarily. Since knowledge work can't be monitored or evaluated visually, we need to embrace performance measurement systems that clearly communicate goals and intentions—systems that are built on the basis of trust.

What Is Trust and Why Is It Important?

Trust is about reliability and confidence in a relationship between two people. It is about believing that you can give up control and yet expect a certain outcome, of a particular quality, at a designated time. It isn't technology or distance that is pushing the limits of trust, it is the nature of knowledge work itself. Knowledge work is often invisible and frequently uncertain. It is so complex that teamwork is more powerful than solo work. Strong relationships are more important than ever before. According to Deborah L. Duarte and Nancy Tennant Snyder, authors of *Mastering Virtual Teams*, "Although trust is, to some extent, based on individual tolerances and experiences, people tend to trust others who perform competently, act with integrity, and display concern for the well-being of others."[1]

Management-by-looking-around doesn't work for knowledge workers (even if they are on site every day). Trust is essential in the knowledge economy and has significant payoffs for employers in terms of attraction, retention, and performance of employees. "Today's mobile workers look for an employer of choice—one they can be proud to work for and whose leadership they trust," said Bruce Pfau, director of organization measurement at Watson Wyatt and author of the *WorkUSA 2000* study. "This sense of trust in senior leadership is really a key factor in commitment—which is a key factor in creating economic value for the organization." The survey of 7,500 workers—at all levels in all industries—found that companies with employees who reported high levels of trust in senior management had a 108 percent three-year total return to shareholders. Companies with employees who expressed low trust levels had a 66 percent return. Respondents reported that seven factors drive their level of trust in senior leadership: promoting the most qualified employees, gaining support for the business direction, explaining reasons behind major decisions, motivating workforce to high performance, acting on employee suggestions, providing job security, and encouraging employee involvement.[2]

Employees want to be trusted, too. In a 1999 study of 2,300 workers representative of the U.S. workforce, Walker Information and Hudson Institute found that 41 percent of employees did not feel that their organization trusted its employees. Trust in employees was reported to be one of six key factors that affect employee commitment to an organization. The other factors were fairness at work, care and concern for employees, satisfaction with day-to-day activities, reputation of the organization, and work and job resources.[3]

Without trust, remote and mobile work strategies fail. Suspicion, doubt, and micromanagement can destroy working relationships.

There have been cases where managers of remote workers scheduled so many on-site team meetings to check on progress that employees ended up commuting to the office almost every day anyway. Or the manager calls the remote workers so frequently during the day that concentration is disrupted. Yes, a distributed workforce tests the limits of trust, but trust is a valuable component of any organization regardless of geographic dispersal. Imagine how much potential you are wasting by not trusting your employees to work where and when they are most effective.

Should Everyone Be Trusted to Decide Where and When to Work?

While I was writing a column on virtual office trends a few years ago, I reread Charles Handy's *Harvard Business Review* article about trust and virtual organizations on my way to a routine dental appointment.[4] As I was sitting in the dentist's chair having my teeth cleaned, I glanced up at a familiar small sign: "You don't have to floss all your teeth, only the ones you want to keep." It hit me that with a little alteration, the phrase could express my feelings about the importance of trust in the virtual workplace: "You don't have to trust all your employees to work where and when they are most effective, only the ones you want to keep."[5] If you want to attract, retain, and motivate talented individuals, you must treat them well—and that begins with trust.

I know of corporate committees that spend a lot of time debating selection criteria in search of the perfect checklist to assess who would be a good remote and mobile worker and who would not. I recommend that you not waste too much time on this type of exercise. Instead, start from the premise that most people can and should be trusted to make the right decisions about where and when to work. You may argue that it would be impossible for some employees to work from anywhere but the corporate office—

and you may be right. If a job involves greeting visitors in a reception area, the person filling that post would be wise to choose to be in the reception area during office hours when guests arrive. In addition, a significant number of workers would choose to continue to go to the office each day rather than perform their work from home or another location. In the 1999 Telework America National Telework Study, when workers were asked if they would like the opportunity to work from home on a regular basis (one or more days per week), 70 percent said they would not.[6] Just imagine how different their attitude would be, though, if they chose to go to the office every day rather than feel that it had been mandated by management.

Keep in mind, I am only suggesting that you trust your employees to make the right choices. You would not be trusting them to never come to the office again. Most remote and mobile workers, whether they work from home five days a week or five days a month, do meet with their managers and colleagues periodically. The main point is that you should not have to dictate to employees when and where to work—with a clear understanding of their mission and role in the organization, they should be trusted to make the right choices.

The most significant obstacle to this level of trust is that we have become accustomed to seeing workers every day (or at least to the illusion that we see them every day). Because we are comfortable with this arrangement, we believe it is the best and only way to guarantee high performance. Even though the technology is available to work from almost anywhere, doubts about employee behavior keep us from fully exploiting the value of new tools. In a technology-savvy, geographically dispersed virtual organization like The Promar Group, this is not the case. Promar staff have never had the luxury of working from the same office and this has been one of their biggest advantages. This business and technology advisory firm could not exist without strong bonds of trust. Its structure, which pushes the limits of trust further than any other type of organization, offers good lessons for more traditional organizations that need to enhance trust within their own companies.

The Promar Group: A Virtual Organization Built on Trust

When asked about the importance of trust among the staff of The Promar Group, Chairman and CEO Bill Weiss says, "I've trusted our future to their abilities. My reputation and that of Promar are our most valuable business assets. We have to hire people that I know will represent the firm well to clients and investors when I'm not there at the meeting." The full-time members of this twenty-year-old unconventional, virtual organization have all been executives in major corporations such as GE, Steelcase, and Saatchi & Saatchi, where going to the office was part of the work routine. All of them, that is, with the exception of Bill. A computer science major, he was one of those eager young college kids who are not only very familiar with new technologies but can foresee business opportunities possible with them. He had already started several multimillion-dollar businesses before he even graduated. Weiss also understood enough about corporate life (his father was a director at IBM) to know it wasn't for him.

Why is Promar set up as a virtual organization rather than a traditional company? Weiss estimates that "at least 25 percent to 50 percent of human resource capital in North American companies (depending on their size and 'construction') is spent on the politics of getting key decisions made instead of focusing on executing the right and speediest decisions for the marketplace." In the fast-moving technology business, taking an extra three or four weeks to come to a decision can mean the difference between gaining the first-to-market advantages and playing catch-up. He has no desire to join the corporate hierarchy even though he has business colleagues who thrive in that environment. Weiss enjoys designing the future of business with clients and implementing the new designs too much to get slowed down by conventional ways of doing things. His recruits to Promar have come to the same conclusion after working in corporations for many years.

Trust is what holds the staff together, not geographic proximity. The nucleus is dispersed around the globe—Tokyo, London, Washington, D.C., and San Francisco. Bill Weiss still lives in the town where he spent most of his young adult life, Cary, North Carolina. These locations are based somewhat on business strategy, being close to key markets, but also reflect where the individuals and their families want to live. It doesn't matter whether they rent office space in their home city or work right from their home. It is essential, though, that every staff member is accomplished at being mobile and knows how to stay connected to global clients and teammates even when working remotely.

Weiss and his executive associates want to help their clients develop, produce, and deliver new strategies that capitalize on technology and that will earn them substantially more money. They make decisions; they don't get bogged down in politics. Sharing business goals and avoiding internal strife are key to maintaining trust. Weiss describes the nucleus of well-seasoned executives (other consortium members are added as needed) as a "lean, highly efficient team." Every member of this team has been carefully selected in a somewhat informal way. Typically, Bill has a chance to see the person in action with a client (usually working on the same or a parallel project) and they develop a personal relationship outside of work. He learns about their personal goals and motivations and, if they are in line with Promar's mission, eventually he suggests that they consider joining him. A good, trusting relationship has already developed between Weiss and a new associate before someone is brought on board.

Trust within the team is supported through focused structure. Promar usually takes on only six clients per year, but the financial commitment is high (to have a positive result for the client). All the team members understand their role and contribution they are expected to make. If a team is missing deadlines or clients are missing their financial targets, it becomes apparent very quickly. There is no room for "time wasting"—results are monitored closely—so infighting and doubts about performance would be obvious to the team and would be addressed immediately. Furthermore, these people came to work with Promar because they wanted to get things accomplished and didn't want to get caught up in the old trappings of large corporations—there is a built-in incentive to avoid unproductive behavior. The fact that their clients—Toshiba, Ericsson, Lotus, and others—maintain long-term relationships with Promar is proof that the system works.

While clear timetables and project goals ensure that all team members are working toward the same results, Weiss uses face-to-face time together to build and reinforce bonds of trust and respect. At least five times a year, the members of Promar's nucleus meet for review and strategy sessions. These gatherings are sometimes linked to client meetings to minimize travel, but the locations vary so that the team gets a chance to experience the range of global markets firsthand. Outside of these gatherings, team members collaborate using cutting-edge technologies that give them access to each other and their sensitive data. With the exception of some remote locations, The Promar Group always has at least a conversational connection to clients, investors, and teammates.

What is the payoff of this virtual structure? Promar's team members benefit from the freedom their virtual organization gives them to earn more money than they would in a large corporation and the flexibility to integrate their personal and work lives. Clients benefit from access to Promar's team of experts, who are experienced at executing key business strategies, not just giving advice. When Promar associates encourage a client to take advantage of emerging technology, they have typically already used it within their own team—their clients can trust that it is a reliable tool. Similarly, Promar's virtual structure is a good role model for clients. According to Weiss, "In some cases, we have helped establish this as a rigor that was embedded in launches of new business for global corporations."

Achieving a High Level of Trust in an Existing Organization

We see from the Promar example that trust is built through relationships, reinforced through project structure, and reinvigorated by face-to-face interaction. Can traditional organizations realize some of the same benefits of this virtual organization? Yes, but we need to recognize that we often will not have the luxury of starting from scratch and building good, trusting relationships as Bill Weiss has done with The Promar Group. He only hires trustworthy associates. Many managers have inherited employees they did not hire—and possibly would not have hired. What should you do if you need to develop or enhance trust in an existing situation? Fear of the unknown, of giving up a current system that appears to be working, is the primary threat to trust-based relationships. We need information and communication to calm those fears and build the trust we need to take full advantage of remote and mobile work strategies. The remainder of this chapter is devoted to a discussion of action steps that would help a traditional organization overcome misgivings about trusting employees to work off site.

Expand Your Definition of Trust Beyond the Manager-Employee Relationship

Begin by recognizing that the issue of trust is much more complicated than just managers trusting the people reporting to them. Consider the many levels of trust that are critical to business success:

- *Trusting your clients (internal and external)* to communicate clearly, to give honest feedback, to cooperate with you, to treat you fairly, and to compensate you appropriately.
- *Trusting your leaders* to be good role models, to set and maintain direction, to know how to evaluate your performance, to reward results rather than face-time, to listen to constructive

dissent and new ideas, to hire other high-quality employees, to give you a good understanding of your roles and responsibilities, to give you challenging work, and to give you the tools and encouragement to excel.

- *Trusting employees you are managing* to do a good job, to make smart choices about where and when they should work, to ask for help when they need it, to accomplish the goals you set together, and to manage their time well.

- *Trusting your colleagues* to use your time effectively, to work with you to produce a quality product or service on time, to respect your point of view, to share ideas openly, to do their share of the work, to pitch in when you need help, and to be accessible.

- *Trusting yourself* to deliver high-quality results, to redefine effectiveness, to know when and where you are most productive, to manage employees appropriately (if you are a manager), to make wise decisions about whom to trust, to detect when changes are needed, and to adapt to a constantly evolving business environment.

- *Trusting your suppliers and service providers* to maintain confidentiality, to fulfill commitments, to deliver quality products and services on time, to cooperate with you if the scope of work changes, and to charge you a fair price.

Assess the Quality of Trust in Existing Business Relationships

Now take this expanded definition and evaluate the concept of trust within the context of your own work and of your organization. How do you define trust? What makes you trustworthy? Have you ever violated a colleague's trust? How have you successfully regained that person's trust? If someone loses your trust, how can they regain it? Warning: these can be very tough issues to confront. Trust is a very personal subject. You may find that you want to avoid some questions (take note of which ones) and some may require a lot of thought. It may be best to mull these questions over in your mind for a few days before jotting down your answers. Keep in mind that your colleagues may have different answers than you do.

Think about all the business relationships you currently maintain with clients, suppliers and service providers, leaders, subordinates, and colleagues. Where is trust the strongest? What is the benefit of a trusting relationship to you and your organization? Trust can make it easier to get along on a day-to-day basis, enhance a good working relationship over time, and enable the team to produce better results.

Now consider how location affects those business relationships. Which people are located within walking distance of your office? Which ones are off-site? Two of the groups mentioned here are typically managed remotely—clients and suppliers or service providers. You may also be managing contract workers or outsourced workers. You are probably working on teams with colleagues who are in other cities or countries. How do you know they are performing? How do they know you are performing? How comfortable are you with this style of remote management? How would managing your own employees remotely be different from dealing with these remote groups?

Make a list of your employees you would not trust with the freedom to choose where and when to work. Describe the reasons for that mistrust in very detailed terms. If there were specific incidents where the employee missed a deadline or misused the allotted time, make sure it is on the list. At some point in the process, you should be willing to share this information with the individual and have an honest discussion about how the situation can be corrected.

At Merrill Lynch, where there are 2,300 workers who work from home two to three days a week, employees fill out an application to request permission to telework. The form gets submitted to their manager and the Alternative Work Arrangements Team at the same time. If the manager denies the request, the Alternative Work Arrangements Team counsels that manager to give the employee a detailed explanation about how to change the situation and win approval to telework. They also ask the manager to set a date when the employee can reapply and be reevaluated. Yes, this can be an awkward situation for a manager. It is never pleasant to deny an employee request. As discussed in the chapter on Principle #1: Initiative, this is one of the downsides of a voluntary program: "inappropriate" workers may ask to participate and then the manager is in the position of turning them down. Nonetheless, it can have a constructive effect on the working relationship, as Merrill Lynch has found. Merrill Lynch sees this as a positive outcome of the program because communication about performance is opened up. There is a team in place to help managers through these discussions and, usually, when employees reapply, they are accepted. These difficulties are worth overcoming because successful remote and mobile work strategies "contribute to making Merrill Lynch an employer of choice in this competitive environment," according to Bernadette Fusaro, vice president of Global Work/Life Strategies at Merrill Lynch.

Fully Embrace a Results-Based Performance Review Process

When people wonder, "How will I know they are working?" if employees are permitted to work from somewhere other than the office, it is good to ask, "How do you know they are working now? How do you judge their performance today?" Results-based performance measurement has been in place in many organizations for a long time. But, typically, it has never been fully tested or truly relied upon. Many extraneous issues still get factored in at review time, such as attendance and hours worked.

The relationship between a course instructor and a class of students is the most straightforward model of results-based evaluation I've experienced. Clear direction is given about a term paper or project and a deadline is set. The instructor has established criteria for evaluating the product that have been discussed with the students. Student grades are based solely on these criteria. It doesn't matter how much time someone spent on the paper, where they did the work, or when they wrote the paper. What matters is the quality of the result and their ability to meet the deadline. This is much the same way we are evaluated by our customers and clients. Either we have met their expectations or we have not. Customers don't say, "Well, since you spent such a long time on it and worked late into the night, I guess it'll meet my needs." Clients measure our performance by results, not by process or other irrelevant factors. This is how we need to measure the performance of employees.

The key to success in maintaining good, trusting relationships with clients, strategic partners and suppliers, contract workers, and outsourced providers is having clear, documented criteria. Employees need the same level of understanding about their work. They need to trust that their manager and leaders have a direction and can articulate it. Employees should have a clear picture of how their role fits into the organization and its overall mission. They need to know what the deliverable is and how it will be judged. Without this, remote work will exacerbate existing performance problems, not solve them.

Understand More About How You and Your Employees Work Today

Even though it should not factor into how employees are evaluated, it is often helpful to take the time to analyze how and where you and your employees spend time currently. This process helps build trust because it dispels misperceptions about how much time is spent on which kinds of activities and where employees accomplish their work. Often, for instance, managers overestimate the amount of time employees spend in meetings or other collaborative activities and underestimate the time that is already spent working from somewhere other than the office. Unveiling current work patterns often helps managers realize that they currently trust workers to do some of their solo work out of sight of management and colleagues.

I've developed a very simple matrix, the Job Activities Analysis Survey—Part 1 (Short Version)(on page 61), that can be used to understand perceptions about time and place use.[7] (You will see several components of this tool throughout the book that build on or expand upon earlier information.) The matrix can be easily tailored to suit your particular needs; it can have more choices or fewer choices, different headings, whatever you need. The survey should be set up on a spreadsheet so that all the numerical calculations are automatically made quickly.

Here's how it works. First, estimate the number of hours you typically work in a week. Whatever that number is, say forty hours, should ultimately equal the sum of all of the cells in the matrix. Then think about where you do your work (at your office or off site, for instance) and how your work is performed (solo or with other people, for instance). To fill in this chart, you'll eventually have to get to a finer level of detail. Does the work you do with other people happen in planned meetings or impromptu discussion sessions? Does your solo work involve a phone, a computer, or other materials?

There are many ways to fill out the chart and no right or wrong answers. Don't get too caught up in being accurate down to the last minute. Most people fill in the cells in hour or half-hour increments. Some people find it best to start by filling in the totals by place (last full row on chart). For instance, say you know that you spend about thirty minutes every weeknight and on Saturday working from home. That's six days a week for half an hour each

How much time do you spend on these activities, in these places, in a typical workweek?

Activity	Location of Activity				
	On-Site Workplace	Client Site	Home	Other Off-Site Location	Total
Formal meetings (scheduled in advance)					
Informal collaboration					
Phone calls (including teleconferences)					
Independent work that requires a computer (including e-mail)					
Independent work without a computer					
Other (please describe)					
Total work hours					
Hours spent commuting					
Hours spent traveling for work					

Job Activities Analysis Survey—Part 1 (Short Version)

day, or three hours per week total. You would put the number 3 in the "Total" row, under the column headed "Home." Maybe the three hours is roughly equally split between checking e-mail and returning voicemail messages. So, you put 1.5 in the row labeled "Phone calls" and 1.5 in the row labeled "Independent work that requires a computer." Continue filling in the chart until it totals forty hours or whatever your average number of work hours is per week. If your schedule fluctuates greatly during the year, fill out a chart for each scenario (busy season, high travel, low travel, and so on). After you've accounted for all forty hours in the workweek, complete the two final parts, total time spent commuting to and from work and total time spent traveling on company business that is not counted in your work hours.

Again, do not be too concerned about taking this to a high level of accuracy. This is a starting point that represents your perception of your current work patterns (which may or may not be close to reality). After you've filled in the matrix and can see the totals for the columns and rows, take a look at the percentage of time you spend on each activity and in each place. How much of your time do you spend working with other people (the sum of the first two rows)? It is unusual for this figure to be more than 60 percent to 70 percent even for managerial and other highly collaborative jobs. How much time do you spend on site as opposed to off site? Salespeople and consultants typically spend the most time off site (three or more days per week), but few knowledge workers perform 100 percent of their work at the office. Most employees do some work from home, especially during evening and weekend hours.

Now ask your employees to fill out the chart. You should see some significant differences between their charts and yours. In many cases, nonmanagerial workers spend less time interacting with other people than managers. Nonmanagers usually spend more time on solo activities such as working on the computer, reading reports, and making phone calls.

It is helpful to have everyone fill out the chart independently, then meet for a group discussion of the results. Sometimes it is useful to see if there are a few prototypical workstyles in the group or to consolidate all the matrices into one average profile for the department. Take a few minutes in the beginning to review the compiled information with the group. Do the similarities in profiles make sense? Are differences due to type of work or personal style? What do employees feel are the positive and negative aspects of their current profile? Carefully examine the percentage of time you and your employees work from off-site locations today. This figure usually surprises everyone when they realize that people are already trusted to work remotely for some portion of time.

These group discussions are instrumental in building trust because doubts are removed (or at least minimized) about how work is currently performed. The subsequent conversations about how these work patterns may change when remote and mobile work strategies are implemented should help overcome fears about meeting deadlines and commitments differently in the future. Everyone needs to trust that the work is going to get done. Consider the specific goals of your proposed remote and mobile work program. If you want employees to improve relationships with clients, talk with the group about your goal for the amount of time they should be at client sites. Should it be 10 percent more or 20 percent more than today? Discuss how that would affect the time use profile. As a consequence, which activities or places would decrease under this plan? (Note that unless you intend to ask employees to work more hours per week, an increase in one area must be offset by a decrease in others.) If your goal is to give employees flexibility to work from another location (such as home), ask them how much time they'd like to spend off site as opposed to on site. Look at the amount of time spent commuting now and discuss how this time could be used more effectively. Review the amount of time already spent working from home combined with the total amount of time engaged in solo activities that could be performed from anywhere (phone calling, computer work, reading, and so on). Can these hours and these activities be aggregated into one day and performed from home or another remote location? On the flip side, can all the face-to-face interaction (whether planned or unplanned) be aggregated into the days that would be worked on site?

Try to estimate how each person's activity profile would change as a result of remote and mobile work. The more detail that is discussed as a group the better. This gives everyone in the department a chance to gain insights into workstyle differences from seeing the other profiles. The interchange of ideas about how time and place of work could be used more effectively always yields creative approaches. More important, the process of setting goals together regarding new ways of working will reinforce bonds of trust among the members of the group.

Conduct Workshops Before People Begin Working Differently

Before employees are sent out to work in a different way, they need to attend education sessions to prepare them for successful teleworking. David Fleming, telework program consultant for the State of California, is very experienced at leading these types of workshops. He has found that detailed conversations between managers and employees are essential to building the trust needed for an employee to be an effective remote worker. He generally recommends three separate workshops: one for teleworker candidates, one for managers and supervisors, and a joint session that brings both groups together. Each workshop lasts two to three hours, for a total time commitment of four to six hours per participant.

First he meets with the prospective teleworkers (about fifteen people in each session) to discuss options to address, mitigate, or eliminate concerns about working from home or another remote location. One exercise focuses on specifically identifying each job task as either teleworkable or non-teleworkable. Then, Fleming asks them to suggest ways the "non-teleworkable" tasks could be performed remotely. For instance, if "attend staff meetings" is placed on the non-teleworkable task list, they discuss the possibility of occasionally participating in these meetings via teleconference, using telephone-bridging services.

In the second session, Fleming meets with managers of the prospective teleworkers. As much as 80 percent of this session is a dialogue about dealing with managers' fears, issues, and concerns. They are asked to perform a job-task analysis to identify what they perceive as their prospective teleworkers' teleworkable and non-teleworkable tasks. Fleming asks them, too, to rethink their pre-conceptions about non-teleworkable tasks.

In the third joint session, the managers and telecommuters compare the list of job tasks. A fair amount of time is used to compare and contrast the teleworkers' and managers' list of tasks. The goal is to reach an agreement about which tasks are suitable for remote work. Fleming has heard many participants say that the workshop provided an opportunity for often-neglected quality communication between the workers and their supervisors. The workshop concludes with the managers and teleworkers planning a typical workday, work-week, or workmonth, complete with expected deliverables and a clear idea of what constitutes successful performance. Following the workshop, this documentation can be used by both groups when they evaluate the success of the telework initiative and can be updated and modified as job responsibilities change.

Reinforce Trust in Leadership by Committing Resources to the New Work Initiative

At Merrill Lynch, employees have learned they can trust that they will get the tools and support they need to work remotely. More than 18 percent of Merrill Lynch's 1,900-person Private Client Technology division works from home one to four days a week. The program was launched in 1996 as part of a commitment to being the employer of choice and improving recruiting and retention of information technology professionals. Based on pilot projects that had been conducted in 1994, leaders knew that they had to provide good technological support and training for these remote workers to succeed. An eight-person cross-functional team ensures the success of the telecommuters through a carefully tested implementation process.

After an employee's request to work from home has been approved, a member of the Alternative Work Arrangements Team (which is headed by Janice Miholics) meets with the employee. A technology interview is conducted to determine hardware and software requirements and level of support the person may need based on their knowledge of the systems. The team then sets about configuring the appropriate system that will meet their needs and fulfill Merrill Lynch's technical specifications. The team also arranges for the installation of two phone lines in the employee's house that will be billed directly to Merrill Lynch.

After completing classroom training, telecommuters spend the first two weeks of their new work arrangement in one of three simulation labs (located in Somerset, New Jersey, Jacksonville, Florida, and New York City). Here they receive hands-on guidance from the team about their new hardware setup, remote access, equipment installation, and tech support. Then they are left alone in the lab to work in the same way they will from home. This gives them a chance to see what it will be like to work remote from their manager and colleagues and think about planning ahead. For example, some trainees don't bring enough work the first day or they forget an important file.

This two-week period gives the employees a chance to build confidence that they can handle working remotely and that tech support will be available when they need it. It also provides a nice transition time for the manager and employee to become accustomed to working apart. "Most important," says Miholics, "the investment in this process and training facility conveys management's commitment to optimizing productivity and flexibility." Her team provides ongoing support and collects feedback. They maintain an active schedule for updating hardware and software. Twice a year they hold focus groups with managers and telecommuters to make sure the arrangement is still working and to look for ways to improve it. Periodically, they survey the group to monitor productivity, job satisfaction, and other business measures that continue to show positive results.

Recognize That Behavior and Results Have to Change

Trust should build over time as work is performed differently and positive outcomes become more apparent. When IBM implemented its Mobility Initiative, it involved a major change in the way managers and employees worked. Traditionally, the sales and support staffers started each day by going to the office for an hour or so. During the day, they'd go out for client meetings or service calls and usually stop back at the office between appointments. Then they ended the day by wrapping up paperwork at the office. Managers were used to seeing their employees frequently during the day. For the Mobility Initiative to be effective, though, managers had to learn to trust their employees to use their time wisely. And managers had to trust themselves that they could learn to do their jobs differently.

Strong direction from the top helped people through this transition. The goals of this mandatory remote and mobile work strategy were ambitious: be more responsive and accessible to clients, reduce sales costs, and improve productivity of the sales force. The plan was implemented after Lou Gerstner became IBM's new leader in 1993, layoffs happened for the first time in the history of the company, and major change was essential.

IBM's sales managers were hit with three major changes at the same time: mobility, downsizing, and a reorganization to a product or industry-specialist focus as opposed to a geographic focus. The branch office system was abandoned and many managers were far away from their newly assigned employees. Being able to manage remotely had become a critical skill. The smart managers realized they had to use technology to develop an entirely new way of working. They recognized that if employees worked from home first thing in the morning, they wouldn't waste time traveling to the office through rush hour traffic. Then sales and support people could go directly from home to customer sites. Equipped with more powerful portable technology, they could download information and prepare quotes at the client's office and be much more responsive. Collaboration via Lotus Notes and teleconferences substituted for half-day staff meetings and were a much more effective use of time. One of the most significant changes for the sales force was dictated by Gerstner himself: he eliminated time cards in the sales area saying, "we trust you to keep track of sick days and vacation days." Hierarchical managers who couldn't adapt to this new system were shifted to managing groups that still went to the office each day.

According to Bob Egan, managing principal for Mobile and Wireless Competency in IBM Global Services, the payoff has been tremendous. The sales teams spend 25 percent to 50 percent more time at client sites and customers say they are much more satisfied with the level of service they receive. Revenue per employee increased—growing 10–12 percent per year with only half the sales force. Mobile employees report working nine hours more per week with less impact on personal and family life. Their morale is higher and they are less likely to leave IBM than nonmobile employees. In 1996 alone, $75 million in real estate costs were saved. By that time, ten thousand people were part of the Mobility Initiative and no longer had dedicated offices at an IBM site. Instead, shared workstations at a ratio of 1:4 were available at centralized office locations. This facilitated a reduction of 2 million square feet of space in the United States. Monitoring and communicating the success of the Mobility Initiative helped spread enthusiasm and increase involvement. When people see that a program is working, trust builds quickly.

By 2000, IBM had sixty thousand participants in the Mobility Initiative worldwide (this includes an estimated thirty thousand sales and sales support people, twenty thousand services people, and ten thousand headquarters staffers who voluntarily telework).

This means that roughly 20 percent of the 300,000-person IBM population no longer have a dedicated workstation or office on site. About 50 percent of the staff have remote access capability and work from home or another remote location some of the time.

Don't Leave Unions Out

Some major corporations who were early adopters of telework strategies for nonunionized employees have shied away from extending these new work options to workers represented by unions. Likewise, unions have not always made telework a top priority at the bargaining table. One of the best examples of a remote work program for unionized employees is the U.S. Department of Labor. The initial interest in Flexiplace came from the union side during bargaining talks in 1991 and 1992. Of the 16,000 workers in the Department of Labor, 11,500 are bargaining unit employees represented by the American Federation of Government Employees (AFGE) Local 12 and the National Council of Field Labor Locals. After the union voiced initial interest in telecommuting, both sides agreed to create a Flexiplace task force with union and management representation. This group then did the groundwork for pilot programs that began in 1994.

Supervisors decided whether or not their groups would participate based on mission accomplishment needs. Once the supervisor had elected to get involved, the employees were free to volunteer to be part of the year-long pilot study (extended to eighteen months). There were two pilot programs: the national office, which involved 240 workers; and the field staff, that involved 353 participants. There was mandatory training for supervisors and telecommuters. Typically, flexiplacers worked one to two days from home and three or four days in the office. Supervisors and employees then completed a survey at the end of the pilot program to evaluate the benefits and problems of the arrangement.

Employees reported that they could get more accomplished in an eight-hour day at home because there were fewer interruptions and there was less wasted time chatting at the coffee machine, for instance. Supervisors agreed that work got done faster and quality improved during the pilot projects. This was a pleasant surprise for some supervisors, who started out viewing Flexiplace as a program that only benefited the worker. While employees worked the same number of hours per week, the average time spent commuting dropped from 12.22 hours per week to 6.93 hours per week. Incidentally, the group of six hundred employees who participated in the pilot was just about evenly split between male and female. Clearly, this was a program that could offer advantages to many union members.

In 1996, based on the positive findings, the unions and management recommended that this be adopted as a permanent program. By the end of 1998, both unions had negotiated and agreed to a handbook and guidelines that detailed the implementation process for Flexiplace at the Department of Labor. According to Gail Guest, work-life program specialist, the important lesson of this example is *take your time.* Proceed carefully while involving everyone in the process. Since they've successfully built trusting relationships and valuable results in the pilot phase, unions and management are now poised to benefit from improved attraction and retention of staff and better work-life balance.

Chapter Summary: Trust

For remote and mobile workers to succeed, management control needs to be replaced with a healthy sense of trust. Without trust, remote work doesn't work. More important, without trust, even on-site work is not as productive as it could be. This chapter has covered ways to develop and maintain good working relationships without seeing employees five days a week at the office.

WHAT CHANGE AGENTS NEED TO TAKE RESPONSIBILITY FOR:

- Assess the state of trust in current business relationships.

- Acknowledge shortcomings in trustworthiness and identify ways to correct the problems.

- Structure the remote and mobile work initiative to gradually build comfort with new work relationships.

- Provide clear direction to employees and assess performance through results.

- Understand where and when workers spend their time today.

- Show that leaders can be trusted to change their own ways of working and support the change efforts of others.

- Conduct education sessions to help managers and employees work through potential problems.

- Monitor behavior change and business outcomes and communicate results to all staff.

- Address the concerns of all employees including those represented by unions.

WHAT ALL EMPLOYEES SHOULD ACCEPT RESPONSIBILITY FOR:

- Review your existing work patterns to understand how and where you spend your time.

- Talk with leaders and colleagues about reasons for changes you'd like to see in these work patterns.

- Meet performance commitments you've made with managers, colleagues, and clients to maintain a high level of trustworthiness.

- Trust yourself, your leaders, and your colleagues to make smart choices about when and where to work.

Joy

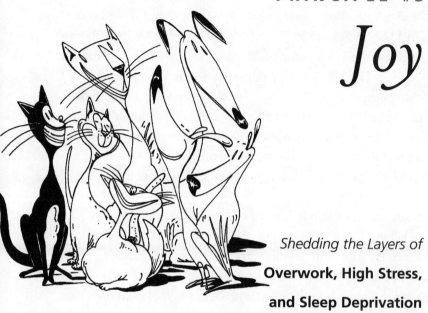

Shedding the Layers of

Overwork, High Stress,

and Sleep Deprivation

Joy.
It's beyond balance.

It's way beyond balance. The popular phrase, "balancing work and family," implies that work and family are opposing forces *and* that there are only two priorities to satisfy. It sounds as if it is a struggle to handle both without letting one overwhelm the other. "Integrating work and life" is a little more inclusive, but there is an underlying assumption that working doesn't involve living and that it still comes down to an either-or choice. We need to set higher expectations and reward different behaviors if we are to capitalize on the real promise of technology—improved productivity and more leisure time. Consider the difference if the primary goal were joy rather than balance or integration.

Face it. We are more effective workers when we are well-rested, well-fed, physically fit, and generally happy. It just makes sense. When I board a plane to fly to or from New York City, I like to believe that the pilot and copilot really love their work, are not stressed out, and are not sleep deprived. It is important to me that they are operating at peak performance because my life is in their hands. Why should we have different expectations for our own employees? Maybe our lives are not potentially in danger when we interact with other workers, but we would all get a lot more accomplished if we had a different image of the "effective worker."

What are the traits of an effective worker in your organization? A person who is willing to travel a lot? An early riser who gets to the office before 7 A.M.? The person who skips lunch and stays late into the evening? The worker who commutes a long distance to get to work each day? Jot down the names of your employees who begin each day filled with excitement and eager to get started on a new project, but who also get their work done by five or six in the evening and go home for dinner. Is your list long or short? How are these people viewed by you and others? Look back at your answer to Question 12 on the Work Naked Checklist in the first chapter: "If you are having fun and are well-rested and physically fit, you must not have enough work to do." Is that true or false at your company? If you think this is a false statement, you can skim the rest of this chapter and go quickly to the next. Maybe in your heart you believe it is false, but the attitude at your company is that those workers are slacking off and are not dedicated to the organization. If that is the case or if you are a firm believer that work should be grueling and physically taxing, read on—these mind-sets are the toughest obstacles to getting the most out of new ways of working.

A joyful attitude toward work is essential to the long-term success of a remote and mobile work strategy. If you give people the tools and encouragement to work anytime, anywhere and then continue to reward workaholic behavior, your employees are being set up for overwork and burnout. Let's take a look at one way two people have created a work situation that blends well with their lifestyles. This gives us a sense of what a joyful approach to work and life could look and feel like at a small scale.

Crafting an Enjoyable Way of Working

Nancy and Bart Mills roll out of bed around 8:30 in the morning, eat a light breakfast, and then make the ten-step commute to their home office in Manhattan Beach, California. By 9 A.M., they are talking with editors or writing up their celebrity interviews to be published in the *Los Angeles Times*, the *New York Daily News*, or one of the other outlets for their journalism. By this time, their counterparts—full-time staffers at newspapers—have probably been jolted out of bed before dawn by a loud alarm clock, gulped down coffee and toast, and endured a slow, frustrating commute to the office (especially in Los Angeles). Who do you think is in a better frame of mind to begin their work for the day?

Since 1972, Nancy and Bart have built a business together as journalists covering the movie industry. They've always shared an office, sometimes even a computer, and worked from home. The two Mills children, Bonnie and Kevin, are now adults and have moved away, but while they were growing up, they never came home to an empty house. Nancy and Bart have the flexibility to schedule interviews and movie screenings during the times of the day or evening when traffic is tolerable. When they were raising their children, this flexibility allowed them to make sure one parent was there to send their son and daughter off to school and to welcome them home at the end of the day. Nancy and Bart must have been good role models—both children have started their own businesses that they run from their homes. Lately, Nancy and her son have collaborated on a novel series of cookbooks, including *Help! My Apartment Has a Kitchen, Help! My Apartment Has a Dining Room,* and *Chocolate on the Brain* (published by Chapters/Houghton Mifflin).

Both Bart and Nancy say they "miss the social aspects of working at a newspaper and going to the office every day," but they've made up for that loss of camaraderie by being involved in the Cornell Alumni Association in Los Angeles, getting to know their neighbors, and playing on local athletic teams. They don't miss the time-wasting interruptions and petty politics that plague traditional work settings. Nancy estimates that they write two or three times more stories per week than the typical staff journalist. All in all, they are pleased with the trade-offs they've made. When they compare themselves to friends who are also in their mid-fifties, Nancy and Bart feel they have more control over their lives, are aging at a slower rate, complain less, and are generally happier. Nancy enjoys the fact that her children have been able to observe firsthand that "you can take a different path, take risks, love your work, and be successful."

Why Should Business Leaders Be Concerned About Bringing More Joy to the Workplace?

Bart and Nancy Mills are good examples of effective workers who are content with their work-lifestyle. Unfortunately, many of today's workers would not describe their situations in the positive terms the Millses used. By many measures, employees in the United States are working more hours, sleeping fewer hours, and feeling more stress. This is not a context where high performance can flourish over the long term.

The amount of time spent at work and the workload has been increasing. A landmark study by the Families and Work Institute reported that between 1977 and 1997 the average workweek increased from 43.6 hours to 47.1 hours. Those who say they "never seem to have enough time to get everything done" increased from 40 percent in 1977 to 60 percent in 1997.[1] A 1999 survey of workers by Roper Starch for *Fast Company* reported that people were spending an average of roughly fifty-six hours working per week when they totaled the following three categories: forty-one hours were worked at an office or somewhere else outside the home; six hours were spent working from home; and nine hours were spent thinking about work during nonwork activities. Half of the respondents characterized this as "too much time" spent working or thinking about work. And only one in four of those surveyed said they loved their job.[2]

Workers are discontent and stressed out. In a 1999 Gallup survey of over a thousand adults, 34 percent described themselves as "not satisfied" with the amount of on-the-job stress they experience. Another 44 percent were somewhat satisfied with on-the-job stress, but only 21 percent said they were completely satisfied with the level of stress they experience at work. Those who were completely satisfied with on-the-job stress were much more likely to report high levels of job satisfaction as well.[3]

Work can have a negative effect on the health of your employees. A 1997 study by the World Bank of its employee health insurance records found that those who routinely traveled for business were responsible for 80 percent more claims than those who stayed put. The business travelers' complaints included intestinal problems, vascular problems, respiratory infections, backaches, and other issues involving occupational stress and anxiety.[4] According to Dr. Peter Schnall, there is considerable evidence linking job strain to cardiovascular disease. Schnall estimates that the economic costs of job strain, including absenteeism and lost productivity, could be several hundred billion dollars per year.[5]

Today's workers are tired and this limits them from performing up to their full potential. The National Sleep Foundation's 1999 Omnibus "Sleep in America Poll" surveyed a thousand adults about sleep habits, problems, and beliefs. The researchers reported that adults sleep an average of about seven hours a night during the workweek (an hour less than the eight hours that most sleep experts recommend). Only 35 percent of adults sleep eight or more hours per night during the five-day workweek. A surprising 62 percent of respondents experienced a sleep problem a few nights per week and 30 percent of respondents said that stress affected their ability to sleep well. Further, 40 percent of adults say they are so sleepy during the workday that it interferes with their daily activities.[6] According to Dr. James B. Maas, who conducts sleep research at Cornell University, "if you've had adequate sleep, things like warm rooms and dull meetings will make you bored, mad, uncomfortable, and restless, but not sleepy."[7] If you get sleepy in these situations, you are suffering from underlying sleep debt that may have been accumulating over a long time. Gradually, it may seem that your body gets used to it, but this is not a good thing. Maas says, "The truth is that most of us are functioning at a level far from optimal, far from the level of alertness that enables us to be energetic, wide awake, happy, creative, productive, motivated, and healthy human beings."[8]

Almost half (46 percent) of all workers have children living with them at least half of the time.[9] It is these children who are responsible for the loudest wake-up call regarding the state of the current worker. Ellen Galinsky, president of the Families and Work Institute and author of *Ask the Children,* reports that when children aged eight through seventeen were asked, "If you were granted one wish to change the way that your mother's/your father's work affects your life, what would that wish be?" 34 percent wished that their mother would be less stressed or less tired by work and 27 percent wished the same for their father. Parents in the study misjudged what the children's responses would be: they predicted that the children would ask for more time with them.[10] In fact, 70 percent of all parents in the National Study of the Changing Workforce said they feel they don't spend enough time with their children.[11]

Nancy and Bart Mills do not experience many of the problems described by other workers. But does that mean that the only solution is to start your own business and run it from home? No, there are many examples of companies where a healthy work environment has been created. Often these are cited in *Working Mother's* "100 Best Companies for Working Mothers" list or *Fortune's* "100 Best Companies to Work For in America." One large company where people love going to work is SAS Institute, headquartered in Cary, North Carolina.

One Example of a Joyful Company: SAS Institute

When Jim Goodnight and John Sall left North Carolina State University in 1976 to co-found SAS Institute, they knew they wanted work to be an enjoyable experience for the handful of employees who would endure the long hours of the start-up phase with them. This philosophy has not wavered as SAS has grown to a 6,800-person, highly profitable software company. From the beginning, it has had a flexible work schedule and thirty-five-hour workweek. Since 1976, SAS employees have also had access to free food and drinks on site and their families have been welcomed at numerous company picnics and parties. When one of the original employees had a baby and was feeling the struggle of motherhood versus the job she loved, on-site day care began. Today, five hundred children go to SAS's state-of-the-art Montessori day care program.

The value placed on employee health and well-being is obvious when you understand what is provided at the headquarters facility. Walk onto the two-hundred-acre, twenty-two-building site and you may think you're visiting a college campus. Casual clothes and knapsacks abound. If it is a nice day, you'll see people working on laptops at picnic tables or meeting with colleagues on a well-groomed lawn. If the people you've come to see aren't in their private offices (everyone has one), the cafeteria, or one of the well-stocked break rooms, they may be out on the running trail, in the fitness center, at the health clinic, or visiting their kids at the day care center. An on-site Wellness Center features massage therapists, seminars on a variety of health topics, and an ergonomics lab where staff evaluate the best equipment and furniture arrangement for employees.

Even with all these great on-site services, SAS leaders don't try to hold employees captive there. Results matter, not the number of hours people spend in their offices. They trust that employees are adults and will exhibit adult behavior when there is a conflict between work and personal life. About 50 percent have the ability to work off site—from home or on the road. It is left to the discretion of managers and their staffs to agree on an appropriate work routine.

Leadership counts. John Sall is frequently seen in the cafeteria eating lunch with his family. Goodnight and Sall get to work at 8:30 A.M. and call it a day at 5 P.M. They still get involved in the programming work. There are no executive dining rooms or special parking spaces to distinguish them from their colleagues. The corporate culture they've created, though, does distinguish SAS from its competitors.

There is an academic feel to the SAS Institute culture. From the private offices to the entrepreneurial spirit and high energy, it is very different from more traditional companies. This is not a company built on the command-and-control military structure. People love to work there. And very few leave. SAS has never had an annual turnover rate higher than 5 percent even though the average turnover rate in the industry is 20 percent. The corporate culture is described as relaxed while being committed to creativity, quality, and innovation. The culture of SAS Institute is based on this philosophy: "If you treat employees as if they make a difference to the company, they will make a difference to the company."[12] When I surveyed SAS Institute leadership about the top three business strategies that allow them to maximize their competitive advantage, the response was (in priority order):

1. Respond faster to market changes and customer demands.

2. Increase customer satisfaction.

3. Attract, retain, and develop high-quality talent.

And, indeed, all three of these are inextricably linked. The unusually low turnover rate means teams can maintain good working relationships over time and that helps get products out faster. Customers develop long-term relationships with SAS support teams, who have the benefit of knowing the history of the customer.

All these qualities have paid off from a business standpoint. Since the company was incorporated in 1976, SAS Institute has had double-digit growth in percentage of revenue increases every year. SAS topped the billion-dollar mark in 1999, strengthening its position as the largest privately held software company in the world.

What Are Other Companies Doing to Come Close to SAS Institute?

Unlike many of the other companies on *Fortune*'s "Best Companies to Work For" list, SAS Institute has embraced work-life integration from the very beginning. Other employers have been trying to play catch-up. In response to high attrition and the demands of a changing workforce, many companies have been adding family-friendly programs and on-site amenities since the early 1980s. In general, when potential solutions to work-life conflicts are embraced, companies seem to favor amenities and benefits that bring employees to the work site or make it easier for employees to stay there. The 2000 Society for Human Resource Management (SHRM) *Benefits Survey*[13] reported that the following family-friendly benefits are offered by companies:

BENEFIT	PERCENTAGE OF EMPLOYEES
Employee assistance program	66
Flextime	51
Wellness program	49
Compressed workweeks	27
Telecommuting	26
On-site fitness center	19
Stress reduction program	19
On-site child care center	3

Companies typically address the "life" side of the work-life issue rather than deal with changing the way people work. Furthermore, even when these programs are offered, they are often not used. According to the Families and Work Institute 1997 study of employees' views, 40 percent felt that using flexible schedules or taking time off to deal with family issues could jeopardize their advancement in the company.[14] Your company could offer the same amenities and services as SAS Institute, but the effect would not be the same unless the attitude behind the programs was the same. Ernst & Young took this into account and developed a different approach when it set a goal to become the "employer of choice."

How Ernst & Young Is Changing Attitudes and Behavior

High turnover became a concern of Ernst & Young's leaders in the early 1990s when clients complained about how staff losses and subsequent replacements affected the quality of service. At the time, approximately one in four workers left the firm each year (25 percent turnover is typical for professional services firms). When CEO Philip Laskawy commissioned a retention study in 1994, the firm discovered that women were leaving E&Y at higher rates than their male counterparts. Subsequently, the Gender Equity Task Force hired Catalyst to analyze the situation and pose solutions to improve retention of female employees. In 1996, Ernst & Young formed the Office for Retention, headed by Deborah Holmes (who had led the Catalyst consulting team), and by 1998 the office was staffed by eight people with diverse skills and backgrounds such as organizational development, communications, and change management.[15]

Deborah Holmes's passion for her work is rooted in a career-changing experience early in her work life. After graduating from Harvard Law School, Holmes went to work for a New York City law firm. She was frustrated to learn that few people in her chosen profession understood the "connection between happy employees and happy clients."[16] Disillusioned and unhappy with the work-styles rewarded by law firms, Holmes went to work for the Families and Work Institute to consult with companies who wanted to change that paradigm. Eventually, she moved to Catalyst, a not-for-profit organization that researches and advises companies on issues facing women in the business world. The move to Ernst & Young was exciting for Holmes because she "finally got to be in charge of implementation."

Through surveys, focus groups, interviews, and task forces, Holmes's group learned that one area that affected all employees and their commitment to Ernst & Young was what they termed "healthy life balance." The life balance initiative has this goal: "Developing a culture that encourages Ernst & Young people to maintain a healthy and fulfilling balance in their lives while contributing fully to the firm."[17] Rather than focus a lot of attention on amenities and services that attempt to resolve issues in employees' personal lives, Ernst & Young has focused on redesigning the work itself. The underpinnings for this approach came from a 1996 Ford Foundation study by Lotte Bailyn that impressed Deborah Holmes. The message she took away from the report, "Relinking Life and Work: Toward a Better Future," was this: if you regard work-life issues as a lever for changing the way work is done rather than a competing need, you can come up with outcomes that are better for people's lives away from work and better for the work itself. The process and the solutions reflect a belief that people are creative and ingenious about solving these concerns if you let them enter into the discussion.

Recognizing that some of the pressure to overwork comes from within E&Y rather than from clients, emphasis has been placed on strategies that promote flexibility and autonomy (allowing employees to make life-workstyle choices that suit them best). A variety of tools have been made available to managers and team leaders through the Life Balance Matrix, a Lotus Notes database of best practices describing ways to organize work differently that have been tested by teams at E&Y. These strategies include the following:

- *Life Balance Survey.* All client-serving team members complete this survey at the beginning of each project. The questionnaire, which takes about twenty minutes to fill out, asks about work and personal goals and commitments. The belief is that the more you know up front, the more you make people welcome in a whole sense, the better they'll perform and the fewer the surprises that will arise later. The results of the survey are used in two ways: the information forms the basis for a conversation between the manager and each individual on the team, and the consolidated team results are discussed by the entire team in a meeting. The survey results provide a way to jump-start an honest conversation about non-work priorities whether they be volunteer work, hobbies, family, or other avocations. The group discussion of life balance issues allows teams a way to avoid conflicts between employees' needs and client commitments. This tool has been key to breaking down the barrier between appropriate and inappropriate subjects to discuss with managers and colleagues.

- *Codevelopment of client expectations around life balance.* Using the information gathered in the life balance survey and discussions, the team leader addresses these goals for healthy life balance with the client. Together, they work out a way to meet everyone's goals while meeting the client's expectations.

- *Utilization committee.* For office-based employees, an oversight committee reviews workload commitments to ensure that each employee is being used effectively while not being overcommitted on several projects. Employees are also urged to go to this committee if they feel their workload is too great.

- *Freedom from e-mail and voicemail on weekends and vacation.* Employees are discouraged from checking e-mail and voicemail on nonwork days, creating a separation between work time and personal time.

The matrix is organized so that users can search for both office-based and client-based solutions. In 2000, 73 percent of Ernst & Young's thirty-four thousand U.S.-based employees were client-serving while 27 percent were office-based practice support personnel. New tools are added to the matrix as they are developed and tested. For each tool, there is a detailed description, an example of a team that has tested it, and contact information for team leaders who would be willing to discuss their experiences with the strategy. These tools were developed by a cross-section of several hundred employees working in teams over a nine-month period. The role of the Office for Retention was to facilitate this process and make the tools available across the organization through the database structure. This process not only brought out the most creative solutions, it was essential to building commitment to the concept.

While the Life Balance Matrix is intended for team leaders and managers to use, the Flexible Work Arrangements (FWA) Database and FWA Roadmap were developed to put some of the tools directly in the hands of the employees. Through surveys and focus groups, Holmes's team learned that many employees were reluctant to request a flexible work arrangement. To dispel myths about who used these tools, why, and how it was working, E&Y built a database of 550 profiles of FWA users. Like the Life Balance Matrix, each profile describes the arrangement, the benefits, how the employee negotiated the arrangement with the manager, and contact information so people can reach the person profiled to discuss their experiences. The profiles give examples of the following types of strategies:

- Telework—working from home one to two days per week.
- Flexible hours—this could be nontraditional start or finish times for the work day, compressed workweek, or reduced

time during a less busy season. Employees still work
the same number of hours annually as other full-time
employees.

- Reduced schedule—may include reduced hours or days
  worked or responsibilities assigned.

- Seasonal schedule—work full-time part of the year and then
  have three to four months off.

The database is used by four hundred people per month on average and is updated on an ongoing basis. The FWA Roadmap walks a person through the process of requesting one of the flexible work arrangements. This allows the person to build a solid business case and open up the best conversation with his or her own manager.

In addition to these on-line tools for managers and employees, an active program to promote good role models for healthy life balance was developed. Through discussions with staff nationwide, Holmes's team generated a list of employees that colleagues felt displayed a good sense of work-life integration. Management was then asked to designate the top performers from the list. The stories of these top-performing, well-balanced individuals were then publicized within Ernst & Young to dispel the myth that you can't be committed to work and have a healthy sense of balance.

What is the payoff? Ernst & Young realized a savings of $9 million, based on a 2 percent decrease in turnover for women, in a three-year period from 1997 through 1999. These practices also give the company a competitive edge from a recruiting standpoint. Have E&Y managers reached their goal of being the employer of choice? Holmes feels that they will always be working toward this goal because it is a moving target. They will continue to have conversations with employees about needs that are not being met. They also plan to continue constant testing, surveys, focus groups, and interviews to find out which tools are working and what can be done to improve existing strategies.

Changing the Situation at Your Company

You could replicate the strategies used by SAS or Ernst & Young, but you may not experience the same levels of success at your company. For example, you could provide all the same amenities as SAS Institute or implement the same kind of on-line databases and tools as Ernst & Young, but you'd be missing two important elements. In the case of SAS Institute, it is not about the amenities, it is about the attitude behind them. At Ernst & Young, it is less about the tools and more about the fact that these tools were developed by the employees. Attitude and involvement, though, can be addressed in your company's own unique way. You need to tailor the response to solve the particular problems your employees are experiencing.

In general, what do employees say they want out of work? In McKinsey's 1998 study, "The War for Talent," workers defined a "great job" as one with freedom and autonomy to make decisions, a solid relationship between daily activities and business results, a challenge that can be met (rather than being overwhelming), new projects on a frequent basis, and good relationships with colleagues.[18] In "The American Dream," a Roper Starch Survey of two thousand U.S. adults, researchers found that half of the respondents would choose a low-paying job they love over a high-paying job they hate. A full 38 percent would choose more time over more money.[19]

Does your company offer positions that would meet the McKinsey study criteria for a "great job"? How many people in your company would say they love their work? Is your company a joyful place to work? Gather and analyze some of the following data (which your staff probably already collects) to find out what problems exist at your company:

- Turnover rate
- Cost of turnover (cost of recruiting, hiring, and training replacements)
- Absenteeism
- Cost of absenteeism
- Types of flexible work options offered
- Number and types of people using flexible work options
- Commuting distances (using home zip codes, you can map employee home locations versus office assignments)
- Client or customer satisfaction and turnover rates
- Level of innovation (percent sales from new products, number of new patents, and so on)
- Employee satisfaction and morale
- Other results from employee surveys—especially negative responses

Take a careful look at this quantitative data, especially at trends over the last two to five years. Have the measures shown improvement or further decline? What has been done to reverse negative trends? If steps have been taken to improve satisfaction or performance levels, find out what worked and what did not work.

Attrition is an especially costly problem. Has turnover been increasing or decreasing? How does your turnover rate compare to your industry competitors and your neighbors? Get a better idea of why people are leaving and where they go after your organization. The people who want flexibility but are afraid to participate in corporate programs are often the workers contributing to high turnover rates. Laraine Zappert, clinical associate professor of psychiatry and behavioral sciences at Stanford University's School of Medicine, has studied female MBA students who graduated from Stanford's Business School between 1931 and 1995. Those who graduated between 1975 and 1985 expressed the most concerns about workplaces not accommodating flexibility and autonomy. Many women with small children left traditional companies and either did not go back to full-time work for a while or started their own consulting practices.

If your employees are leaving to start their own businesses or become free agents, you should definitely take a closer look at that trend because you are probably losing valuable entrepreneurial talent. It is estimated that there are 25 million free agents in the United States.[20] This group includes freelancers, self-employed people, solo consultants, and contract workers and is expected to continue to grow at a fast pace. I've interviewed a lot of free agents and there is one consistent trait—they really love their work. It is a joy to speak with them. What's behind this trend? According to Dan Pink, author of *Free Agent Nation: How America's New Independent Workers Are Transforming the Way We Live*, "The key reason people leave traditional jobs isn't usually money or prestige or promotions. It's most often the urge to take control of their lives—whether that means control of their time, control of their freedom, control of their health, or control of the quality of their work. The flow of work may remain the same. But as free agents, they're in charge of the faucets—and that can be amazingly liberating for many people."

Understand How Remote and Mobile Work Strategies Can Make Work More Enjoyable

We saw in the profiles of SAS Institute and Ernst & Young that it is important for leaders to believe that new ways of working can improve employee satisfaction. If you haven't yet had a personal experience that persuaded you, there is now very good research available to convince you and your colleagues of the benefits of allowing employees to choose where and when to work. Increased satisfaction, improved performance, lowered stress levels, and reduced absenteeism are just a few of the outcomes these surveys have linked to these new ways of working.

In the 1997 AT&T National Survey of Teleworker Attitudes and Work Styles, conducted by FIND/SVP and Joanne H. Pratt Associates, 73 percent of the twelve thousand workers surveyed said they were more satisfied with their personal and family life since they started doing some work from home (19 percent were neutral, only 2 percent were less satisfied). Of those who were more satisfied, more than 80 percent credited the following factors for the increase in their satisfaction: better relationship with spouse or significant other, better personal morale, fewer sick days, better relationship with children, better balance of work and personal life, and less personal stress. Job satisfaction improved as well; 71 percent said they were more satisfied with their job than they were before they started working at home. When asked how working from home has affected their career, 63 percent said positively (another 33 percent said no effect). Those whose careers were positively affected reported that they have been given greater responsibility, received greater recognition for work, and were more productive.[21]

In AT&T's 1999 Employee Telework Survey (an internal study of the estimated eighteen thousand managers who work from home once a week or more), 68 percent said they were more productive when working at home and 79 percent were more satisfied with their personal and family lives than before they began teleworking. They also reported being more satisfied with their careers (79 percent).[22]

A study conducted by the Radcliffe Public Policy Institute at Fleet Financial Group in 1997 found that employees using telecommuting and flextime strategies experienced a 35 percent reduction in insomnia and other sleep disorders.[23]

The 1999 Telework America National Telework Survey (conducted by Joanne H. Pratt for the International Telework Association and Council) focused specifically on how telecommuting helps people balance their work and personal lives. Having the ability to work from home allows employees to use fewer sick days and personal days while attending to issues that arise unexpectedly. In addition to using these days for their own illnesses, employees often must use sick or personal time to deal with the following types of issues:

- Personal needs such as routine doctor or dental appointments, to let workmen into the house, deal with car repair.
- Children's illness, school function, after-school activities, and so on.
- Problem with day care arrangements.
- Spouse or elders living in household need assistance driving to medical appointment or dealing with an emergency.

According to the study, personal and family responsibilities during the work day typically average about forty-five incidents per year for a total of 165 hours during a typical year. Incidents amounting to 52 hours of this total can be scheduled in advance and, therefore, are less disruptive. The majority of teleworkers in the study said they were likely to work at home on the days that they knew they would have to attend to a personal matter. If they did not have the ability to work from home, these workers would have taken sick or personal leave or shortened the workday by going in late or leaving early. Their work-from-home arrangement allows them to take time out during the day to deal with these issues and then make up the hours later in the evening or on the weekend.[24]

Obviously, remote and mobile work strategies cannot solve all problems faced by employees. Working from home should not be used as a substitute for day care, for instance. However, it can alleviate some of the hassles surrounding day care arrangements such as drop-off times and pick-up times that don't mesh well with commuting and work schedules. New parents' fears about leaving their children with a nanny may be alleviated by working from a home office a few days a week and being accessible to the nanny and baby. Parents of older children and teenagers find benefits from being able to work from home during those after-school hours when typically their children would be home alone.

At different times in their lives, workers may find it is useful to avoid traveling to and from the office every day to go to work. For example, workers who are recovering from surgery, undergoing chemotherapy, or caring for a spouse, parent, or child who is ill can continue working full-time from home if they are equipped and supported properly. In some cases, these employees might have to go on disability or quit their jobs if they didn't have the freedom to work from home. However, the most significant advantage to remote and mobile work is that it can be made available to most employees and many employees can benefit from it, even if they don't have a special problem that is interfering with work.

Tauna Jecmen works for WaveBend Solutions, LLC, a technology consulting firm that is a wholly owned subsidiary of BDO Seidman, LLP. She is the national human resources director for this 250-person firm and works from her home in Phoenix, Arizona, when she is not traveling to one of the ten cities where WaveBend has offices. Her reason for living in Phoenix instead of Chicago (the office she originally reported to) is simple: she is just as passionate about being a competitive runner as she is about her work. A warm climate is important for her training regimen. On a typical work-from-home day, Jecmen wakes at 5 A.M., runs eight to ten miles with a group of friends, and is ready to get to work at 7:30 A.M. so she is available for phone calls with colleagues in the Eastern time zone. Some days, she breaks at noon for swim practice at a local pool or a bike ride and is back at her desk by 1:30 P.M. where she works until 6 or 7 P.M. She usually travels three days of the week for three weeks of the month to meet with colleagues or employees. Her job at WaveBend is to ensure that people find meaning in their work and develop strategies to improve the quality of work. Tauna Jecmen is a proponent of alternative work arrangements and a good role model for the consultants she serves.

Understand the Linkages Between Employee Satisfaction and Corporate Performance for Your Business

Be realistic. If there is no clear link between employee satisfaction and corporate performance, it will be difficult to change the way people work in a significant way. Some corporate leaders are willing to trust their gut feeling that more satisfied employees will result in more satisfied customers and higher sales. A more rigorous approach can be more persuasive and informative about how one factor affects another. For example, Sears has developed a sophisticated yet simple model of the employee-customer-profit chain. Through extensive research and statistical analysis, the company has documented that a 5-unit increase in employee attitude drives a 1.3-unit increase in customer impression, which drives a 0.5 percent increase in revenue growth. In 1998, a 4 percent increase in customer satisfaction translated into more than $200 million in additional revenues for the year. This is a predictive model designed to support the company's goals of being a compelling place to work, to shop, and to invest. Its leaders know which factors they need to survey employees about to come up with the best index of employee attitude. They have similar measurement methods for customer impression and revenue growth and all are monitored continually and used to update the model.[25]

Unfortunately, Sears is part of a small group of companies who measure employee satisfaction levels and use the information to improve business performance. According to Brian Morgan and William Schiemann, leaders of a study sponsored by *Quality Progress* magazine and Metrus Group, "Although there is clear evidence that employee commitment and satisfaction have an impact on customer satisfaction and financial performance, less than two in 10 companies use people measures to predict these key business outcomes. In fact, most companies do not measure performance on those people issues that are predictive of customer satisfaction."[26] The people dimensions that are considered predictors of customer satisfaction are as follows: customer focus, performance management, teamwork, senior leadership, supervisor effectiveness, clarity of direction, employee commitment, employee satisfaction, respect, empowerment, and organizational learning. Many companies do not measure these factors and some that do collect the data do not use it strategically.[27]

While remote and mobile work strategies have been shown to improve employee job satisfaction in both case studies and national surveys, you will need to determine what that means for your company. The level of commitment to change and investment of resources will be affected by the perceived influence of new ways of working on overall financial performance. Therefore, these links need to be understood in the context of your organization.

Address Underlying Conditions and Attitudes About Work

When you determine that remote and mobile work strategies would have a positive impact on employee satisfaction and performance, you need to encourage people to use these workstyles in advantageous ways. Be willing to have a conversation with employees about the pressures on the job; ask employees, "What takes the joy out of work for you?" Find out their perceptions about what behavior gets rewarded and whether that behavior actually contributes to high organizational performance. Be willing to listen to their ideas about attitudes that discourage them from working at home or another remote location. Would it show lack of dedication, for instance? Would it be difficult to get promoted without having high visibility with management?

Discuss feelings about how a "joyful job" would be structured. Should work be hard or easy, challenging or comfortable? What words would be an appropriate way to describe work: inspiring, joyful, fun, rewarding? Surely, you can't make employees love their work, but you can set the expectation that they should and you can structure jobs to be desirable and enjoyable. The real difference at SAS Institute is that there is an expectation that people will love their work—and that their work can be accomplished in a thirty-five-hour workweek. At your company, should employees be able to accomplish their assignments in a forty-hour week? If not, why not? How many hours should it take employees at your company to do their work? Are they aware of that expectation? As downsizing reduces the number of employees in companies, the workload for each individual often increases. The resulting feeling of being overwhelmed is counterproductive and no amount of remote work could solve that problem.

Business leaders should not be expected to solve employees' nonwork problems, but you should be aware that they may be having an impact on the work of other employees. As Arlie Hochschild pointed out in *The Time Bind*, a study of why employees were not using flexible work arrangements in a "family-friendly" company, some employees use work as a refuge from problems at home.[28] It may not be your responsibility to push these employees out the door at the end of the day, but you should make sure these workaholics are not keeping other employees at the office needlessly just to have company. Also, be aware that they may be stirring up crises at work to have an excuse to stay there and avoid going home.

Evaluate whether you and your colleagues are ready for people to be happier or at least less stressed out about work. How would you react in this situation? I work from an apartment in a brownstone on the Upper West Side of Manhattan. During warm months, I often work from my outdoor deck garden. If I'm on the phone when a noisy plane flies overhead, I explain to the caller that I'm working outside. At that point, many have said, "Oh, it must be nice to take off on such a lovely afternoon." The fact that I'm outside on a nice day leads people to conclude that I'm *not* working even though I am discussing business with them on the phone.

The flip side of this type of misperception occurs in many offices. Often, frenetic, unproductive activity gets misconstrued as a sign of high performance. The "whirling dervish" who travels constantly, never has more than two minutes for a serious discussion, and is always racing from one meeting to the next is thought of as a hard worker. Underneath all that activity (especially if someone brags or complains about it) there is frequently very little real productivity. Performance has to be measured by results, not appearance or hours worked.

Dispel the myth that remote and mobile work strategies are for people in special situations. Employees shouldn't need a reason to use these options. When having the freedom to work where and when they are most effective is extended to all employees, it sends a clear message that workers are trusted to act as adults and make wise choices. Many may still choose to work at the office each day, but they will go there with a much different attitude knowing they had a choice.

Invite employees to share their thoughts about solving these problems. Articulating that these problems exist should go a long way toward eliminating them. Work together with employees to change those conditions and mind-sets. At Ernst & Young it has been helpful to make tools available to managers and employees about what works and how it works. Employees also act as resources to each other to guide them through the new work experience.

Monitor and Measure Effectiveness

Employees' feelings about their work and corporate performance should be monitored to determine how well remote and mobile workstyles are working. We are accustomed to surveying workers about "employee satisfaction," but it may be time to change our terminology. Many companies have switched from focusing on customer satisfaction to a desire to "delight our customers." Employee satisfaction needs a similar redefinition. Recent national surveys have queried respondents about how much they love their work—this is probably getting closer to measuring joy at work. We could also ask how often employees wake up feeling like they can't wait to get to work or when was the last time they got really excited about a project assignment. The measures should be tailored to fit each corporate culture. When the critical factors that relate to employee joy are understood, surveys should be designed to address this limited set of issues rather than ask about a wide range of topics. Data can then be collected quickly without demanding a lot of time from the employees.

If employees run into problems when working in a different way, the problems should be caught early so that they don't have a negative impact on client relations and overall financial performance. The two most important problems to catch early on are overwork and work at home interfering with family life (the second often stems from the first). Working too much can be overcome by having clearer definitions of goals and objectives. Without the routine of leaving work at a certain hour each day, many employees do not have a good sense of when they have accomplished their work. As discussed in the chapter on Principle #2: Trust, focusing on results rather than hours worked or the false appearance of productivity is the best solution for this problem. Periodically, leaders should ask, "Are we rewarding the person who is well-rested, well-fed, physically fit, and generally happy?" If it is true that you get what you reward, you have tremendous power to change the way people in your organization work.

Chapter Summary: Joy

Without a belief that work should be enjoyable and fun, employees may not take advantage of remote and mobile work strategies or they may use the ability to work anytime, anywhere to overwork. Developing a more positive attitude about work-life integration is a gradual process, but has been shown to have significant advantages, including improved employee satisfaction levels and reduced turnover.

WHAT CHANGE AGENTS NEED TO TAKE RESPONSIBILITY FOR:

- Evaluate how an "effective worker" would be described at your company.

- Understand how happy employees are with their work and personal lives.

- Talk with employees about attitudes and work behaviors that take the joy out of work.

- Determine where the company can help solve problems employees are experiencing.

- Set a good example of work-life integration that reflects the belief that effective workers are well-rested, well-fed, physically fit, and generally happy.

- Work with employees to make changes in attitudes and work practices.

- Set higher expectations for how employees should feel about their work.

- Change the way work is structured so that more employees can love their work.

- Monitor and measure performance levels and make changes when needed.

WHAT ALL EMPLOYEES SHOULD ACCEPT RESPONSIBILITY FOR:

- Explore your feelings about whether work should be hard, easy, challenging, invigorating, joyful, fun, and so on.

- Give honest feedback to management about why work is or is not enjoyable.

- Evaluate your own goals and priorities regarding work-life integration.

- Be realistic about the types of concerns your employer can help resolve and which ones you need to take responsibility for.

- Be willing to strategize with colleagues and management about creative ways to bring joy to the workplace.

Individuality

Shedding the Layers of

Conformity,

One-Size-Fits-All

Routines, and Fixed Work Hours

Mary Lou Quinlan broke the rules.
She didn't conform.

And because of the risks she took in 1998, a lot of people came out winners. Mary Lou had been the president and CEO of N.W. Ayer & Partners (a three-hundred-person advertising agency that is part of Bcom3 Group Inc.) for five years when she decided she needed to step back and rethink her career goals. Just before her forty-fifth birthday, Quinlan realized that she had been spending more and more time on frustrating management tasks that she didn't enjoy and less time on the creative activities she really loved. An overwhelming feeling of sadness pervaded her typically energetic, enthusiastic personality. Her husband and parents told her they were worried because she seemed tired and unhappy, so when a friend suggested she take some time off, Mary Lou took the advice.

She asked Roy Bostock, chairman of Bcom3, for a five-week leave and was granted it. By the end of that leave, she had decided to step aside as CEO of Ayer. When Quinlan told Bostock about her intention to resign, he wanted to know what she planned to do next. Her goal was to start a marketing strategy business that would talk with and listen to female consumers in an entirely different way. Recognizing Quinlan's talent for leadership, Bostock convinced her to build her business within Bcom3 rather than seek venture capital and go out on her own.

That business has become Just Ask A Woman, a virtual organization that has successfully challenged the rules about how marketing strategies should be created. Instead of gathering data about customers from dry, boring ten-person focus groups, Quinlan plays host to groups of twenty-five women in a free-flowing discussion of their opinions using a talk show–style format. The clients are right in the room, not behind a two-way mirror, and direct interaction is encouraged. Quinlan doesn't follow a prepared script of questions; she lets the participants go on tangents that often yield the best new marketing ideas.

Mary Lou has no regrets about her decision to opt for creativity and content over being at the top of the hierarchy. Just Ask A Woman is structured as a virtual organization where a small team of four full-time employees are wired to a wider ring of experts who work as free agents. Quinlan builds relationships with experts who are well-rounded people that bring a unique perspective to the specific project at hand. Because these free agents tend to work faster and are more committed to the work, Quinlan finds she needs fewer senior producers, assistant producers, and writers on assignments now. She is happier dispensing with bureaucracy and getting things done quickly and effectively—which has obvious benefits for clients, too. She's back to enjoying time with her husband, family, and friends at their weekend home in Bucks County, Pennsylvania, just ninety minutes away from her Manhattan apartment.

Quinlan has the freedom of a free agent combined with the support of a large organization. Bcom3 found a way to let a talented ten-year veteran take on a new role within a traditional organization rather than lose her.

In the industrial era, factory output could be improved by minimizing the idiosyncrasies of manufacturing workers so that they almost became interchangeable parts meshed into the system. In the knowledge economy, workers' individuality can sustain a company's competitive advantage. According to Bartlett and Ghoshal, "The most basic task of corporate leaders is to unleash the human spirit, which makes initiative, creativity, and entrepreneurship possible."[1] Many knowledge workers still conform to a routine that was based largely on manufacturing work. Even though most employees no longer need access to heavy machinery, there is still a strong attitude that working the same hours in the same place is the best way to perform solo or collaborative work. Teamwork has received so much attention that the contribution an individual makes to an organization gets obscured. Often, the unique qualities of each person get buried beneath the bureaucracy of the traditional company. Fortunately, that didn't happen with Bcom3 and Mary Lou Quinlan. But as Quinlan has observed, "The ego of the parent company has to be strong enough to let people test new, nontraditional roles." These new roles include leading a virtual organization or testing out a new way of working while performing the same job. In both cases, management needs to broaden its view of work and the function of the individual.

Uncovering Individuality Through Remote and Mobile Workstyles

The most significant obstacle to individuality in the corporate environment is the mind-set that there is one right way (and only one right way) to perform work successfully. For years, management has enforced a routine that requires workers to commute to an office location where they work for eight or more hours a day, five days a week. In fact, this is not the most productive routine for everyone. But it would be just as shortsighted and limiting to mandate that all employees must work from home on a full-time basis. Even working from home for just part of the week is not the best solution for all workers. That's why it is important to let employees decide for themselves where and when to work and to recognize that there are several different types of workstyles that can be productive.

The Job Activities Analysis Survey: Part 1 (see the chapter on Principle #2: Trust) gives us a good idea of the ratio of solo work to face-to-face collaborative work we perform. The total amount of time we spend on solo work is made up of activities such as phone calls and independent work on a computer (or using other tools) or reading reports and other documents. The percentage of time for solo work varies considerably depending on job responsibilities, but even the most team-oriented knowledge workers spend at least one-third of their time working on their own. This is the work time that could be better leveraged by letting each employee choose the best setting for that type of work. The appropriate place for face-to-face collaboration (whether formal or informal) should continue to be agreed upon by the participants and may be the office, a client site, restaurant, conference center, or other location.

I have defined three basic types of solo workstyles based on workplace preference: those who are more comfortable at home, those who prefer the office, and those who enjoy a public setting like a café, restaurant, or outdoor area. Interviews with all types of workers and a survey I conducted of more than five hundred Autodesk employees revealed a strong relationship between these three solo workstyles and where people preferred to study when they were in school. Those who now perform a significant portion of their solo work from home usually studied in their dorm room, apartment, or home. Generally, workers who have the freedom to work where they want yet still gravitate toward an office environment for their solo work preferred to study in the library. Students who spent a lot of time studying in the student union, coffee shop, or an outside area on campus have probably found similar settings where they can set up a laptop and work for a while.

Why is this important in the virtual workplace? For most knowledge workers, college was their first experience of having the freedom to choose where and when to work. For many, college was the only time in their adult life when they had that level of autonomy. Conforming to the traditional corporate 9-to-5 routine has left many workers without a good sense for where and when they would perform best. Reaching back to remember our habits in college can shed light on where we would be happiest doing our solo work now. Think back for a moment: when you were in school, where did you prefer to study? When did you prefer to study? Why did you choose that place and those times? What did you like about it? Keep these reasons in mind as we review the three types in more detail to understand the differences between them and get a sense of the implications for you and your employees.

The next three stories profile individuals who exemplify the type of worker who prefers each of the three workstyles, followed by a discussion of the relevant input received from the Autodesk survey. Autodesk, a leading developer of design software and multimedia tools, is headquartered in San Rafael, California. It was a good company to study because nearly all of the 3,100 employees have had the freedom to choose where and when to work since its founding in 1982. According to Walt Spevak, senior director of corporate real estate at Autodesk, the company's "Future Work Now" initiative is designed to encourage and enable employees to work from home and other off-site locations.

Solo Workstyle Type 1: More Comfortable at Home

When Kelley Dallas graduated from the University of Tennessee in 1993, she went from studying in a dorm room to working out of her home as a salesperson for Armstrong World Industries. She'd never known the "structure" of going to the office for an eight-hour workday and after two months of training, she was relocated to Chicago (a city she had never even visited before). She had to make the transition from college to work, get used to a new city, and figure out how to work on her own. Dallas learned a lot from the other, more experienced staff assigned to the Chicago area about how to provide the best service to clients and how to organize her own schedule.

Her typical week started by using Monday to get organized. She'd work from home making phone calls to set up appointments for the week, doing paperwork, or planning longer trips to see clients that required an overnight stay. Usually, she'd be up by 7 A.M. and would make all phone calls in the morning since many of her clients were construction contractors who started work at 7:30 A.M. Kelley knew herself well enough to know that late afternoons were not her most productive times so some days she'd exercise at the local health club or run errands during that time. Then, she'd get back to work in the evening, another of her peak performance times, sometimes doing her best work from 10 P.M. to midnight.

The other four days of the week she usually had client appointments and her day would start at about the same time, she'd check voicemail and e-mail, shower, have breakfast, and then get on the road (after rush-hour traffic had subsided). At first, Kelley went to client appointments with colleagues or her manager and she would spend about half a day every two weeks at the local Armstrong sales office or showroom where she'd make copies, pick up samples, and talk to her manager. Eventually, Armstrong closed the sales offices and had managers work from home as well. After that change, she would spend time with teammates and her manager either going on sales calls together or meeting three or four hours every other week at colleagues' homes, in coffee shops, in the atrium of a downtown building, or other public places.

During the seven years Dallas was with Armstrong (before going back to graduate school), she relocated from Chicago to Milwaukee and then to San Francisco. For many of her college peers, the workplace was an important part of their social life, especially if they had moved to a new city after graduation. Did she find her independent workstyle lonely or isolating? No. Like many salespeople, Kelley is very gregarious and welcomed the challenge of creating a new network of friends in new places. She joined the local co-ed sport and social club, and even if her territories were in suburban areas, she would live downtown where there were more young people and after-work activities.

The more experienced she got, the more comfortable she became with her own routine. As long as client satisfaction remained high, she enjoyed the flexibility of running personal errands between meetings (even though her friends who worked at more traditional jobs thought she should feel guilty). Dallas was maximizing her productivity through scheduling. For instance, some of her colleagues were early risers who would meet with clients at 7 A.M., but since that is not the best time of day for her, Kelley would schedule her first meeting for later in the morning. Having clear goals and good performance measures kept her dedicated to her work without overworking. Kelley and her teammates would set goals together and hold each other accountable by discussing progress in those biweekly meetings. On her own, she felt good about what she had accomplished each week when, for instance, she had successfully established appointments that were project-related and resulted in specifications, she had helped customers work through issues, and her sales numbers were on target. While there were no formal surveys to measure client satisfaction, she and her manager would make frequent visits to clients to get their feedback on the service they were receiving.

The best part of working remotely for Kelley Dallas was that she had total control—there was no one looking over her shoulder or micromanaging her. She felt trusted. And that was motivation enough for her to be a top performer.

Kelley Dallas is typical of people who prefer situations where they can do some of their work from home. They generally like to integrate their work and personal lives, switching back and forth several times a day between their job-related work and housework, hobbies, or other personal activities. They like the privacy working at home allows, and they really appreciate having the flexibility to check e-mail before breakfast and just before they go to bed. They work when they are feeling most productive. They take breaks from work to do the laundry, garden, or go for a bike ride, and they enjoy being part of their neighborhood and community. The boundary between work and personal life is intentionally blurred.

In the Autodesk survey, 62 percent said they preferred to study in their dormitory, apartment, or home when they were in college. When asked why they chose these environments, the respondents reported that they liked being able to have complete control over the environment (lighting, music, temperature), take breaks for sports or other activities, work whenever they wanted (even at unusual times), have access to food, get other tasks such as laundry and cooking done while studying, avoid going out in bad weather, stop and start without having to close everything up and reopen it later, have no commuting time, and dress comfortably. In general, most said there were fewer distractions in their dorm, apartment, or home. Some of the representative comments included "I was comfortable in my surroundings with music in the background and no interruptions," "I always feel better in a quiet, relaxed environment where my stresses don't feed off other people's stresses," and "Work was always available. Ideas could be acted on immediately."

Solo Workstyle Type 2: Go to an Office for Solo Work

When Michele Foyer decided to start her own communications firm, she did what she thought every free agent did (especially in San Francisco)—she set herself up to work from her apartment. She had the freedom to work in whatever way she wanted, so she should work from home, right? Foyer had left corporate life so she could dispense with the activities that were "not essential to the task at hand." These distractions from the real work included the office politics, the dress codes, and the commute between home and office.

After a while, she realized that she missed the visual stimulation of commuting—seeing new things she wouldn't otherwise pass by. She also found working from home too lonely and isolated even though she spent some of her time out visiting with clients. Finally, after about a year, Michele had to admit to herself that running her business from home just wasn't working out for her; that was a big surprise and disappointment. It felt like she was going against the grain of the trend toward working from home. At first she worried that her only alternative would be to go back to a corporate situation, but she really didn't want to give up the freedom and flexibility of being on her own. Then she tested some other workplace options. She tried sharing space with a client and then working alone in her own leased office space. Finally, she discovered a situation that works very well for her: she rents office space that is large enough for her to share with another person in a building that offers support services for small business tenants—copy and mail services, conference facilities, and tech support. Her current officemate is a journalist from France covering Silicon Valley trends. Even though the work they do is quite different, Foyer enjoys the intellectual stimulation and the diversity of hearing another point of view.

Now she can walk or ride a bus to her office (either way, it takes about forty-five minutes from home to office). She has a great view of the hills and the city and is in a hot neighborhood in San Francisco where many Internet and multimedia companies are located. Foyer follows a pretty regular routine where she goes to the office each weekday at about the same time. While she does about 10–15 percent of her work from home, she only works there in the evenings. Sometimes she takes her laptop with her to work in a café near the office or she goes to a nearby museum or bookstore when she needs a break.

Michele has been the principal of Foyer Communications since 1994 and has built a successful, creative practice. The process of finding the most productive work situation has taught her a lot about herself and what she needs to perform well. When she was in a corporate setting, there were too many people and she craved being alone. When she was alone, she needed more contact with other people. She's found a nice balance now, but recognizes that her needs may change over time and she will continue the refining process to ensure peak performance.

Michele Foyer exemplifies those workers who prefer to do their solo work in an office setting. This helps them maintain a separation between work and personal life, which is key to their productivity. It enhances their motivation and performance to be surrounded by other people engaged in similar activities. Even though most office environments are not as quiet as a college library, those who prefer these environments have a lot in common.

In the Autodesk survey, 24 percent of the respondents said they had preferred to study in the library, lab, or studio when they were in school. They appreciated the fact that they couldn't be distracted by the phone, television, food, or housework and they could study uninterrupted. The environment set the tone for the activity. Their own words give us great insight into these study habits: "Everybody was doing the same thing as me—studying," "It's like going to work—when you're at the library it is time to study," "I liked to finish my work at school and feel free of homework obligations once I got home, so I could pursue my other interests," and "I needed a change of location to focus on studying (as my 'office' provides now)."

Solo Workstyle Type 3: The Coffee Shop Regular

Jeff Mauzy works in three types of places when he is not working at client sites. A principal with Synectics, Mauzy and his fifteen colleagues consult with corporations on creativity and innovation techniques and travel about 50 percent of the time. On nontravel days, he starts the day by working from his apartment in Cambridge, Massachusetts. After getting through his "must do" list of phone calls and e-mail messages, he settles in to write proposals or work on the book he's authoring about creativity. Most days, from around 10 A.M. until noon, he camps out at a coffee shop about a mile from Harvard Square, where he gets some of his best writing done. The other regulars who hang out there at the same time are of "like philosophical mind" and include writers, psychologists, and physicists. Jeff finds that it is comforting to have others around in a setting where interaction can be controlled. It is obvious when someone is lost in work and does not want to be disturbed. Discussions with this diverse group of people have added new dimensions to Mauzy's thinking and writing about creativity and innovation. The coffee shop fulfills a need for affiliation and is a good option between the isolation of his home office and the organization's office where there is sometimes "too much affiliation."

Although Mauzy appreciates the opportunity to be with "like professional minds" at the Synectics office, he finds that sometimes there is too much gossip that would be distracting if he worked from there on a full-time basis. These days he goes to the office (where he does not have a dedicated workspace) specifically to interact with his colleagues. Typically, Jeff goes there in the midafternoon and sets himself up in one of the shared offices or meeting rooms arranged as large living rooms, or in the café. The Synectics office is used for staff interaction, facilitation of innovation workshops with clients, and as full-time work space for the support and administrative staff. Since the consultants spend so much time traveling or working from other locations, none of them have their own offices anymore. He spends a few hours talking with colleagues before going across the street to work out at the gym. Eventually, he heads back to the office in the evening when it is much quieter and he can get more work done in a focused way. In total, Mauzy spends about 10–15 percent of his work time at the Synectics office.

Jeff Mauzy is a good example of the third major type of worker, the one that gravitates toward a coffee shop, restaurant, or other public setting to do solo work. When they were in college, you would have found these people in the student union, local café, or an outdoor area around campus. They prefer to be surrounded by background noise and activity that does not relate directly to them or the work they are doing. Although it is not like being at the office where chances are they'd be around colleagues they know, most of the "coffee shop workers" report that there is an opportunity for social interaction if they want it.

In the Autodesk survey, 14 percent of respondents said their first choice was to study in the student union, a coffee shop, an outdoor area, or some combination of similar places. Their reasons for choosing these places included "Moderate level of random noise in coffee shop was less distracting than isolated tiny noises in a library," "Café gave me privacy while lessening the sense of isolation," "It lacks the distractions you find at home, but there is access to a snack and coffee," "Small amount of hustle and bustle in cafes creates effect of 'white noise,'" "An ideal outdoor area provides me with a range of relaxing distractions allowing the mind to wander while contemplating the task at hand," and "The feeling of less constriction seems to free up my thought processes. Additionally, background noise in outdoor areas seems less intrusive."

What Is the Value of Understanding These Three Types of Solo Workstyles?

All three types have one trait in common: when they need to concentrate on solo work, they seek out the place that has the fewest distractions. Where they differ greatly is in what they perceive to be distracting. A distraction to one person may be a convenience or source of stimulation to another. There are no right or wrong choices here, just differences in perceptions and preferences.

We need to recognize that it would be nearly impossible to design one corporate workplace that would satisfy everyone's solo workstyles (unless we went back to the old concept of a company town). Even if you gave a dorm room–studier a private office at work where they could play their own music, control the lighting and temperature, and wear whatever they wanted, they would still be happier doing their solo work at home. Why? Because in a corporate workplace, you can't give a person the ability to work whenever an idea occurs to them (including the middle of the night) or garden in their backyard when they hit a roadblock in their work (unless they live really close by). Likewise, it would be tough to find a way to make working at home the most productive arrangement for a library-studier. Blurring the line between work and home life causes stress for these people no matter how distinct the separation between the home office and the rest of the house. They would have a greater tendency to overwork, feel isolated, and have trouble getting motivated to work in a home office arrangement.

Well-designed corporate campuses that offer outdoor areas, traditional work areas, and cafeterias and coffee bars could certainly provide comfortable solo work places for library-studiers and coffee shop–studiers. But does that mean that these non-dorm studiers are condemned to long commutes to the corporate office in order to be productive? No. People who liked to study outdoors or in public settings could probably find a place closer to home that fits their requirements for the ideal place for solo work. With the right equipment, they could be very productive. Library-studiers who want to shorten their commute but are not productive at home are perfect candidates for using a telework center. This is an alternative work site located closer to where employees live (usually in a suburban area if the main office is downtown) that provides a professional work environment for those days when a worker does not need to go to the assigned work site for meetings or other collaborative activities. (Telework centers are described further in the chapter on Principle #8: Workplace Options.)

Some managers may fear that if they let employees do their solo work in the most suitable location, the corporate offices would become ghost towns occupied by a few library-studiers. First, remember that we are only addressing solo workstyles. All types of workers would still go to their assigned work site or client location for face-to-face collaborative work. Even though the majority of Autodesk survey respondents (62 percent) characterized themselves as dorm room–studiers and 90 percent said that their current job responsibilities permit them to do some work from home, on average they only spend 13 percent of their time working from home. In general, 67 percent of the respondents reported that they spend some time working from home during regular business hours, but a much smaller number (22 percent) work from home for one or more days per week. Many Autodesk employees are software developers, architects, and engineers; their work is highly team-oriented and requires frequent formal and informal collaboration in person. They need to be at the office to accomplish their work.

While all the respondents reported a high level of satisfaction with the workplaces they use now, the highest levels of satisfaction were found among those who spent 60 percent or more of their work time at home and described themselves as dorm room–studiers. Even though their work is highly collaborative, there are probably some Autodesk employees who are performing solo work at the office that they would prefer to do at home. When work is very team-oriented, it is not unusual for an employee to attend a scheduled meeting every day of the workweek. If it is easier to commute to the office for a whole day rather than a partial day (just to attend a meeting), people who would rather do their solo work from home often end up working at the office between meetings. This makes it hard to optimize solo work time. Autodesk has discovered one way to get around this obstacle. At the San Francisco office of Autodesk's Discreet division, the leader declared Wednesday and Friday to be "no meeting days." Since these days are set aside for solo work, employees can spend the whole day working from home if they want. They know they won't miss out on a meeting by not being in the office. The survey showed that, on average, employees of the San Francisco office spend 37 percent of their time working from home, which is significantly higher than the 13 percent average for all sites.

The freedom to work where and when you are most effective is an integral part of the Autodesk culture (as is bringing pets to work, dressing casually, and having no regularly scheduled office hours). The company describes itself as one where "we honor individuality and foster diversity," which it believes "fuels our creativity as a company."[2] This culture has earned Autodesk recognition as one of the "100 Best Companies for Working Mothers" by *Working Mother* magazine and one of *Fortune*'s "100 Best Companies to Work For in America."

Why should managers take the time to bring out the individuality in each of their employees? Imagine how much potential is squandered when employees cannot select the appropriate time and place for their solo work. When we realize that there is no one-size-fits-all approach to workstyle and give employees the freedom to make smart choices about where and when to work, we reveal other benefits including creativity, peak performance, self-management skills, and improved relationships with colleagues. These four outcomes contribute significantly to an organization's ability to sustain its competitive edge. Let's look at each one in more depth.

Creativity

Teresa Amabile, a professor at the Harvard Business School who has been studying creativity since 1976, comments that "creativity is undermined unintentionally every day in work environments that were established—for entirely good reasons—to maximize business imperatives such as coordination, productivity, and control."[3] Her contention is that creativity is essential to all parts of a business (not just research and development or marketing) and can flourish under the right organizational conditions. One way to enhance creativity is to give people freedom regarding process but not goals. According to Amabile, "Autonomy around process fosters creativity because giving people freedom in how they approach their work heightens their intrinsic motivation and sense of ownership."[4] But this will only work well, she warns, if the goal is clear and does not change constantly: "Employees may have freedom around process, but if they don't know where they are headed, such freedom is pointless."[5]

Jeff Mauzy, a leading expert on creativity in business, points out that while organizations see the value of creativity, they often emphasize training for teams to improve group innovation skills. He sees enormous potential in helping companies focus on the personal creativity of individuals. Mauzy writes, "Creative people have conscious and unconscious strategies and ways of thinking that help them access fresh ideas. They walk away from the problem, sleep on it, turn it upside down, think in metaphors — all patterns of thought that do not come naturally to those accustomed to working in results-oriented business environments."[6]

The freedom to change places and activities has a significant effect on personal creativity. Think for a minute about when and where you are most creative. Is it while you are sitting at your desk in front of your computer? In a conference room meeting with colleagues? Or do you come up with some of your best ideas during one of these activities?

- Driving a car
- Flying on a plane
- Listening to music
- Walking along a beach
- Showering
- Swimming

- Jogging
- Playing with children
- Cooking
- Doing housework or yardwork
- Staring out a window
- Talking with friends or family
- Meditating

Business settings and activities are not always the places where great ideas get generated. Mihaly Csikszentmihalyi, a social psychologist at the University of Chicago who has studied creativity, notes, "When ordinary people are signaled with an electronic pager at random times of the day and asked to rate how creative they feel, they tend to report the highest levels of creativity when walking, driving, or swimming; in other words, when involved in semiautomatic activity that takes up a certain amount of attention, while leaving some of it free to make connections among ideas below the threshold of conscious intentionality. Devoting full attention to a problem is not the best recipe for having creative thoughts."[7]

Sometimes creative thinking occurs during the most mundane tasks. For example, many of my best thoughts occur when I'm doing the dishes. (This book would have taken much longer to write if I had a fancy kitchen with a dishwasher!) I've noticed, though, that when I'm struggling with how to organize the various components of a presentation or something I'm writing, the answer usually comes to me in the shower (pardon the pun, but maybe it has something to do with the "flow of ideas").

Anat Baron, owner of Ducks In A Row Entertainment Corporation and founder and CEO of TravelFanatic.com, distinguishes between these "big idea" work patterns and her "get it done" mode of work. Ideas for new businesses occur in the course of her daily routine and she tries to jot them down quickly on Post-it notes, which she carries with her everywhere (even at the gym). She can't force this kind of creativity; inspiration happens when it happens. But when she has to be creative on demand, when she needs to produce a business plan, for instance, Baron has to consciously focus her attention on the task and give herself a deadline. For these tasks, she usually needs to be sitting in front of a computer. Much of this work is done at night and on the weekends from her home office because the workday is typically filled with phone calls and meetings.

The portability of technology gives some people the freedom to find even more subtle distinctions in what gets their creative juices flowing. Lisa Belkin, who writes about the intersection of jobs and personal lives every other week for the *New York Times*, works from home—where she has both a desktop computer and a laptop. She has two different contracts to write for the *Times*: the "Life's Work" column, a regular feature in the Workplace section, and special articles for the Sunday magazine section. In addition to her work for the *New York Times*, Belkin is also working on a novel. The magazine pieces take about two months to research and three to four weeks to write; she always writes those articles at her desk, in her own home office, on her desktop computer. The column and novel, though, are usually written on her laptop. Lisa finds that she writes in a more conversational tone when she sets up her laptop at the local Starbucks or Barnes & Noble or even if she pulls it into bed with her. She feels she can write more about herself and in a more intimate way when she is not in her office sitting in front of the computer.

People come up with novel ways of solving problems when they have more freedom to shape their workstyle. Phyllis Weiss Haserot, president of Practice Development Counsel, found a unique solution to her need for a part-time secretary and assistant and a part-time child care provider. When her son, Zane, started school at age three, her nanny was no longer needed full-time. The nanny had started taking typing classes and was thinking of getting a full-time office job. Phyllis suggested that she continue caring for Zane, but fill the time when he was in school by doing office work from Haserot's home office. The situation worked out so well for everyone involved that after the first nanny left, Phyllis advertised to find someone with previous office experience who was interested in the same work split. As her son got older, the ads she placed emphasized the office assistant role more and mentioned that the job also involved "picking up a child after school." Throughout Zane's childhood, even though Phyllis spent most of her time working from her outside office or visiting clients, someone was always there with him after school to prepare his dinner, review his homework, or take him to activities.

Peak Performance

Studies of teleworkers find that productivity improves when people have flexibility to adjust the time and place of work. One reason for this improvement is that they can work at their own peak performance times. Everybody has their own times during the day when they are energetic, thoughtful, or tired. Some like to get up early in the morning. Others work well late at night and prefer to sleep later in the morning. People who have a lot of control over their workstyle typically do not use an alarm clock on a regular basis. They generally get sufficient sleep and wake at a time that is comfortable for them. Employees who commute long distances to offices with fixed work hours do not have that luxury.

Again, there isn't one right answer here. You probably have a mix of early risers and night owls on your staff. According to Michael Smolensky and Lynne Lamberg, authors of *The Body Clock Guide to Better Health*, 10 percent of us are early birds, 20 percent are night owls, and the remaining 70 percent are more flexible and can be alert either early in the morning or late at night.[8] Learn to use these variations in style to your advantage. For instance, if you are on the West Coast, assign an early riser to cover coordination and communication with the East Coast. If you are on the East Coast, find a late riser to work with the West Coast.

Throughout the day, we have peaks and valleys of energy needed for work. Talk with employees about their own rhythms and how that fits with their job responsibilities. Remember Kelley Dallas, the former Armstrong salesperson profiled earlier, who arranged her schedule to make phone calls in the morning when she knew her clients were accessible. But she didn't have face-to-face meetings with clients until later in the morning when she was at her best. These seemingly small adjustments make a big difference in performance, especially when client relationships are involved.

Dallas and some of the others profiled in this chapter report that when their energy is low from a work standpoint, they don't try to force themselves to produce. Sometimes they use this time to exercise, which has two advantages: it maintains their physical fitness and overall health, and it gives them an energy boost to resume working when they are finished. It is in the organization's best interest to encourage employees to work at the times of the day when they feel they are most productive and to coordinate those individual patterns to provide the best coverage and service to clients collectively.

Self-Management

Managing oneself is one of the most important keys to success in the twenty-first century, according to Peter Drucker. He advises that knowledge workers "will have to place themselves where they can make the greatest contribution; they will have to learn to develop themselves." Drucker goes on to suggest that workers need to ask themselves, "Who am I? What are my strengths? How do I work?"[9]

This valuable self-awareness is one benefit of remote and mobile work strategies. Not only do workers discover when and where they are most productive and creative, they also learn about other strengths and weaknesses. For example, once someone gets away from interruptions at the office, they may discover that they still can't concentrate on their solo work at home or wherever they choose to work. This, then, becomes a problem that they need to solve themselves and not something that can be blamed on distracting coworkers. The office, it seems, is full of excuses for why we can't get our work done (if we are looking for excuses). But when we have more control over our work setting, it allows us to see a problem differently and the potential solutions become clearer.

Thomas Davenport, author of *Human Capital: What It Is and Why People Invest It*, discusses the value of autonomy and its impact on high investment and high returns. "Workers with the freedom that autonomy implies can formulate principles for personal behavior and then act accordingly. Autonomous workers invest more human capital than their less autonomous counterparts because they work free of restrictive rules and regulations."[10] Autonomy encourages people to take responsibility for their performance.

Edward Vielmetti, a remote worker for Cisco Systems, has learned how to use place and technology in unique ways to optimize his performance. As a consulting engineer in the office of the chief strategy officer, he collaborates with fifty or more other people in his group who are scattered throughout the country and the world and much of the communication takes place by e-mail or phone. Since he's chosen to live in Ann Arbor (where he's lived since graduating from University of Michigan in 1988) rather than San Jose (where he would have to cope with what he sees as long commutes and high cost of living), he works from a spare bedroom in his home when he is not traveling to a Cisco site. Most mornings, he takes his laptop to a local coffee shop after downloading his e-mail at home. Free from the distractions of the phone and the Internet, he concentrates on cleaning up his e-mail in-box for an hour or more. After he has responded to requests, written new outgoing messages, and sorted and deleted messages, he goes home to do work that requires a connection to the Internet and make phone calls. By that time, his colleagues in San Jose have started their workday and his manager (in Austin, Texas) is still available for real-time collaboration. His handling of two tools—the phone and the Internet—that are sometimes a distraction to him and other times provide a vital link to colleagues, demonstrates good self-management skills.

Improved Relationships with Colleagues

When workers are given the opportunity to focus on where and when they do their best solo work, teamwork and client service usually improve as much as their individual contribution. Take the case of Jerry Schrepple, who jumped at the chance to participate in the Department of Labor's Flexiplace pilot in 1994.

After using flextime for a few years, Jerry Schrepple was very pleased to try any alternative that would minimize his forty-minute commute from Arlington, Virginia, to his office in downtown Washington, D.C. As an attorney adviser on the Employees' Compensation Appeals Board, Schrepple writes draft decisions on workers' compensation issues—a task that is well-suited to being performed from home three days a week. He meets his quota (twelve cases per month) and finds time to go to the driving range or batting cage at lunch time or take care of doctor's appointments and grocery shopping during less crowded times and off-peak traffic on the roads. Since his wife works a flexible schedule as a realtor, they get to spend much more time together during the week.

But the unexpected benefit that proved to be a pleasant surprise for both Jerry and his supervisor, Valerie Evans-Harrell, was the change in relationships with his colleagues and management. Schrepple looks forward to going into work on Tuesdays and Thursdays where he shares an office with a colleague who also works from home three days a week. He doesn't get bored there anymore and rarely gets frustrated with his colleagues for interrupting him as he did when he was there forty hours a week. His two days on site are sufficient time for him to pick up new assignments, do research, and finalize reports as well as fulfill his duties as a union steward for the American Federation of Government Employees Local 12. Evans-Harrell, division chief supervisory attorney, has noticed an improvement in morale among flexiplacers, in part, she feels, "because they don't have to be here every day to deal with the day-to-day nuances of the office."

More than half of Evans-Harrell's then thirteen-person group volunteered for the Flexiplace pilot when it began and they've all been successful and more productive. They work from home two or three days a week, but come to the office on different days of the week so the entire group is rarely together. This allows her to get more work done because there are fewer employees just dropping by to ask one question. Typically, flexiplacers keep a list of questions that all get discussed with Evans-Harrell at one time when they come into the office. She's a big supporter of the Flexiplace program because it improves morale and productivity and notes that, most important, "Happier employees translate into improved service for clients."

Managers Need to Take On New Roles

If workers are managing themselves, what is the role of the manager? Employees still need managers who set goals and clear the way for individuals to do their best work. They need guidance about how much time they should be spending on their individual work as opposed to collaborating with teammates. They need help figuring out which work patterns would make them most productive.

Leaders need to give workers the freedom and autonomy to make workstyle decisions and ensure that one person does not impose their workstyle preference on another. Probably the most common example of this phenomenon in a traditional company is the early riser boss who monitors employees' arrival times and evaluates performance based on how early they get to the office. When remote and mobile work strategies are implemented, don't let a library-studier mandate that everyone has to come to the office or a dorm room–studier dictate that all employees should work from home. This is a tough new role for management: you must lead by letting go. Managers should make the transition to remote and mobile forms of work by giving employees room to test out different options, support to make mistakes, and time to ease into a new situation.

Encourage employees to shape their work context to their life context and recognize that the life context will change over time. For instance, some parents find it difficult to work at home when their children are very young and they have in-home child care. When the children go to school, parents may find it more convenient to work from home some of the time. Likewise, some single parents prefer to work from home during those after-school hours when their children are at loose ends. Then when the children go off to college, the same employees sometimes find it is too isolating to work from home a lot. For these reasons, it is important that you not lock employees into working in one particular way.

As a corporate leader, you need to think about how you can best use the freedom to work where and when you are most effective. Let's look at the workstyles of two leaders at Jupiter Communications to see how remote and mobile work has affected their own work patterns.

Marc Johnson, vice president of marketing and media research, spends about 75 percent of his time working from Jupiter's New York City headquarters. Kitty Kolding, vice president of strategic accounts, works from her home outside Denver, Colorado, for about 75 percent of the workweek. Both manage employees who are free to work where they want, but perform very different tasks.

Since 1996, the staff of Jupiter Communications, an Internet research company, has grown from 50 to over 400 employees.

Roughly 250 work from the New York City headquarters and the remaining 150 work from other locations around the world. In total, more than 60 percent of the employees have the flexibility to work where and when they are most effective. According to Amy Bromberg, vice president of human resources, the employees who answer the phones, compile press kits, and perform other administrative tasks do not have the same flexibility to work remotely as the others do. There are no formal rules or policies about flexibility at Jupiter; employees are trusted to make the right decisions for themselves. Bromberg feels this gives the company an important edge over the competition in terms of attracting and retaining the most talented employees.

Kitty Kolding manages salespeople who are expected to spend 50 percent of their time at client meetings. Most them work from home during the remaining time although they are free to use a Jupiter office if one is nearby. She enjoys working from her home office because she can control distractions more easily than in a traditional office setting. While she often works long hours, from 7 A.M. until 7 P.M., Kitty usually works in sweatpants and takes breaks to visit with her husband who works from his home office just down the hall. Since Kitty and her husband are both in sales and can work remotely, they recently moved out of the costly San Francisco area to Denver, where they prefer the quality of life. Kolding sees some of her employees as often as once a month at the conferences that Jupiter hosts for clients and she typically talks on the phone with each of her fifteen direct reports every few days. Regardless of where she is working, Kolding is very clear about how she measures her own performance:

1. *Responsiveness to my team:* That is, how quickly I get back to my people when they need me. If it's not the same day it has to be within twenty-four hours, otherwise I don't think I am doing a good job. When I am here and not traveling, I almost always make that time frame, which makes me feel good.

2. *Responsiveness to my peers and superiors:* My ability to respond to their requests/needs, to attend their meetings in person or by phone, stay in contact with all the people I need to in order to keep all my plates spinning. If I am doing this in a timely manner, I consider myself to be effective and productive.

3. *Our sales numbers:* Just a straight measurement there. I need to hit our monthly and quarterly new business and renewal business totals all the time. I can motivate my people and assist in making that happen if I am focused on it. If I'm not, our numbers suffer.

Like Kitty, Marc Johnson also feels it is important to be accessible to the twenty analysts and research associates he manages, but to do that, he needs to be in the office. His staff spends about half of their time in the New York office; the remaining time is spent with clients or working from home or another suitable location. They are a mix of early risers, commuters, and late risers who have the flexibility to figure out when and where they do their best writing. Many find they write well in the morning from home or a café and then they bring their draft research reports to Johnson to get his feedback. He encourages them to think creatively about how to work independently and sometimes kicks people out of the office if he sees that they can't concentrate in that setting. This level of freedom is valuable, Marc believes, because "it takes away the focus on anything other than results. It's clear that you don't score points by staying late or coming in early." It is also his role to support collaborative research. Since ad hoc discussions are a challenge to arrange in a company where so many people are mobile, he has organized two standing meetings on Tuesdays and Thursdays. These are used for brainstorming and presenting ideas to get feedback from the group. Participants often circulate their presentations ahead of time and usually 20 percent of the attendees call in to the meetings from remote locations.

Johnson didn't always spend the majority of the workweek at the office. Before he was promoted, his primary responsibilities as a research analyst involved generating research reports on particular Internet strategy issues and responding to client inquiries about the subjects. A lot of his writing was done between 9 P.M. and 1 A.M. at a pub next door to his apartment. But as a manager, Marc's job is to give people feedback on research instead of creating it. Since at any one time, 60 percent of his staff might be in the office, he needs to spend a lot more time there to be available for face-to-face meetings with them.

The way Johnson, Kolding, and the Jupiter staff have been working is certainly working out well for the company. In 1999 it launched a successful IPO and it continues to show good revenue increases that keep investors happy. A new headquarters lease signed in early 2000 provides expansion space for an additional 1,300 employees over the fifteen-year term.[11]

Chapter Summary: Individuality

Leaders need to uncover and support the individuality of each employee. Helping employees discover the best work pattern for themselves can yield improved creativity, performance, self-management skills, and relationships with colleagues and clients. There is no one-size-fits-all work routine: autonomy and freedom are the new tools knowledge workers will use to achieve their full potential.

WHAT CHANGE AGENTS NEED TO TAKE RESPONSIBILITY FOR:

- Create a culture where there is freedom within structure.
- Recognize that workers will be better individual contributors and better team players when they have more autonomy.
- Realize that your role as a leader will change as your employees take on more responsibility for their own work.
- Give employees room to test out different options and ease into working in a new way.

- Avoid policies and agreements that lock remote and mobile workers into fixed work schedules.

- Check in with employees often to make sure they are using the optimal work arrangement for themselves.

WHAT ALL EMPLOYEES SHOULD ACCEPT RESPONSIBILITY FOR:

- Understand the details of where and when you perform your best solo work and tailor your workstyle accordingly.

- Improve self-management skills.

- Explore new places and activities that enhance your creativity.

- Monitor your performance and rethink your workstyle when necessary.

Equality

Shedding the Layers of

Hierarchy,

Status Symbols,

and Dress Codes

A few years ago, I worked with a client whose primary goal was improving collaboration and innovation.
The leaders of this seventy-year-old company knew that to regain their competitive edge, they had to encourage creativity at all levels of the organization.

They had already taken steps to flatten the hierarchy and remove obvious obstacles to communication between executives and employees: they were moving toward a more casual dress policy, had eliminated reserved parking spaces, and were doing away with job titles. During one of the group discussions I facilitated, we were purposely pursuing some pretty silly tangents to generate more ideas about how to break down the barriers between the ranks.

Someone came up with the idea of having Friday-afternoon water balloon fights between leaders and their subordinates. The group had been getting pretty charged up about the impact of this kind of activity when the highest-ranking person in the room said, "I'd have a hard time explaining the shareholder value of water balloon fights." The room fell silent. One very courageous employee quickly replied, "How would you explain the shareholder value of giving very large, expensively furnished private offices to executives who travel most of the time?" The lively discussion that followed raised some good points about the messages conveyed by the physical setting, the value of status display, and the purpose of some of the traditional rewards of rank.

Look around your own work environment and think about your company's policies. Does rank have its privileges in your organization? Who, if anyone, has access to the following?

- Private bathrooms
- Executive dining facilities
- Reserved parking spaces
- Large private offices
- Corner offices with the best views
- Customized furnishings
- Flying first class instead of coach
- Country club memberships
- Executive health club
- Company cars

Some may think of these as rewards for working hard and climbing the corporate ladder. From a shareholder's perspective, how many of these status symbols or privileges really contribute to individual performance, team performance, or company performance? Maybe you believe that these kinds of rewards affect your ability to retain talented employees. Again, from a shareholder's point of view, how valuable could someone be if they are staying at your company simply because they don't want to leave behind their corner office? Take a moment to think about the messages being sent to your employees, your clients, and your shareholders. Consider the impact these status differentials may have on morale and collaboration.

Is your company trying to become more hierarchical or less hierarchical? Are you encouraging more teamwork or less teamwork? Is your corporate culture becoming more formal or more informal? The physical setting and system of privileges should be conveying a message that is consistent with the business direction. If your company has been moving toward a more egalitarian culture, equality should be a higher priority than status.

Why Is Equality Important in the Virtual Workplace?

A company that is still strongly tied to hierarchy and the associated symbols of rank such as office space is not one where remote and mobile work can truly flourish. Measurable results must take precedence over appearance. Many of these long-established status cues have become obstacles to free-flowing communication and teamwork; they set one group apart from another. Some of these perks keep people tied to physical space as an entitlement rather than seeing it as a corporate resource to be used wisely. Ultimately, it means that money is being wasted on expenditures that do not necessarily contribute to higher performance or morale. Successful remote and mobile work strategies typically require a rethinking of resource allocation from real estate to technology.

I am not suggesting that all employees should be treated exactly the same way or that workspaces should be bland, one-size-fits-all configurations. I am encouraging you to decide very consciously when it makes sense to differentiate. Don't continue to do things just because "we've always done it that way" or it's the way others think a company should be run. The growing numbers of free agents, virtual organizations, and Internet start-ups have challenged the conventional ways of organizing business. They share a desire to get away from the formality and bureaucracy of large, traditional companies.

Julie Chon, who joined iGoAbroad.com just as it was getting started in early 2000, had been unhappy with her corporate jobs because she felt pigeonholed into a narrowly defined role. She and her nine colleagues at this Internet company love the autonomy they have to learn new skills, discover hidden talents, and build areas of expertise. Like Julie, the other employees are young (out of college only three or four years) and enthusiastic and they treat each other as equals. When they work long hours in their down-town Manhattan office, the employees wear what they want, share a large open work area, and maintain a collegial atmosphere.

Free agent and founder of a virtual organization called the Chartered Facility Management Group, Inc., Subodh Kumar has strategic partnerships with a number of experienced professionals but no full-time employees. His colleagues work from their homes, which are located in four states in the United States (California, Oregon, Arizona, and Utah), as well as in Austria, Australia, and India. While there is no formal requirement to bring in work for the others, they all back each other up and work well together as a team on client projects. This type of organization allows Kumar to avoid all the things he hated about corporate life: wearing a suit every day, commuting during peak traffic in Los Angeles, getting bogged down in bureaucratic decision making, and wasting time on administrative overhead. He enjoys being on a level playing field with his colleagues where they share the desire to deliver strategic results for clients while having fun.

The experiences of Julie Chon and Subodh Kumar illustrate the advantages of small organizations for knowledge workers, but the same qualities can be found in a few large organizations. Let's take a look at how Cisco Systems has scaled up while avoiding some common problems of large organizations.

A Good Role Model: The Non-Hierarchical Culture of Cisco Systems

"We're all in it together" is a phrase that I've heard over and over again, in several different contexts, from employees at Cisco Systems. There is a true sense of teamwork and commitment among these workers. It is no coincidence that hierarchy and status symbols have been eschewed since Cisco was founded in 1984. Throughout its history, as it has gone from Silicon Valley start-up to a staff of more than forty-two thousand, Cisco has been through reorganizations aimed at avoiding the bureaucracy that can accompany hierarchy in large companies. When John Chambers became CEO in 1994, he led a major decentralization effort. "Chambers wanted, above all, to be closer to the customer, so he eliminated layers of management between himself and his customers."[1] He knew that giving employees more decision-making power would help Cisco keep its agility and leadership in the Internet networking market. This high level of autonomy extends to the workplace as well. More than 80 percent of Cisco's employees have the freedom to work where they want. Equipped with laptops and remote access to the network, many work from home one or two days a week.

When they go to the office, Cisco staffers are not surrounded by reminders of rank in the organization. The environment is professional, but it is also expressive of one of the most well-known Cisco qualities: frugality (there is a "frugality policy" posted on the company's intranet). The corporate offices are filled with one-size offices, one-size open plan workstations, and reconfigurable team areas. According to Marina van Overbeek, a planning and design manager with Cisco, "Managers with more than eight direct reports have the option to reside in a private office, but some decide to use it as a meeting room and choose to sit with their team in open plan. The difference in workspace size and enclosure is more about function (need for confidential conversations) than status." The CEO has the same size office as a Cisco manager.

Roughly one out of every six Cisco employees works in a nonterritorial office environment where no one has a dedicated workspace—and the number is growing daily, according to Chris Ross, workplace strategist at Cisco. Sales or sales-related personnel and tech support workers who are typically out of the office 70 percent of the time have access to shared workspaces in the field offices. Each employee has their own kiosk for files and book storage, but they do not have their own desk or chair. The field offices are planned at a 2:1 workstation-sharing ratio, but the density can be pushed higher to accommodate the rapid staff growth the company has been experiencing. Marina van Overbeek says that the goal is to use Cisco's resources rationally and appropriately—not to push people out to client sites. Fact is, there is high demand for customer-related space in the field offices and relatively low demand for dedicated employee workspace. In the New York City office, for example, there are several large training rooms in the Customer Conference Center along with three testing labs and two demonstration labs where clients can view their proposed installation.

When Cisco employees are traveling outside the office, there are no class distinctions either. Chambers's predecessor as CEO (now chairman of the board), John Morgridge, jokingly encouraged his colleagues to fly "virtual first-class" by picking up slippers and a mask as they walked through the first-class cabin on their way back to coach.[2] Morgridge felt that setting an example was important: "Someone flies first class, no one else does; he gets a suite, no one else does. You can run the company that way, but don't expect employees to be excited about it."[3] You'll only see Cisco staffers in first class if they've used frequent flyer bonuses or their own money to get an upgrade.

Cisco employees are trusted to make smart decisions about where to work, what to wear, and how to use their time wisely. The focus is on results, not appearance or status. Employees understand the formal reporting relationships because they are illustrated as part of the intranet-based staff directory. At Cisco, this organizational structure does not need to be reinforced with traditional status symbols. The result of this culture of equality is an environment where communication and teamwork flourish. "There is a strong spirit of cooperation," says van Overbeek. "Everyone bands together to accomplish big tasks. People love their work and the work is very rewarding."

From a corporate performance standpoint, Cisco Systems is a growing, profitable business. Its annual revenues have increased from $69 million in 1990 to $12.2 billion in fiscal year 1999.[4] The employee turnover rate is low, 8.4 percent,[5] which is unusual for a high-tech company based in San Jose, where competition for talent can be fierce. From the shareholders' point of view, there is also good news. Cisco went public in February 1990 at a split-adjusted price of about 6 cents; in August 2000 the stock price was hovering around $65 per share.[6]

Moving Away from Status Differentials and Toward Equality

Cisco is in the fortunate position of growing up without attachment to the traditional status symbols seen in many other companies. But what if you have to make the transition away from a conventional organization with the old trappings? What if you want to eliminate the status symbols?

Although most large organizations are not yet at the point Cisco is, throughout the 1980s and 1990s, the look of corporate America has been changing dramatically. Companies have been moving away from being formal and hierarchical to informal and more of a networked organization. The way people dress has changed, the way offices are designed and assigned has changed, and "ownership" of the work environment has changed. In each case, there were early adopters and there continue to be laggards, but there has been progress overall. Let's take a look at each change in more depth.

The Evolution of Dress Codes

Warning: If your company has not yet relaxed its dress code, don't expect to shift to remote and mobile work quickly. Think of it this way: if a company hasn't given up control over the way workers dress, how can managers be expected to give up control over where employees work? In both cases, you must be committed to the idea that results are more important than appearances. For years, it had been acceptable for the "quirky scientists and engineers" in the research and development division to wear whatever they wanted to work. Everyone else, though, was generally expected to wear a business suit to the office. In 1983, when I went to work for IBM as a summer intern, a female colleague gave me some advice about clothing that left quite an impression. (I was a graduate student at the time and for five previous summers had worked as a camp counselor, so I must have looked like I needed some direction on this subject.) She told me it was important to wear a suit jacket every day—even with a dress (luckily I didn't have to invest in five suits). The jacket, she said, would differentiate me from the secretarial staff. Until then, I had no idea that there was such a strong dividing line. Luckily, this has been changing over the past fifteen years or so.

It's not absolutely clear how the casual business attire trend got started in corporate America, but one of the earliest examples of a strategic change of dress code came from Saturn, the unconventional subsidiary of General Motors. At the Saturn plant in Tennessee it is virtually impossible to differentiate the blue-collar workers from the white-collar workers. Why? Because ever since they started operating as a company in the late 1980s, all employees have been able to wear khakis and golf shirts during the entire workweek (not just on Fridays).

Adopting a casual dress code may not seem like such a dramatic change, but at the time, it set Saturn apart from the rest of the auto industry—where the line between labor and management was reflected in the difference between casual clothes and suits. This sent a strong message internally about commitment to a real partnership between UAW and GM management. When Saturn leaders showed up for Auto Show press conferences wearing sweaters and slacks instead of suits and ties, it reinforced their external message that they intended to build and market cars in a different way. As they were searching for ways to rethink the production process for small cars, Saturn's early fact-finding team observed that "equality is practiced, not just preached" in the successful companies they visited in 1984.[7] The casual dress code is just one way Saturn has reinforced that equality.

Like many companies, Chase Manhattan Bank very gradually changed its dress code over a ten-year period. Early in 2000, the transition to a casual dress code for every workday at every Chase site was finally completed. The official policy statement begins, "In keeping with the premise that a more casual work environment mirrors the more flexible, informal organization that Chase is becoming, business casual dress is an option every day of the week including at our Corporate Headquarters at 270 Park Avenue."[8] This is big news! The change started in the early 1990s when "casual Fridays" were introduced as one of the incentives to get employees excited about moving from their Wall Street building in Manhattan to a new development called MetroTech across the river in Brooklyn. When visiting managers saw that the casual dress policy worked at MetroTech, it started spreading to other Chase locations. Eventually, the casual dress policy was extended to every day in the summer and then to all year long. The 270 Park Avenue headquarters—the last holdout—finally implemented the policy in 2000. Even though each business unit sets its own standards, employees are generally trusted to use good judgment when deciding how to dress for client meetings.

According to Cynthia Doyle, vice president, corporate human resources, "Chase is giving employees the same level of flexibility in other areas as well including work hours, job description, and career development. It's one more way we can compete with dot-com companies and others who are vying for talented workers." In addition to dress codes, Chase offers other options to help with retention. More than 20 percent of Chase's seventy-five thousand staffers use one of the following flexible work arrangements: flextime, compressed work schedule, part-time, job sharing, and work at home or telecommuting. These arrangements have been offered since the early 1990s. Flextime is still the most popular, but as awareness and comfort with telecommuting grows, more and more employees request authorization to work from home for some portion of the week.

Even though casual business attire has become acceptable in many offices, clothing choices still present a small hurdle to managers who are skeptical about work-from-home programs. For whatever reason, it makes some people very uncomfortable to think that a colleague may be working from home clad in pajamas and slippers. They feel it is unprofessional or shows lack of discipline. In an informal survey of fifty home workers conducted by June Langhoff, author of *The Telecommuter's Advisor,* only 13 percent reported wearing pajamas while the majority (62 percent) said they prefer very casual clothes such as jeans, sweats, or shorts. This is one of the real advantages for employees who spend some time working from a home office: they can dress more comfortably than they can in the corporate office. This saves them money (on the clothes and dry cleaning) and time (normally spent primping for the office). As long as workers produce the same or better results, clothing shouldn't matter. Employees should be trusted to make these decisions for themselves. A more relaxed dress code doesn't cost a company anything, but it surely goes a long way toward changing the tone of an organization.

Minimizing Status Symbols in the Office Environment

Up until the early 1980s, most corporations assigned space on the basis of rank. Each time a person was promoted, they were entitled to a larger office with more and higher-quality furniture. Some companies had an elaborate system of status symbols: managers could have one office wall painted a different color from the dull beige of everyone else's; at director level, two walls could be painted an "accent color"; at the highest levels, artwork would decorate the office walls. There were also differences concerning who was assigned to an open plan workspace versus an enclosed office. Was the person entitled to an interior office (no windows), a one-window office, a two-window office, or a corner office? Facilities managers worried when too many people were "out of standard," meaning they had moved into an office that was meant for someone of higher rank.

In 1982, when Union Carbide moved its headquarters from 270 Park Avenue in Manhattan to a custom-designed building in Danbury, Connecticut, it was one of the first large companies to successfully challenge the traditional means of allocating space and furnishings. The building was designed to give virtually every employee (there were about three thousand at the time) a private office with a window. All offices were the same size (roughly 180 square feet) and could accommodate meetings with the occupant plus three other people. Every employee had a chance to select furniture from thirty predesigned packages that varied in terms of function and image. One office type, for instance, was lime green, glass, and chrome with very little storage for files while another featured a very traditional wood banker's desk with an oriental rug and lots of bookshelves.[9]

Union Carbide's leaders had two reasons for endorsing this unusual plan: they wanted to create a more egalitarian corporate culture, and they needed to reduce the facilities costs associated with rearranging walls and furniture every time someone was promoted or a division was reorganized. (They had been spending about $1.5 million a year on these move costs at 270 Park Avenue.) The new headquarters was heralded for making it possible to "move people, not partitions." The cost of moving people's boxes when a change had to be made was far less than what it used to cost to move walls. And, most important, it was good for employees and the overall corporate culture, too. In a detailed workspace survey that I administered as part of my master's thesis research, Union Carbide's employees in Danbury reported very high levels of satisfaction with their work environment and almost no dissatisfaction with the lack of status differentials.[10] Clearly, Union Carbide leaders had succeeded in achieving their goals. It was a landmark design because it recognized that all employees need privacy and the ability to meet with small teams of colleagues and that they deserve access to daylight and views and some control over the furniture, layout, and color scheme of their workspace.

Many companies have made great strides over the last two decades in minimizing the number of different workspace sizes. Nonetheless, it is still considered newsworthy to make a radical change where employees are treated as equals when it comes to the office environment. The latest example came from Alcoa, whose then recently opened headquarters in Pittsburgh, Pennsylvania, was featured in a December 13, 1998, *New York Times Magazine* article titled, "Place: And the Walls Came Tumbling Down."[11] The title tells it all.

Alcoa's four hundred-person staff moved from a high-rise building with small floors and lots of private offices to a six-story structure where everyone received an eighty-one-square-foot open plan workstation (nine feet by nine feet) that was no more than forty-five feet from a window. The building was designed for continuous teamwork and collaboration where—according to Paul O'Neill, Alcoa's chairman, who oversaw the project—"Everyone is important. . . . Power status does not seem to me to be a very good basis for designing a space or spending money . . . I am not for that."[12]

When O'Neill reorganized the company in the early 1990s to flatten the hierarchy and encourage more teamwork, he realized that its 1950s building presented real obstacles to improved communication.[13] He hired The Design Alliance, a Pittsburgh-based architectural firm, to help him solve that problem. When it became clear early in the design process that there would be some resistance to giving up private offices, O'Neill led a bold experiment, according to David L. Ross, The Design Alliance's principal in charge of design. In 1994, four years before the entire staff would move to the new building, O'Neill, eight other Alcoa executives, and their administrative assistants moved to the penthouse floor (formerly a boardroom), which had been redesigned as a mock-up of the proposed new open plan environment. They discovered pretty quickly that a kitchen with a six-seat table became a focal point for informal conversations. They found it was easier to stop by someone's workspace and get a quick decision made than wait for a formal meeting to be scheduled through administrative assistants.

Executives weren't the only ones to evaluate the demonstration office; all employees were welcome to walk through the new test floor to evaluate the design and give feedback to the team. Ross says several features were changed in response to these reactions. They increased the translucency of some of the panels surrounding the workstations to improve privacy for those who needed it and eliminated some fully enclosed phone rooms because they were never used. Most important, for over three years the executives showed that this new work environment would be very beneficial to the operation of Alcoa and that encouraged buy-in at all levels of the company. It would have been very difficult to make a strong case for needing a private office when the leadership team had been working well in open plan.

As David Ross describes, "The workstations are designed according to what you do, not who you are." Treating people as equals does not mean treating them the same. This was not a one-size-fits-all approach to the work environment. As at Union Carbide, employees were given choices about furniture layout, type of chair, number of guest chairs, and amount of storage in their assigned workstation. They also have access to many other workspaces beyond their own workstation including team meeting areas, conference rooms, and a coffee bar with seating area on each floor, as well as a cafeteria and outdoor terrace where the tables are wired for laptop connectivity. The result is a very flexible environment that reduces the cost of rearrangement and recabling that also sends important messages about equality and openness to the staff.

Rethinking the Need for a Dedicated Workspace

Another way to foster equality is to rethink office ownership. In the late 1980s and early 1990s, accounting and management consulting firms like Andersen Consulting and Ernst & Young began evaluating the value of the traditional one-to-one ratio between employees and workspaces. Recognizing that some employees worked at client sites three or four days a week while their assigned offices sat empty, leaders couldn't bring themselves to lease even more space (to accommodate staff additions) that would be vacant most of the time. When companies like IBM, American Express, and AT&T implemented virtual office programs that improved the mobility of sales and sales support personnel, allowing them to spend more time with customers, their leaders also realized that everyone didn't need their own dedicated workspace. These organizations arrived at solutions where a mobile or remote worker had access to a workspace only when they needed it. Given names such as Just-In-Time officing, hot-desking, free address, and hoteling, these approaches were all considered nonterritorial office strategies because there were fewer workspaces than people and a way of sharing those places (usually either reserved in advance or assigned on a first-come, first-served basis). In some cases, support staff delivered files and other materials to the office an employee would be using for the day. In other cases, employees were responsible for moving their files to their selected work area. Some used in-house portable or cellular phones while others rerouted phone calls to the assigned desk.

In 1991, a Cornell research team studied the value of seven different approaches to nonterritorial offices and generally found that the arrangements were cost-effective and acceptable to the users.[14] The most successful cases were ones where the new, shared workspaces were higher quality and decidedly better than the old, dedicated workspaces. Further, they recommended, "Some of the cost savings from reduced space requirements must be allocated to providing new common areas (e.g., project, meeting rooms) and new technology (e.g., laptop computers, fax machines, car phones)."[15] Most important, they advised that employees should be involved in shaping, testing, and refining new approaches to the workplace.

Deloitte & Touche's approach to nonterritorial officing follows the Cornell guidelines and is one of the most sophisticated in terms of both the solution and the process used to develop and implement it. "SmartSpace™: It Makes Good Sense" is the motto for a strategy being put into practice by Stephen Silverstein in the New York metropolitan region. Silverstein, the director of real estate, facilities, and office services for Deloitte & Touche, was brought on board in 1997 to lead the development of a new workspace strategy that would be flexible enough to accommodate staff growth (between 1997 and 2000 headcount grew by 50 percent) and support professionals appropriately while using real estate rationally and effectively.

At the time he was hired, the New York region had a very traditional approach to the office environment. Everyone had personal workplaces except the entry-level professionals, who used a drop-in area when they were in the office. Senior managers, partners, and directors had private offices with windows; some managers had enclosed offices while others were in open plan workstations with the professional and administrative staff. Because of the rapid staff growth, some staff doubled up in workspaces. Still, at any one time, Silverstein observed that 40 percent of the space was not occupied because staff members were out at client meetings or working off-site.

SmartSpace provides virtually all of the four thousand staffers in the region access to a wide range of work settings that vary in size and enclosure, but that do not relate to status. Administrative assistants are the only employees who enjoy long-term ownership of their workspace—because all of their work is performed on Deloitte's premises. Everyone else participates in a *hoteling* arrangement where space is reserved in advance through an intranet-based reservation system. Even the partners use a system called "reverse hoteling" that makes their offices available to others when they are off-site. Professionals have their own high-end "lockers" that provide locked storage for their coats, essential files, and other work materials they need to access on a regular basis. (A lot of files have been moved to basement storage that is far less expensive.)

What makes this arrangement desirable from an employee's point of view? They've been given the tools to tailor their workspace to the specific tasks they are performing each day. In SmartSpace, professionals have equal access to a variety of well-designed collaborative and solo workspaces. There are five different workspace sizes: 24 square feet, 48 square feet, 96 square feet, 144 square feet, and 188 square feet. Some of these are fully enclosed (yes, even the 24-square-foot ones), others are partially enclosed, and some are grouped in a team arrangement. The solo workspaces (24 and 48 square feet) can be reserved for as long as six weeks at a time, depending on a person's work requirements, while the collaborative spaces (96 square feet or larger) are available in increments up to forty-eight hours. Professionals are not forced to move every day, but they have the option of changing their workspace or location as often as they want. The reservation system includes a floor plan that allows professionals to see who will be working where for the day so they can reserve a workspace near a particular colleague or team if they need to collaborate. Silverstein says people can also exercise preferences for proximity to the café, bathrooms, reception area, and other fixed features of the floor plan. The on-line floor plan also shows the furniture layout for each room, which gives employees the ability to select the best arrangement for each activity. Some of the collaborative rooms are furnished with lounge seating for informal discussions and others have a more traditional private office or conference room layout.

Professionals can also select the most appropriate location for each day's work. While every "hoteler" has an assigned locker at only one site, they are free to work from any of the sites in the region including Stamford and Hartford in Connecticut, Parsippany in New Jersey, and Jericho (Long Island) and Manhattan in New York. Depending on the location of a client site or the employee's home, it might make more sense to work from another Deloitte & Touche office for the day. Phone calls can be routed to any workspace at any site and laptops are easily connected into the network from all locations (including home).

What does Deloitte & Touche get out of SmartSpace? In addition to providing a more productive environment for work, SmartSpace is one more way for Deloitte & Touche to meet its goal of being an employer of choice. Employees have the tools and flexibility to achieve work-life balance. This is one of the reasons Deloitte & Touche has been on *Fortune*'s "100 Best Companies to Work For in America" list as well as *Working Mother*'s "100 Best Companies for Working Mothers" list.

Another benefit is that "SmartSpace breaks down the hierarchy and the feeling that 'if I can't see you, you're not working' of some managers," according to Stephen Silverstein. In this scenario, managers give up control over where their employees work (whether in the office or off-site) and become comfortable relying on the follow-me phone number system to find team members when they need them.

From management's perspective, one of the key advantages of this workspace strategy is that staff additions can be accommodated without leasing additional space, which reduces the overall space per person. This results in significant cost savings. When all of the million square feet of office space in the region has been converted to SmartSpace, Steve Silverstein estimates that the organization will have saved 100,000 square feet. This translates into a first-year cost savings of $20 million (based on avoidance of build-out costs, rent, and operations and maintenance costs for 100,000 square feet) and a total of approximately $66 million when the annual cost savings are projected over a typical ten-year lease program.

In addition to the advantages at both the individual and organizational levels, a great deal has been learned about the employees' unique work patterns through the highly participative process used to develop and implement the new workspace strategy. Silverstein's first move when he began in 1997 was to organize the Alternative Officing Steering Committee, with a dozen senior leaders from Human Resources, Information Technology, and the major business functions such as Audit, Tax, Consulting, and Change Leadership. This group met once or twice a month, depending on the phase of the project, to listen to the project team's recommendations and provide guidance and decisions when needed. Ongoing involvement from Steering Committee members demonstrated that senior management was committed to the project.

Through interviews and focus groups with all levels of professionals, the project team learned a lot about how employees worked and how those workstyles may change in the future. Based on what they heard, they categorized employees as nomads or settlers. Nomads are out of the office at least 60 percent of the time; settlers spend more of their time in the office. Overall, more than half of the workers are considered nomadic, but the mix varies by business unit and level of professional. The combination of different size spaces on each floor and at each location depends on the specific characteristics of the business units assigned there. The first groups that moved into SmartSpace were the more nomadic ones.

Early on, a strong identity was developed that linked the Smart-Space slogan and a recognizable logo with the initiative. This identity was then carried through on every announcement sent out to inform workers of the progress and is very visible on the reservation system and protocol booklets left in each room. In-person presentations are made to each group when they are beginning the process and a video has been developed to get the word out to all employees. Employees are kept informed and involved throughout the transition process. Two weeks before they move to Smart-Space (or when they get hired), employees attend a three-hour training class to learn how to optimize their use of the work environment. During the move and first week of occupancy, Silverstein and his team are on site to answer questions and help employees get acclimated. This process has led to very high levels of employee satisfaction.

The solution that Deloitte & Touche has embraced may not be the best approach for every organization, but others can learn a lot from the process and the design solution. Most important, it has been tailored to the particular workstyles and culture of that company. Deloitte & Touche staff have successfully implemented a strategy that eliminates ownership of individual workspace while giving employees access to a network of high-performance work environments.

Using Corporate Resources Wisely to Support the Virtual Workplace

Equality is a symbolic as well as a financial precept. How do you determine the best way to spend company money to support the work of your employees? Often a trade-off between investment in real estate (workplaces) versus information technology (connectivity) needs to be made when remote and mobile work is involved. When employees spend more than half of their time out of the office, you can save money on office space, but you may need to spend more on equipment or telecommunications. By changing the operating cost mix to focus more on the digital infrastructure and less on traditional physical assets, "The total value of the enterprise is enhanced by increasing the speed, agility, flexibility, and customer intimacy of the enterprise," advises Michael A. Bell, research director of GartnerGroup.[16]

In most companies, the information technology infrastructure and the real estate and facilities are managed by two different groups. The costs of these two functions are traditionally monitored separately and rarely compared on the same spreadsheet. Increasingly, as mobile and remote work options become more prevalent, we need to change the way we track and make choices about how money is spent in order to enable employees to do their best work and to retain them. The Institute of Management Accountants (IMA) has endorsed a system called "Workpoint Cost Accounting" that was developed by the International Development Research Council, KPMG Peat Marwick LLP, Peter Valentine of Comsul Ltd., and Commonwealth Advisors. The premise of the Workpoint Cost approach is that "The worker is supported by a combination of elements for which management is challenged to find the right blend beyond just the scope of real estate-related decisions."[17] It shifts the focus to the individual worker and away from buildings or equipment. This system also makes it easier to see the trade-offs between real estate and information technology and to build a good cost model for mobilizing the workforce.

"Workpoint cost is the total cost incurred by an organization to provide space, technology, equipment, support, connectivity, and other services to its workers in order for them to complete their operating tasks and support their business unit mission."[18] There are five categories of costs: direct space, direct support and equipment, connectivity, indirect space, and indirect support and equipment.

The originators of Workpoint Cost Accounting developed a model that calculated the average costs for an office-based employee as compared to an employee who spent the majority of the week working from home. In both cases, the total annual cost per employee came to approximately $25,000. However, the distribution of those costs varied significantly. For instance, remote workers consumed fewer dollars in the direct space category because they used a shared work area when they went to the office. However, their connectivity charges were higher because they had an ISDN line to their home that was paid for by the company. They also had higher indirect support charges because of their use of the expanded information technology help desk.

This type of cost model can be useful in determining the current total cost to support an employee—it is helpful to know whether your company is spending more or less than the average of $25,000 per year per employee. The information can then inform decisions about how much money will be spent to support remote and mobile workers in the future. Most companies find a way to provide equipment for home offices. They may let workers take older desktop equipment home, supply them with a laptop, or purchase a new desktop system for home use. Most companies are also willing to pay for an additional phone line or high-speed line into employees' homes. But fewer provide desks, chairs, and file cabinets for home offices.

Regardless of what is provided by the company, most corporate leaders want to see some kind of payback for these investments. Usually, the major cost savings come in the form of reduced real estate expenditures. But as companies engage in the war for talent, they see that there is significant payback in the form of reduced turnover and increased employee satisfaction and productivity. When figures are attached to these "soft cost" issues, the benefits of remote and mobile work always outweigh the costs. To build a comprehensive cost model, you must explore all the potential costs and benefits and be willing to make trade-offs between them. The goal is to use corporate resources rationally and to invest in technology and workplaces that enable all workers to be effective.

Chapter Summary: Equality

Remote and mobile work can thrive in a culture where employees are treated as equals and resources are used rationally to support high performance rather than reinforce rank in the hierarchy. Leaders need to help employees view workspace as a tool rather than an entitlement and learn to make smart choices about investments in technology versus real estate.

WHAT CHANGE AGENTS NEED TO TAKE RESPONSIBILITY FOR:

- Focus on performance and not appearance.

- Evaluate whether existing status differentials add value or not and eliminate the ones that are superfluous.

- Don't ask others to give up status symbols until leaders set the example first.

- Trust your employees to dress appropriately for the work they are performing.

- Evaluate the total cost of supporting the work of an individual employee in terms of direct and indirect infrastructure expenditures.

- Analyze the advantages of spending money on technology versus on physical settings.

WHAT ALL EMPLOYEES SHOULD ACCEPT RESPONSIBILITY FOR:

- Be honest with yourself about what contributes to your productivity as opposed to conveying status.

- Talk with management about the tools and support you need to be a high performer.

- Be willing to give up "ownership" of workspace if you use it less than 50 percent of the time.

Dialogue

Shedding the Layers of

One-Way Communication,

Misunderstandings,

and Idea-Hoarding

Open, honest communication is important in any company, but it is essential in a world of remote and mobile work.
Let's consider for a moment the purpose of communication in a business setting.

The most important reasons are to give direction or inspire action, to generate a good understanding of the business context, to avoid "reinvention of the wheel" and to learn from others' experiences, to give and receive input that will improve decision making and its end result, and to build and maintain relationships. In general, the goal is to optimize individual performance and the contribution each makes to others' work. The premise is that employees

will be more motivated and better equipped to do a good job if
they have accurate information and a forum for collaboration.

A common fear about remote and mobile work is that it will
cause a breakdown in communication and teamwork at a time when
more is needed, not less. Corporate leaders want to increase collaboration because they believe it will result in improved innovation, shortened time to market, and ultimately in higher profits.
These are all very important goals, to be sure. It's absurd to imagine any manager saying, "We need to limit communication," or
"There is too much knowledge sharing going on around here." Unfortunately, corporate leaders often have only a vague idea of how
improved collaboration should look and feel. Because of this lack
of clarity in their own minds, they do not convey explicit goals to
employees in terms of expected behavioral changes—and therefore cannot measure the effects.

Managers typically fill this information vacuum by latching onto
business practices and trendy tools that they think will improve
communication, but may or may not be useful. They may try
scheduling more formal meetings and inviting more participants.
But if these are not well-run meetings where each attendee has a
clear role, aggravation and wasted time could be the only outcomes.
Some managers try to improve communication by increasing the
amount and frequency of the information they send out through
newsletters, e-mail, videotapes, and so on. In some cases, employees get so overwhelmed by the amount of data that they stop reading any of it. Management may initiate a "suggestion box" program
or other strategy designed to encourage employee input. Often,
these strategies get little response and the few employees who do
send ideas or complaints grow frustrated when they do not get any
feedback from management or see changes being made to address
the issue. Some companies have tried radically changing their physical office space, believing that taking down walls to create an open
plan environment will result in more open communication. When
not implemented carefully, however, open plan offices can have
the opposite effect: I've visited workplaces where staffers wear head-

phones all day to avoid distractions and noise. Some companies have invested in expensive groupware or other technology tools designed to facilitate exchange of information. Many of these systems are grossly underutilized and end up becoming sophisticated e-mail programs. The problem with these various attempts to facilitate communication is that while they may boost the flow of information, they rarely increase the amount of valuable dialogue among workers in a comprehensive, systematic way. This is where real progress can be made.

What Is Dialogue and Why Is It Important in the Virtual Workplace?

Dialogue is two-way communication where positive and negative issues can be discussed freely. The ability to convey and listen to constructive criticism and talk about mistakes and doubts are essential elements of dialogue. The give-and-take that is required does not mean the communication has to be in person or even happening at the same time; dialogue can be asynchronous and still be successful. Traditional one-way communication techniques can be easily transformed into opportunities for dialogue. For example, most corporate announcements sent to all employees by memo or e-mail could be accompanied by e-mail addresses or phone numbers of contacts who can answer questions and take input in response to the message. If the contents of messages are truthful and there is a genuine commitment to an interchange of ideas, dialogue can flourish.

Unfortunately, in many organizations, employees have learned over the years that positive news is conveyed by management through official channels and negative information or what some consider "the real story" is carried over the company grapevine. When prospective remote workers voice concerns about missing out on "informal communication" when they are not in the office, in part, they are worried about being too far away from the unofficial news network. Usually, there are particular employees who seem to know more than others about what's really happening (or are at least willing to guess). The information exchange happens in person at the coffee machine, in the restrooms, by the smoking area, or as employees pass each other in the hall. Of course, some of what we call informal communication helps build relationships or is job-related, but some of it is gossip and rumor. Many teleworkers say they are relieved to get away from the office rumor mill because it is distracting and unproductive. But until all employees trust they are getting the whole story from management, people will rely too much on going to the office to be fully informed and remote and mobile work strategies will not be used to full advantage.

If telework is implemented before these communication problems are corrected, remote workers will always feel they are missing out on something (because they are) and will gradually become more and more disconnected from the organization. Eventually, teamwork will suffer when virtual workers are not connected through a strong system for dialogue, thus reinforcing management's original concerns about a breakdown in collaboration. Let's be clear: remote work doesn't cause communication problems, it makes existing problems more apparent and exacerbates those underlying difficulties.

What Are the Obstacles to Dialogue in Your Company?

The following barriers to honest, two-way communication in a business environment are important to overcome before implementing remote and mobile work strategies:

- *Avoidance of negative discussions*—information is withheld or massaged so that a positive image is conveyed at all times and there is a reluctance to disagree or raise concerns.
- *Unclear messages*—misunderstandings happen when goals are not explicit and language is not precise.

- *Absence of a communication strategy*—confusion results from lack of clarity about what information is valuable to share, with whom, and how often, and about the role that should be played by each person in the communication process.

- *Idea-hoarding*—when management does not share ideas openly, neither do employees, especially if information is equated with power.

- *Fear of employee involvement*—lack of commitment to participation due to concern that opening discussions to a larger group will slow down the decision-making process and waste employees' time.

- *History of negative experiences*—failed attempts to engage employees in dialogue in the past, such as breaking a promise to guarantee anonymity or punishing an employee who admits a mistake, remain in the "corporate memory" for a long time.

- *Emphasis on hierarchy*—status symbols that reinforce distinctions act as barriers to communication (this is covered extensively in the chapter on Principle #5: Equality).

Not all of these hurdles will be found in any given company (and there may be additional ones in your organization), but it's important to know which ones you're dealing with. These potential obstacles, combined with all the positive aspects of how communication is handled, collectively form what I call the "climate for communication" in a company. One way to assess the climate in your organization is to think about how messages are conveyed to staff and the typical reaction. Consider the gap between what is said by management and what is heard by employees. For example, imagine how your staff would interpret the announcement, "Starting next month, employees will have the freedom to work where and when they are most effective." Here are some possible reactions:

"Yeah right, my manager will never let me out of his sight!"

"Uh oh, now they'll want us to work all the time."

"I bet management wants us to work from home so they can close the offices and save money."

"Hmmm, I wonder if this is another part of that empowerment initiative they talked about last year. . . ."

"That's great! Our leaders trust us to make the right choices. I can't wait to hear more about it."

How many employees would feel comfortable asking: "Why are we doing this?" or "What will this mean for me personally?" Both would be legitimate follow-up questions to this very brief message. Of course, the post-announcement conversations would be affected by who delivered the message and how it was conveyed, but thinking this through should give you a sense of the attitude employees have about official communication. Now put this example in a larger context. Can you think of situations where the gap between what was said and what was heard was fairly large? Is there a consistent pattern of misunderstandings and frustration? Envision a continuum representing the range of climates of communication where one end signifies open, honest dialogue and the other extreme represents a cynical, secretive corporate culture. Where would your company fall along that scale? Here are four descriptions of points along that continuum. Which one comes closest to defining your organization's climate for communication?

- *Type 1:* Comprehensive information is shared with everyone on a timely basis, and participation, questions, and constructive dissent are actively encouraged. Employees consider themselves well-informed about the business and their own performance; teamwork and collaboration flourish.

- *Type 2:* There is talk of an "open door policy," but in reality, management only listens to positive comments and avoids negative feedback. Likewise, a positive spin is put on all messages to employees and bad news usually shows up first in the external press. Employees rarely learn from the mistakes of others.

- *Type 3*: Information is distributed to employees at the last minute; there are few opportunities for involvement in decision making or even having a dialogue about the message. Time is wasted "reinventing the wheel," but there never seems to be enough time to collaborate up front.

- *Type 4*: Participation is discouraged. Decisions are made by only a few senior leaders and there is a lot of infighting between divisions. Management keeps information from employees, and rumors are rampant.

Within one organization, there may be several different climates for communication depending on the leadership style within a particular department, division, or subsidiary. Even so, you can probably define one overall climate for the company. Type 1, where dialogue thrives, should be the goal of any business, but it is critical for organizations that embrace remote and mobile workstyles. If you think that Type 1 is unrealistic and not feasible, consider the two organizations described in the next case study. Both are good examples of a Type 1 climate where bad news and good news are discussed openly within a virtual environment.

Role Models for Healthy, Valuable Dialogue

Will Pape is a major advocate of virtual companies (having founded two of them since 1982), but he warns that "there must be strong business reasons to have staff geographically separated."[1] In both cases, he and his fellow founders opted for proximity to customers rather than co-location of employees, and it proved to be a smart business move. Pape advises that having made that business decision, "Leaders have to make compensatory culture changes to maintain staff cohesion in a virtual workplace." Commitment to open, two-way communication is a crucial element for achieving success.

Will Pape was one of the founders of VeriFone, an organization that grew to a $475 million, four-thousand-person enterprise as a "company without a headquarters" before being acquired by Hewlett-Packard in 1997. When the five founders of VeriFone set out in 1982 to become the leaders of the transaction automation industry, they knew they'd have to do something different to beat the competition. Their first decision, to disperse themselves and their new hires to remote parts of the world so that they were close to clients and emerging markets, was what set them apart.

Following the acquisition of VeriFone by Hewlett-Packard, Pape moved on to help found a new organization, AgInfoLink, Inc., that provides a certified audit trail for beef and other food products. From 1997 to 2000, the company has grown from four to fifty employees who are scattered across five countries: the United States, Canada, Australia, Mexico, and Argentina. Just like VeriFone, AgInfoLink has located employees near the people they need to meet with frequently—whether that is investors, cattle ranchers, or software programmers—and they all have the freedom to work from home or an office.

Recognizing that communication was the key to building a cohesive culture that spanned the globe, VeriFone made a special effort to keep employees informed and engaged in dialogue. One of VeriFone's most effective tools, the "Daily Flash," is being used at AgInfoLink, too. This daily update of key performance measures (in this case, sales and cattle enrollments compared with projections) is distributed to all employees via e-mail.[2] The message is a qualitative assessment by Pape of how well targets are being met; the quantitative data is sent as an attachment. The "Daily Flash" goes out first thing every morning whether it is good news or bad. Reporting wins and losses is important, says Pape, "because it enhances credibility and keeps cynicism down." In more traditional companies, management is sometimes afraid to share bad news, fearing a downturn in employee morale. Pape believes that even though bad news may temporarily raise anxiety levels among the staff, it helps everyone focus on possible solutions.[3] At VeriFone, it was not unusual for Pape to receive six or more e-mail messages a day from employees who challenged his interpretation of the numbers or posed other questions prompted by the "Daily Flash."

When it comes to information distribution, Pape adheres to a "want to know" philosophy rather than the traditional "need to know" approach. He finds that many of today's knowledge workers want to know a lot about company performance, even if it seems not to be relevant to their jobs. Staying informed through the "Daily Flash" and the weekly *Relay Station*, a newsletter that employees contribute to, reassures them that they are part of a growing organization and that they'll have a job for the foreseeable future. Pape is a strong believer that widely circulated, up-to-date information is the best antidote to productivity-sapping rumors. But he also knows that information distribution alone can not eliminate rumors—dialogue is essential. People need to be able to ask questions at any time and they need to get a quick response that they trust is accurate.

A combination of written materials and face-to-face interaction were used to build and strengthen the culture at VeriFone. The leaders took pride in publishing their mission and vision statement in more than five different languages. "The VeriFone Philosophy" was personally written by then-CEO Hatim Tyabji, and covered topics such as commitment to excellence, dedication to customer requirements, promotion of teamwork, individual accountability, and ethical conduct.[4] But a written document can't do it all. The leaders believed that they needed to be visible role models exemplifying the philosophy. Because customer interaction was the highest priority for many VeriFone employees, the leaders spent time in the field to get to know their workers and their customers. Every two months, for one week at a time, the entire senior leadership team would meet at a different VeriFone location around the world. During that week, high-level strategic issues were discussed among the leaders and face-to-face sessions were held with employees and clients in the region. At town-hall style meetings, staffers were encouraged to raise positive and negative questions about the company and the work they were doing. By example, leaders made it clear that it was acceptable to admit mistakes to colleagues and together work on solutions. Through these visits, the VeriFone leadership team sent a strong message that they were a cohesive group that respected each other and the employees.

Employees had other ways to get involved in issues that mattered to them and to voice constructive dissent if they wanted. At VeriFone, Policy Review Committees were organized periodically to evaluate and change corporate policies regarding everything from benefits to technology to travel reimbursement. People could participate at the level they felt comfortable. They could be part of the committee or could just file a comment with the committee. At any time, employees who wanted to check out a rumor or lodge a complaint could log onto the internal network and send e-mail messages anonymously. (To ensure that this system was not misused for harassment, every e-mail was automatically sent to Human Resources, too.) Depending on the issue raised, feedback from management would be given in a public forum (such as a town hall meeting or through e-mail or the newsletter) to dispel the rumor or address the concern in some other way.

At AgInfoLink and VeriFone, dialogue is not just about communication between leaders and employees or leaders and customers, it is also about strong relationships between all employees. There is solid commitment to informal interaction at all levels. Pape sees personal relationships as an important aspect of maintaining corporate culture and cohesiveness. At VeriFone, managers of remote workers were encouraged to plan social time as part of face-to-face meetings. Staying in touch with the work and non-work aspects of individuals was encouraged through use of on-line chat rooms, personal home pages that described hobbies and interests, and spouse and children's use of on-line communication systems like VeriPal (an e-mail pen pal network for employees' children). VeriFone's e-mail system was structured to allow everyone to talk directly to anyone in the company.[5]

At AgInfoLink they are also building strong relationships. Most new employees meet with at least one of the company founders so that the company vision is communicated directly. Everyone gets a directory with employees' photos and a description of each person with serious as well as funny remarks about them. There is a buddy system that pairs new hires (who have probably not worked virtually before) with a veteran virtual worker to shadow and learn how to function in a dispersed company. Spouses are invited to join employees at company dinners so that they understand the mission of this growing organization, too.

One of the most effective ways to maintain open, honest dialogue in a virtual organization, according to Pape, is for the leaders to be good listeners. Being a good listener can be a more important trait than being a good information disseminator. So, he practices "active listening" and checks to make sure he has heard a person's concerns. In group meetings, people feel free to disagree because Pape is open and does not get defensive. He also asks questions of the staff such as, "How close do you feel to where things are really happening?" and "How happy are you?" to understand how well the structure is working. Will Pape knows that if the virtual structure isn't working for the employees, it will not work for customers. He is committed to sustaining the competitive advantage of a well-run virtual organization over a traditional organization: "You can make more customer contacts and be focused on a broader geographic base instead of what is right in front of your nose. With global operations growing simultaneously, it's very hard for competitors to sneak up on you."

Creating a Good Context for Dialogue in the Virtual Workplace

The virtual structure of VeriFone and AgInfoLink forced Pape and the rest of the founders to consciously address communication from the very beginning. If your company does not enjoy the same level of dialogue as Will Pape's organizations, start the transformation by articulating a comprehensive communication strategy. When most traditional companies focus on communication, the outcome is usually more outgoing messages rather than more input coming in. Give more attention to generating dialogue with your employees, clients, suppliers, and other partners. Based on what you've learned about the climate for communication in your organization, develop a strategy to overcome the problems you've observed.

Set Goals and Implement Plans for Achieving Them

First, develop a set of guiding principles for the communication strategy that you are willing to support with action and resources. Let's consider a few examples. If one goal is "100 percent accurate information versus rumor," there must be ways for employees, customers, and other strategic partners to inform management about rumors and methods for leaders to provide accurate information in response. There also has to be a compelling reason for coming forward; stakeholders have to understand why it is damaging to have inaccurate information distributed (formally or informally). As at VeriFone, there should be in-person and electronic forums to discuss these issues and there should be a way to submit input anonymously.

Another guiding principle may be "Employees should know who their colleagues are and be aware of their areas of expertise." There are many ways to facilitate this kind of networking. Some may be more comfortable with in-person meetings while others may prefer access to Web-based directories. Both require that some time and resources be committed to informal interaction outside of the bounds of a particular team or project assignment (although people can get to know each other through formal project work). Although this has long been accomplished through company sports teams and weekly social gatherings, these are usually location-specific. If you want to get geographically dispersed workers to know each other at a personal level, more creative solutions need to be developed. I know of one company that encourages and funds hobby groups. For instance, an employee can start a special interest group devoted to fly-fishing and get employees from across the country to join. The group will have access to company equipment for developing special Web sites, e-mail discussion lists, and teleconferences to facilitate discussion of fly-fishing among its members. Then, once a year, on company time, the members go on an all-expense-paid fly-fishing trip. The rationale behind this is simple and brilliant: when you get a group of people together from the same company for any kind of activity, it is highly likely that they will discuss company business. Since the payoff may not be immediate, commitment to the original goal must be strong.

Other goals could be part of the communication strategy: "We will encourage healthy dissent," or "Everyone should have a chance to participate," or "Employees should feel their input and questions are welcome." These will be specific to each company and will depend on the existing and desired climate for communication. In any case, goals must be backed up with action, resources, and commitment. There must be measurable outcomes that get reported to stakeholders.

Define Roles

From the beginning, everyone needs to understand who should be involved and how they should be involved. Before involving others in an initiative or project, consider the following: who are the stakeholders and what role or roles should they play? The list of possible stakeholders includes

- Leadership and senior management
- Managers
- Employees
- Families of employees

- Clients
- Shareholders
- Community board members
- Neighbors
- Public
- Others

The roles they could fulfill include decision maker, adviser, message deliverer, or someone to be kept informed. In most cases, for instance, senior management plays all of these roles at some point. In many cases, the general public would only be kept informed, but this must be tailored to each situation.

Clearly defined roles help minimize concerns about participation. Making it clear that members of a task force are participating in an advisory way and will be responsible for generating a recommendation to management (rather than a decision to implement) should allay the fears of those who think that decision making becomes cumbersome when the process is opened up. Open, honest dialogue should speed up the process and facilitate better-informed decisions. It should not be used as a way to avoid responsibility for decisions.

It is normal for there to be different deliverers depending on the subject of the message to be conveyed. Be careful to avoid having one leader always deliver the good news and another the bad. Messages should come from leaders that are trusted and experienced in the subject they are discussing and people should be able to get answers to their questions from knowledgeable sources (not necessarily the deliverer). For instance, a CEO may announce a restructuring, while employees get specific information from their manager who has been briefed on the details of the new plan.

Assigned roles may change over time. It is important to define the roles in a written communication strategy and then convey those roles to all the stakeholders. Update this document as roles are redefined or reassigned.

Listen, Be Precise, and Be Consistent and Persistent

As Will Pape advised, being a good listener is one of the most important qualities of a leader. The fast pace of business today often becomes an excuse for not listening. Part of listening is checking to make sure the other person's message has been understood and not misinterpreted. Misunderstandings can be costly and frustrating. Will Pape describes the effect of rumors in the following way: "At the very least they cause people to worry about something other than their jobs; at worst they can destroy a company."[6]

Misinterpretations and rumors can be avoided by recognizing that some commonly used words and phrases mean very different things to different people. For example, *teamwork* is defined in various ways depending on the context and point of view. If three managers use the phrase, "I'd like the work environment to be more supportive of teamwork" during predesign data-gathering interviews, they may mean three totally different things. For instance, one may be thinking that the department needs more and better videoconferencing equipment to support global teamwork. Another may be envisioning a new workplace design that would enable more one-on-one, informal collaboration. Yet another may be planning to spend more time in five- or six-person team meetings and will want to see small team rooms on the new floor plan.

When using words that can be interpreted in a variety of ways, be specific and give examples. When gathering input from people, ask follow-up questions to determine exactly how they are using the word or phrase. If someone says their goal is "more teamwork," for instance, ask these types of questions to clarify the definition:

- Will there be more face-to-face interaction or will some teamwork be supported electronically?
- How much more time will a typical worker spend interacting with others rather than working solo?
- Will some employees be more affected by this than others? How will it vary?

- How many people will be on a team?

- How many teams will each person be on at any one time?

- What will the duration of the teams be? Which ones will be short-term as opposed to long-term?

- How many meetings will be scheduled in advance versus impromptu?

- Will some teams involve clients, suppliers, and so on? Will interaction happen on our site, their site, or virtually?

These types of probing follow-up questions should be viewed as useful rather than time-consuming and frustrating. Avoiding the high cost of misunderstandings can contribute significantly to a company's competitive advantage.

Clear, precise messages need to be delivered consistently to internal and external stakeholders. If employees have to rely on newspapers and television coverage of their company to get the whole story about an upcoming merger, layoff, relocation, or other major event, there is something wrong with internal communication that should be corrected. Even for lower-profile news, inconsistencies between external and internal messages can be damaging to employee morale and willingness to engage in dialogue. For example, if employees see company advertisements promoting remote and mobile work strategies to potential customers when they don't have the same level of freedom in their own jobs, cynicism grows.

In addition to being consistent, communication should be redundant. People like to get information in different ways, and it makes sense to deliver it using a variety of tools. Some absorb information best by reading it, others need diagrams and photos to fully understand a message, while still others get the most out of hearing a description of something new. Messages sink in when we receive them several times in different formats. Web-based technology gives us the ability to cater to everyone's needs.

Determine Who Should Get What Information

Deciding what types of information should or should not be shared with particular stakeholders is an essential component of the communication strategy. What you choose to share will depend on your culture and specific rules about confidentiality. Traditional policies about what is considered confidential and what can be seen or overheard by whom should be challenged when developing a communication strategy. Often, we fall into the "that's the way it's always been" mode of thinking where confidentiality is concerned. You can probably think of information that is not and should not be available to all staff—employee performance reviews and other personal information, for example. Many virtual companies find it useful to share financial data that traditional companies prefer to keep closely held. Keep in mind that if you really want people to understand that financial information, you may have to provide some training or summary explanation for them to reap the full benefits of accessibility to the information.

Ken Anderson, president of Anderson & Associates, Inc. (an engineering-design firm with more than two hundred employees headquartered in Blacksburg, Virginia), has always shared financial information with his staff. Since the company is built on an employee stock ownership plan, Anderson believes that staffers are entitled to see the books and understand the figures. On a biweekly or monthly basis, financial performance summaries go to all employees while a smaller group receives "the hard core numbers" if they have requested it.[7] The Accounting Department gives training sessions every three months so that employees understand the meaning and impact of the numbers. Especially in tough times, it is important to minimize misconceptions about income or expenditures, says Anderson.

Employees' hourly rates are posted on the intranet for all to see (there are no salaried workers). Sure, sometimes people ask the tough questions—"Why is so-and-so making more than I am?"—and Ken

Anderson has to answer them. But he would rather have that discussion than have employees waste time gossiping about it. According to Anderson, "In places where employees don't know all, the
few people who have the information have too much power."

The payoff here is that employees think like owners and ask
smart questions about why money is being spent on certain activities. Since the company was founded in 1968, there has never been
a layoff. Because trust is high, when the workload is low they decide together how to cut back on everyone's hours instead of letting people go.

Anderson's level of openness would not be appropriate for all
companies in all industries, but this case should encourage you to
think about why certain information is considered secret. There
are cases where secrecy is warranted—in the period leading up to
an acquisition or major relocation, for instance. If there are secrets
to be kept, ensure there are no leaks. Secrets getting out little by
little are the leading source of rumors. Make sure everyone who
has access to the confidential information understands the harm-
ful effects of a premature disclosure—and the ever-present risk of
such disclosure. It's useful to note that secrets often leak out unintentionally when they are discussed in a public setting such as
an elevator, restaurant, or airplane where the speakers may believe
they have privacy.

Avoid Information Overload

In some organizations, people are so well-networked that there is
no shortage of information being communicated. Chuck Sieloff,
research affiliate with the Institute for the Future, contends, "On
the one hand, the shift from information scarcity to abundance has
created unprecedented opportunities for knowledge workers to en-
rich their inputs and amplify their outputs across space, time, and
organizational boundaries. On the other hand, the shift has also
exposed their very limited capacity to take advantage of those op-

portunities, creating a form of collective frustration and anxiety which we often label 'information overload.'"[8] Some people feel that even if they could stay on top of all the e-mail, voicemail, and other messages they receive on a daily basis, they still would not feel well-informed. Somehow, the useful information doesn't always get through.

Sieloff advises that we need to shift from knowledge management to attention management by using some of the following strategies. First, determine how much information employees need to know about a particular process or product by asking, "Can we reduce the number of people who really need to understand a topic by embedding their knowledge in automated or facilitated processes?"[9] For example, most of us do not need to understand every detail of how our computer works if good tech support is available. Then, when making information available, make it as concise and targeted as possible (don't assume that everyone wants or needs to become an expert in all areas of the topic). Sieloff predicts that trusted intermediaries who can filter, evaluate, and summarize information will become more and more valuable within organizations. Defining the context of the information is just as important as delivering it and should address its source, reliability, date, and user groups, along with sources for other relevant data. Targeted distribution through self-maintained subscriber lists, for instance, can reduce the amount of e-mail sent to all employees in the company regardless of interest. Sieloff expects to see more sophisticated technology tools for building user interest profiles that understand users' individual needs and gather the appropriate information for them to read.

In February 2000, Sun Microsystems began testing a user profile system to help its sales force find the product and customer information they needed. MySales is a customizable intranet site developed by Sun that works like My Yahoo or other personalization tools used by consumers on the Internet. After the users establish their personal preferences for information, their home pages display links to company documents and external news articles that will help them do their jobs. Their customized home page will also connect them with colleagues who may offer useful information or services to the client. Many of the 3,200 Sun employees who are testing the system already see advantages in terms of reducing e-mail, minimizing time spent searching for information, and generally solving knowledge management problems.[10]

Act as a Role Model

Leaders must communicate differently if they want employees to change the way they interact with others. The following composite example illustrates how the transformation of the climate for communication must begin at the top. As a consultant to a conservative, traditional company led by a new CEO who was frustrated with communication and collaboration issues, I was responsible for defining the problem and implementing solutions to improve dialogue. I started by talking with senior leaders and all levels of employees about the problems. The CEO was convinced that more open communication was the key to turning around the financially ailing company. Since he had come on board, he had reorganized major divisions, eliminated job titles, revamped the compensation structure, and was gradually flattening the hierarchy in an attempt to remove all barriers to interaction. Unfortunately, every initiative designed to improve communication had been met with apathy or outright hostility by the staff.

In individual interviews, I asked the CEO's ten direct reports to tell me about the recent changes, why each had been initiated, and what the effect had been. Very few of them gave me the same explanation of the events or the reasons for them. Most agreed that the changes had not improved communication and teamwork. I asked them if they believed improved communication would actually solve the performance and financial problems of the organization. Not surprisingly, they did not all agree. In fact, several leaders did not even believe that the organization was in financial trouble.

The employees had even more diverse views of the situation. Through a series of discussions with groups of ten to fifteen employees each, it became apparent that the staff did not see the connection between the organizational changes and a desire to improve communication. Many felt that the changes had all been designed to show there was a "new boss in town" and that, eventually, they'd revert to the old way of doing things. Only the employees that had direct client contact were aware of business performance problems; most workers had no idea that their industry was going through a fairly dramatic transformation. As for collaboration, many felt they already worked well with others and some were struggling to get their own work done since they were spending a lot of time in team meetings. A few employees reported that they had taken up the CEO's invitation to write him with ideas about improving work processes and either they did not get an answer or they were criticized for their view of the problem. In general, people were afraid to raise negative issues with this new CEO.

When I reported the findings to the CEO, he was surprised that his top leaders were not completely in line with his agenda. In meetings, they always nodded with approval and never spoke up to disagree. This was one of the major gaps, I pointed out. Since the CEO rarely spoke directly to the staff, his message got lost because his direct reports were not passing it on. In fact, his leaders often sent the signal to their subordinates that they disagreed with the new boss. In part, this was happening because as a group, they had never agreed on the underlying problems they were trying to correct by improving communication.

The first change to be made, then, was the CEO's ability to encourage open, honest dialogue among his leadership team members. He was not asking enough probing questions in an appropriate forum to learn about his direct reports' misgivings about his assessment of the problems. The CEO needed to be a better listener. He needed to let others around him know that he welcomed disagreement. Since his colleagues had been timid about raising objections in a group meeting, the CEO held one-on-one meetings with his direct reports to discuss their concerns. Meetings with the entire team then became much more constructive and, eventually, they all agreed that improving communication and teamwork could help solve their company's problems.

To reach out to the rest of the staff and begin improving the climate for communication within the company, a town hall meeting with all employees was held. The CEO led the presentation and discussion accompanied by his ten senior leaders who sat next to him on the stage. This sent a strong message that they were in agreement as a leadership team and they supported the CEO's initiatives. The presentation made a compelling case for change with financials and case studies of other companies. A strong connection was made between every change that had happened since the CEO came on board. One part of the talk was devoted solely to dispelling rumors that had been collected during the focus group discussions. The CEO asked the employees, "What other rumors have you heard?" Many employees felt comfortable raising concerns in this forum. For example, saying, "I don't believe this rumor, but I think you should know that some people are saying you are going to sell the company" is much easier than asking, "Are you going to sell the company?" The CEO listened closely, asked follow-up questions, and, most important, responded. Following the town hall meeting, significant changes were implemented as a result of the discussion.

An Evolving Process

Implementing a communication strategy starts with transforming leaders' actions—but it doesn't end there. Long-term change takes time and persistence. The climate for communication must be monitored and specific solutions need to be created for each type of hurdle to dialogue in a business setting.

We can learn a lot by examining the experience of Robert H. Buckman, now chairman of the Executive Committee of the Board of Directors of Bulab Holdings, Inc., as he led the transition of Buckman Laboratories from command-and-control management to open knowledge sharing. According to Buckman, "We used technology to widen the *span of communication* and culture change to expand the *span of influence* of each employee. This is where the real power comes in: when people reach out to help people they've never met, we unleash enormous individual potential." His keen eye for obstacles and straightforward approach to overcoming them accounts for his progress in changing the culture at the company over the last twenty-two years. His recognition that the process is never really finished combined with his eagerness to find new ways to exchange ideas, guarantees ongoing success.

Confronting Obstacles One at a Time

Bob Buckman became the leader of Buckman Laboratories (in Memphis, Tennessee) in 1978 after his father, the founder, passed away. He figured out pretty quickly that his father had insisted on approving nearly every decision regarding this company, which had about five hundred employees and provided specialty chemicals to a variety of industries in seven countries.[11] He made up his mind to change the organization and decision-making processes so that customers could be served better and faster. Buckman believed that the old command-and-control organizational model that his father had used to run the company "was copied from the military where the problem was one of managing a high percentage of uneducated individuals."[12] The company needed a different model since, at the time, 39 percent of the employees were college graduates and he expected this to increase. (By 2000, 73 percent of the company's 1,275 associates had a college degree.)

Bob Buckman wanted to lead an organization where openness, shared communication, and quick decision making prevailed. He knew he needed to encourage more dialogue among his increasingly dispersed global staff. At any time, 86 percent of the employees were outside the office serving customers around the world. He wanted a network to link these mobile workers, but not all of his management colleagues saw the wisdom in his strategy. Buckman had to overcome a number of internal obstacles before realizing his original goal.

Early in the 1980s, technology was made available to the general managers that allowed them to share information electronically. This initiative met with a subtle form of resistance: for several months, the general managers used this e-mail system merely to exchange pleasantries rather than real information. To move beyond this, Buckman decided to add salespeople to the network. After all, they were in front of customers on a daily basis and needed better access to the most up-to-date information. They also knew a lot about customer needs that should be conveyed to others back at the office. He was betting that they would use the new system to better advantage than the general managers had so far. This move was not welcomed by the managers. They were concerned that increasing the "span of communication" at the lower ranks would diminish the roles of those in the middle. (At that point, employees were still required to get permission from their managers before calling someone from another division or of a different rank.) Managers then attempted to control usage by limiting the total network fees that could be charged by the associates. Buckman got around this roadblock by having all network charges billed centrally so that managers wouldn't see the costs—and therefore couldn't control them.

Next, managers discouraged use of the network by warning that employees could not judge the quality of the information they were getting (ostensibly because it hadn't been screened by management). At that point, a frustrated Buckman turned to Tom

Peters, the management guru, for advice on how to overcome this annoying resistance. Peters advised that the role of the managers had to change for this effort to be successful. He recommended that managers be turned into mentors whose primary goal would be to help people succeed. Buckman conveyed this message to his managers: they should refocus where they spent their time so they could facilitate the information flow rather than block it. Eventually, managers' attitudes changed and they stopped "getting excited about people sending messages to someone over their heads," says Buckman. Even though his managers had reservations, he says he was never worried about potential downsides to this network that increased accessibility of people and information. It didn't take long for him to see results. "The quality of information improved as we opened up the system," he says. "People only get away with BS-ing someone quietly—smoke-blowers can't function in an open system of communication."

The next challenge was to get all employees linked to what has become known as K'Netix (the Buckman Knowledge Network). There are two important aspects to this system: databases to catalog and store explicit knowledge such as case studies and other work product that could be written down, and e-mail and on-line forums that allow people to exchange the tacit knowledge that is retained in each individual's head and is constantly being updated. Buckman feels strongly about this side of the system. "Since each individual associate is part of the knowledge base of the company, all associates should have equal rights to enter knowledge into the system. To accomplish this we have to change the culture of the company so that every individual feels comfortable influencing others beyond their current boundaries in the organization."[13] He realized that creating a climate of continuity and trust with associates and customers was an essential step in overcoming barriers to communication. Over an eighteen-month period, a Code of Ethics was developed with employee input. This set of principles addresses the central role of the customer, the importance of respecting the individuality of associates, the need for the highest business ethics, and, of course, the need for continuous communication.[14] The Code of Ethics guided the development of the network.

To encourage participation in the on-line forums, the system was designed to be very easy to use—many associates were not technology experts. Systems operators from the Knowledge Transfer Department were appointed to oversee the activity of each forum. They made sure posted questions were answered quickly and then they summarized discussions for the permanent database. Still, some employees were reluctant to join in. To overcome this, Bob Buckman actively participated in the forums and would send messages to people who had not been involved for a while asking them if they needed training or other help with using the system.[15]

In 1994, the top 150 knowledge sharers were invited to a meeting at a high-end resort in Scottsdale, Arizona, to discuss the future of K'Netix. Every attendee received a new, top-of-the-line laptop as a very visible reward for their contribution to the knowledge network. This sparked some resentment from employees who were not selected for the event, but also encouraged much higher participation in the forums. The message was clear: knowledge sharing was a better way to gain influence and recognition in the organization than building power through knowledge hoarding. This one-time event had a profound impact on solidifying the culture Buckman had been trying to create.[16]

But the company didn't stop there. Buckman Laboratories sells to customers in ninety countries, business is conducted in fifteen languages, and half of the associates are outside the United States, so Buckman has put a lot of effort into overcoming language barriers. Translators were added to forums and some discussions are conducted solely in a language other than English.

What topics are associates discussing on K'Netix? There are more than thirty global forums in which all employees can participate and more than twenty-five team forums that have more limited access. Some discussion forums are more social and focus on "water cooler" type conversations or hobbies, while others are strictly business topics. Each month, financial data is posted on the system so that employees have a good understanding of the performance of the company. The company has learned through experience that it needed to set up separate forums with restricted participation for conversations about emerging, unpatented technologies.[17]

In 1997, the network was expanded to include the Bulab Learning Center (developed with Lotus Institute), an on-line training and education program that allows individuals to continuously improve their own knowledge base. Since all associates of Buckman Laboratories have complete and free access to the Internet, the Learning Center gives each an opportunity to take courses for college credit and earn any kind of degree including a Ph.D. These courses are offered through partnerships with twenty universities around the world and the cost to Buckman Laboratories is less than $40 per hour. In 1999, associates logged thirty-three thousand hours of education time, or an average of twenty-six hours per person for the year.

What is the payoff? Each year, 3.5–4.5 percent of revenues is spent on K'Netix and the Bulab Learning Center. Bob Buckman believes it has been a smart investment. One way to measure the value of knowledge sharing is the "speed of innovation," which is defined as the percentage of sales from products that have been developed in the last five years. In 1987, this figure was at 14 percent; in 1999, it averaged 35 percent (an indication that innovation is happening and that clients are willing to pay for it). In 1999, revenues were over $310 million compared to $39 million in 1979. Overall, the speed of response to customers has gone from days and weeks to just a few hours.

There has been an increase in productivity that stems from allowing people to work at their peak times. "The old paradigm— come to office at 9 A.M., turn brain on, work for eight hours, then go home and turn brain off—doesn't work anymore," advises Bob Buckman. Laptop computers and the network Buckman Laboratories uses to connect them allow associates to be effective wherever they are and lets individuals "redefine the personal time equation," according to Buckman. He does some of his best work at 5 A.M., but recognizes that others might be more effective at night. The network facilitates communication regardless of time or place. Buckman likes to stay connected even when he is fishing in Alaska; he strongly believes employees deserve the same freedom. Bob and his colleagues at Buckman Laboratories have learned from experience that when the potential of the individual is optimized, the power of the organization is maximized.

Although they have made tremendous progress and the rewards have been significant, there are four activities that Bob Buckman says they will continually address:

- Getting people comfortable with sharing knowledge
- Increasing the speed with which knowledge goes into people's heads
- Creating a collection of electronic communities for business and personal interests
- Building effective global, virtual teams across the stovepipes of the different operating companies

They will pursue more ways to use electronic tools to collaborate virtually rather than rely on face-to-face team meetings or training sessions. Given the cost and time involved in face-to-face meetings, Buckman prefers that his associates only travel to meet with clients or other outside groups and for critical summits with colleagues.

Over time, Bob Buckman has met all of the requirements for a good communications strategy to promote valuable dialogue. He raises his expectations each time an obstacle has been overcome. He continues to share his learning experiences at Buckman Laboratories with other business leaders by giving speeches, writing articles, and dedicating a Web site to knowledge sharing. His passion and commitment make him an excellent role model for knowledge sharing and dialogue.

Chapter Summary: Dialogue

Globally dispersed virtual work cannot thrive without open, honest dialogue. Identifying the existing and desired climates for communication are the first steps to building a strategy that will overcome obstacles to dialogue in your organization.

WHAT CHANGE AGENTS NEED TO TAKE RESPONSIBILITY FOR:

- Be very clear about what the company will gain by improving communication.
- Understand where the communication gaps and barriers are today.
- Always give employees a way to ask questions and get quick answers.
- Understand how you will measure the cost and the impact of improved dialogue.
- Start at the top by changing the way leaders relate to each other.
- Encourage knowledge-sharing initiatives at all levels within the organization.
- If you want people to share knowledge, provide a way for them to keep their knowledge up-to-date.
- Listen carefully and always look for ways to increase effective communication.

WHAT ALL EMPLOYEES SHOULD ACCEPT RESPONSIBILITY FOR:

- Ask *why* something is happening.
- Bring rumors to the surface to test their accuracy.
- Pay attention to your personal knowledge management: keep improving your own knowledge base so that you have something valuable to contribute to others.

Connectivity

Shedding the Layers of

Geographic Boundaries,

Reliance on Co-Location,

and Misuse of Technology

If your sales force spent only 40–50 percent of the workweek in front of clients and prospects, would business be thriving? American Express didn't think so when it found itself in that situation in 1993.

It wasn't too surprising that American Express was losing ground to Visa and other credit card competitors. Richard Tiani, then vice president of best practices, was charged with improving productivity of the sales force for the Establishment Service Division of the Travel Related Services Company of American Express (responsible for encouraging establishments to accept the American Express card and servicing the accounts that had signed on).

After Tiani's team spent months benchmarking, surveying, observing, and talking with all the parties involved in the sales process, the solution became clear. The division needed to change the process so that salespeople could spend 75–85 percent of their time with prospective and existing clients and respond to client requests faster.[1] This would allow salespeople to sign up more merchants to accept the American Express card and provide more opportunities for card members to use the card. The following changes were made to accomplish the goal:

- Technology was used to improve the mobility and accessibility of the sales representatives and account developers. New laptops were issued with better applications, and voicemail and cell phone service was upgraded. A twenty-four-hour help desk was made available to respond to technical problems that cropped up in the field.

- Low-volume accounts were shifted to being serviced by phone rather than by in-person meetings.

- Paperwork tasks were eliminated, automated, or reassigned to administrative staff.

- Weekly teleconferences replaced in-office staff meetings and sales managers were required to spend more time in the field with their employees and customers. Managers also scheduled one-on-one weekly status phone calls with each field employee, typically spending fifteen to twenty-five minutes on each call.[2]

- Employees' homes were equipped with two phone lines, a fax machine, and a printer. Each employee received $1,000 (plus enough to cover local taxes) to buy a chair, desk, or other essentials for the home office. They were also set up to use local Mail Boxes Etc. outlets for shipping and receiving mail.

- A buddy system was organized and monthly social gatherings (combined with business meetings) were planned to minimize feelings of isolation.[3]

- Since there were very few reasons for sales representatives to "go to the office," many local and district sales offices around the country were consolidated or closed, creating the "virtual office."

- All staff went through training about the new tools, systems, and ways of working.[4]

After pilot testing and refining the program for four months in Atlanta and Philadelphia, American Express implemented the virtual workplace throughout the country in 1994. As a result of these changes, the number of calls per day grew by more than 40 percent and the number of establishments that accepted credit cards increased. Customer satisfaction went up 28 percent and employee satisfaction went up 25 percent.[5] Sales managers spent the majority of their workweek in the field with sales representatives (this increased from an average of 2.5 days to 4 days). Profitability increased 10 percent and productivity was up from 15 percent to 40 percent depending on the region. In total, American Express gained $40 million in incremental new business and saved $3.7 million on real estate costs.

Why You Should Optimize Connectivity in Your Business Network

American Express was one of the early innovators who used mobile work strategies to improve performance rather than simply cut costs. Tiani makes it clear that implementing a virtual workplace program was not the goal at the outset; it came about as a result of rethinking all of the existing links between the various players in the network. Prioritizing face-to-face interaction with customers and leveraging technology brought about significant workstyle changes and resulted in tremendous business improvement.

Optimizing connectivity involves the strategic use of face-to-face interaction and technology to strengthen business relationships.

Although each worker's individual contribution is very valuable, the workers' ability to collaborate with clients and each other has an even more significant effect on organizational performance. The biggest hurdle to connectivity is our inability to creatively rethink the links in our networks. We are used to thinking of distance as a disadvantage, a factor to be overcome. The American Express case illustrates the reality that when we get physically closer to one member in the network (customers), we become distant from another (colleagues). In the American Express case, technology was used to mediate that distance.

Since distance is a fact of life we may as well see it as a positive. Some companies have gone even further to see distance as a true advantage. In a plan to capitalize on the global twenty-four-hour workday, VeriFone located a software quality test center in Laupahoehoe, a rural Hawaiian village twenty-five miles from the nearest town. According to Will Pape, then chief information officer, "We're in Hawaii because we can use time-zone differences to bring products to market faster. But why are we in a rural village? Because Laupahoehoe offers our employees a lifestyle they like. And because technology now makes it possible for us to be anywhere." Pape explains the details of the time-zone advantage: "VeriFone programmers in, say, eastern time zones, near our customers, put software that needs to be tested on the company network when they leave in the evening; engineers in Hawaii pull it down and run the tests while their colleagues sleep. The next morning, the East Coast programmers have their test results."[6]

You can improve the strength of your company's network by thoroughly evaluating the current linkages, your use of technology and face-to-face interaction. Start by assessing your own network of relationships using the Job Activities Analysis Survey—Part 2: Interaction and Collaboration Profile (pages 188–189). Consider all the different people and groups that interact with you in some way and the tools you use to build or maintain those connections.

Eventually, by analyzing the Interaction and Collaboration Profiles on a department or division level, you should get a picture of the profile for your entire company.

When asked what would improve their productivity, many employees cite removing barriers between themselves and the other people with whom they should be communicating. Raghu Garud, Sumita Raghuram, and Batia Wiesenfeld, researchers from New York University and Fordham University, have studied the interaction patterns of mobile and remote workers closely and recommend mapping these relationships onto a spiderweb type of diagram that I call the "World Wide Web of Work." Include family, friends, and community on this web because level of interaction with them may enhance or detract from work relationships. Using this "web of collaboration" and the data from the Job Activities Analysis Survey—Part 2: Interaction and Collaboration Profile, talk with your colleagues about how well the existing situation and tools are working. Which relationships are most critical in terms of helping you achieve good results? Are these relationships being supported well? Are you interacting with the appropriate contacts within the company and outside the organization (or are there people missing from the web)? What is currently inhibiting productive collaboration? Do you have the mobility tools you need to be accessible to clients? Is there sufficient time for family and community activities? Summarize the problem areas and prioritize the importance of finding a solution.

Challenging Traditional Thinking About Connectivity

Once you thoroughly understand the strengths and weaknesses of the current network, turn to discussing how this profile could or should change in the future. As illustrated by the American Express example, consider when an electronic connection may be

Instructions: We would like to understand the nature of your collaborative activities in more detail. Please complete the following matrix by first indicating the typical number of hours per week spent in collaboration with the various players listed in the left-hand column. Then, in the remaining columns, estimate use of the various modes of communication to develop and support those relationships. You may use percentage of time or actual hours; be sure to circle the preferred mode of communication for each type of relationship.

Interaction with . . .	Total # of Hours Spent Collaborating	Mode of Communication (indicate approximate percentage of time on each; circle preferred mode)						
		Face-to-Face	Voice-to-Voice (on phone)	Web-Based Conferencing	Voicemail	E-Mail	Fax	Other (please describe)
Clients or customers								
Potential clients								
Suppliers								
Other external contacts (please list below) _____ _____ _____ _____								

Manager							
Subordinates							
Colleagues within department							
Colleagues in other departments: (please list departments) _____ _____ _____ _____							
Total							

Job Activities Analysis Survey—Part 2: Interaction and Collaboration Profile a better use of time than same-time, same-place interaction. For instance, would handling some relationships via e-mail free up time for meetings with clients?

Traditionally, leaders have assumed that most of their employees should be co-located. The sales force was one exception because they needed to be in field offices relatively close to the customer base (but they still had workspace with their other corporate colleagues). Rarely do we stop to ask, "What value is created by bringing employees together?" or "What are we sacrificing by requiring employees to work in the same location each day?" We need to look at this from a new perspective in order to overcome outdated geographic boundaries and improve all the relationships in our World Wide Web of Work. Like the American Express case study, the examples of work at the *Wall Street Journal*, Roper Starch Worldwide, Putnam Investments, OffSite Works, and GeneraLife demonstrate the many ways companies have broken away from co-location and used distance to realize substantial benefits at organizational and individual levels.

Keeping a Valuable Employee

Since 1994, Sue Shellenbarger has been a full-time teleworker from her home in Oregon while being a full-time columnist for the *Wall Street Journal*, which is headquartered in New York City. Prior to that, she had been with the *Journal* for eleven years as an employee who worked in the newsroom and then for three years as a freelancer who worked from home in Chicago and Oregon. Shellenbarger had good, strong relationships with her editors and they knew from experience that she was productive working from home. It wasn't that big of a stretch when her management asked her to come back on staff full-time even though she had moved with her family to Oregon. Still, this was not an arrangement they had extended to many employees at that time.

Except for taking four to ten business trips a year, Sue does her work on the phone and through e-mail from her home office. Because of this arrangement, she feels she brings a different perspective to her weekly "Work & Family" column than an office-bound writer would. This flexible workstyle enhances her creativity and efficiency. When Shellenbarger moved to the West Coast, she maintained a work schedule that gives her good access to her sources and editors in the eastern time zone and allows her to spend time with her husband and children. Her day starts at three or four in the morning when her family is still sleeping and she can get a lot of writing done. By 6 A.M. she's on the phone conducting interviews or talking with her editors. At 8 A.M. she breaks to send her children off to school and by 2:30 P.M. when they return home, she's finished her working day. Her family gets her undivided attention through the late afternoon and evening until she goes to sleep around 10 P.M.

Yes, she does get lonely for her colleagues. To overcome this, she's become a good "phone friend" and e-mail correspondent. At least twice a year she makes trips to New York to reestablish ties in the office and have in-person meetings with her editor and managing editor. Periodically, she travels for certain stories when she needs to get a sense a place or conduct a very personal interview. For the most part, though, she works solo and believes the advantages far outweigh the disadvantages. "I can do compelling work that I love while still putting my family first," says Sue Shellenbarger. "During the day, I can take time out for my children without inconveniencing my colleagues and boss or compromising my work."

This type of arrangement represents the most comfortable way for many companies to make the transition to remote work. Take a look around your own organization and find out if managers have made special arrangements for trusted employees to work from home on a full-time basis. Talk to the manager and the employee about how well the situation is working. Then find out how many

valuable workers you have lost over the past two to three years because a spouse was relocated or a family moved to be closer to
aging parents, for instance. Review the people and types of jobs
represented in your web of relationships. How many of these roles
could be performed from a distance?

Hiring a Remote Worker

As an editor for Roper Starch Worldwide, Diane Crispell performs
a very collaborative job from her home office in a rural area outside Ithaca, New York, while most of her colleagues work in the
New York City office (a five-hour drive away). She coordinates with
teammates on domestic and international research projects via
conference calls, e-mail, and occasional face-to-face meetings.
Crispell has learned that some people respond better to phone
calls than e-mail so she tailors her style to suit their preferences.
Still, to build and maintain relationships within Roper, she feels
it is important to plan in-person visits where she gets "concentrated
face-time." On average, she travels about once a month; half of
those trips are to New York City to meet with Roper employees
and the others are to attend client meetings.

When she approached Roper Starch Worldwide about working for them, Diane had no intention of moving her family away
from the Ithaca area. Through her work as executive editor at American Demographics, she had built up contacts at Roper and felt
that they would be open to having her work at a distance. Since
she had spent the previous sixteen years making the thirty-five-
minute commute to downtown Ithaca each day, they initially offered to rent office space there for her. Crispell was concerned that
working from home might be too isolating, but wanted to give it
a try. In 1997, she became the first full-time employee at Roper
Starch to be set up to work at home from the start. The company
paid for her computer equipment, phone and answering machine,
and additional furniture she needed (computer desk, filing cabi-

net, printer stand, and bookcase). Roper directly pays for two additional phone lines (voice and modem and fax). She buys her own office supplies and then gets reimbursed.

Diane boasts that she's gained two extra hours on workdays. Along with the elimination of time wasted commuting, she's picked up another hour that would normally be spent chatting with office mates or on other distractions that arise in a traditional workplace. That extra time has not been dedicated to an exercise program as she had originally planned, but has allowed her to calm the frantic pace of a busy home life. "I feel like I'm on more of an even keel now," says Crispell. She keeps roughly the same hours as her New York City teammates and her colleagues have learned they can count on her to produce a quality report on time. From a management perspective, Roper Starch Worldwide gained access to a talented, productive contributor while avoiding relocation costs and office overhead.

Companies that have hired remote workers usually waited until the situation presented itself as was the case with Diane Crispell and Roper Starch. A very talented, experienced prospective employee like Crispell has more leverage to negotiate location issues than an average one. Putnam Investments has taken a different approach to realizing the same benefits that Roper Starch gained by hiring Crispell.

In May 2000, Putnam Investments recruited a hundred new employees to work from home. The Boston-based company, which employs more than six thousand people worldwide, reached out to the neighboring state of Maine to search for remote workers. The hundred new virtual jobs were home-based from the start in disciplines such as customer service, information systems, and management. Putnam Investments equipped the employees' homes with a computer and high-speed Internet access and provided training at Husson College in Bangor, Maine.[7]

Joe Wischerath, executive vice president of Maine & Company, a private nonprofit firm that focuses on attracting businesses to the state, worked with Putnam's management on this initiative. Maine, he says, offers a good labor pool in a large, sparsely populated state with an excellent telecommunications infrastructure. Potential workers are underemployed due to the seasonal nature of tourism, and those in rural areas have been dealing with the decline in the fishing and timber industries. Many Maine residents don't want to leave their rural towns, where some families have lived for generations and where they enjoy the quality of life. When the Putnam Investments' virtual job openings were announced, over two thousand applications from all over the state were received within the first two weeks.

Has your company been successful at hiring and keeping remote workers like Diane Crispell or the home-based workers in Maine? If not, it may be helpful to list all the job types where this type of arrangement would be workable and actively pursue hiring remote workers. Also, find out how many situations your company has experienced where it was not successful at recruiting a talented worker because the candidate did not want to relocate. How long did it take to eventually fill those positions? These voids can be very detrimental to company performance. Take a look at your World Wide Web of Work from a geographic standpoint. Is it tough for your company to fill open positions in certain geographic regions? If the labor pool in certain areas is tapped out, think about whether some of that work could be performed from remote locations if the technological infrastructure was good and the workers could travel for some face-to-face meetings.

Tapping into a New and Expanded Labor Pool

Denise Gore asks her clients to rethink not only where a job is performed but whether the workers really need to be on the company payroll full-time. She is the founder of OffSite Works (based in Nashville, Tennessee), a business that manages home-based professionals for corporate assignments that can be performed off-site.

Since 1994, Gore has successfully tapped into a local workforce that would otherwise not be available to Nashville employers looking for full-time, on-site employees. Of the 120 contractors in Gore's database of professionals, 40 percent have a very long commute from the city, 33 percent are committed to being freelancers, 71 percent have children at home (3 percent are actually home-schooling their kids), 4 percent are disabled or taking care of a disabled family member, and 3 percent are retired or have a spouse who is a retiree.

Gore is convinced that these workers are more motivated and committed than a typical employee and she knows they are very well-qualified. More than half of the OffSite Works personnel have over ten years' work experience. About 65 percent have earned a bachelor's degree or higher (there are even a few Ph.D.'s in the mix) and another 20 percent have an associate's degree. They are computer programmers, graphic designers, transcribers, paralegals, database specialists, and more.

When potential new contractors come to her (usually through word of mouth), they are put through an interview process (always face-to-face), background check, and site visit. Even though Denise is not responsible for the workers' home offices, she likes to see that a separate work area is set aside and offers a checklist of suggestions from ergonomics to safety issues. She always asks candidates, "How does your family feel about you working from home?" and wants to hear how and when they plan to work on assignments (especially when there are small children at home).

Some clients have retainer accounts for tasks that need to be performed routinely (such as bookkeeping, administrative support, and database maintenance). Other clients start with a short-term project to see how well it works. For example, when one company needed to build a database of information about seventy-five thousand contacts as quickly as possible, Gore coordinated a team of twenty contractors to do the work in two weeks. At least one client has contractors working on a nearly full-time basis. National Safety

Alliance, a Nashville-based company that administers workplace substance abuse testing programs, keeps five contractors busy with data-entry work. These contractors have been cleared to access NSA's intranet to verify and update data directly from their home offices.

How is communication handled in this dispersed network? Denise's team works closely with clients to ensure that expectations are understood and contracts include clear directions, deliverables, and timelines. She prefers results-based pricing as opposed to hourly contracts, finding them more effective for everyone involved in the process. Clients fill out evaluations when the project is completed (or on an interim basis if it is an ongoing assignment) and Denise or one of her full-time staffers meets with them in person to monitor their satisfaction. Contractors check in with OffSite Works frequently during the course of an assignment by phone or e-mail. If there is more than one contractor working on a project, Gore coordinates the deliverables. Even though they don't go to the same office building every day, all 120 contractors are linked to each other through e-mail, a quarterly newsletter, and two annual events: a picnic and a Christmas party.

There are significant advantages for all the players in this web of work. Denise Gore runs a company with very little overhead, a small fixed payroll (three full-time staffers help her with marketing, billing, selecting the right team, and ensuring the clients' work gets done), and no burden to find full-time work for every contractor in the database (they are all free to freelance). The contractors are responsible for their own office expenses, including taxes, insurance, and computer equipment.

Gore's clients get high-quality service from a professional staff with a fast turnaround and no ramp-up time. These companies avoid adding full-time employees, the real estate to house them, and the parking lots for their cars (all of which have been in very short supply in and around Nashville). They also avoid the expense of purchasing and maintaining computer equipment.

The contractors get interesting work without spending time marketing themselves or billing clients. They take on as much work as they can handle, work the hours that suit them best, and avoid commuting. Gore says, "We meet all our contractors on their terms." (Which is something that could not be said by many full-time employers!)

Some companies put off new projects simply because there is no vacant office space to house more workers (whether full-time or temporary). Has this ever happened in your organization? Is there work that your company could outsource to off-site contractors on a short-term or long-term basis? The OffSite Works example suggests that, in some cases, we should redraw the boundaries in our web of work so that some work is performed off-site by people who are not on the payroll full time. Gore demonstrates that an entirely new pool of workers opens up when the work can be performed remotely and possibly on a part-time basis. As the baby-boom population ages, employers will need to look for more ways to use retirees on a part-time basis. This is one model that works for any person who does not want to travel to an office location every day and wants to have control over their workload and workstyle.

Total Reinvention of the Business Model

At GeneraLife, seventeen full-time staffers, a savvy group of strategic partners, and a good computer system do the work that would require two or three hundred full-time employees in a traditional insurance company. The self-described "virtual life insurance company" is the brainchild of Michael Conley, president and CEO, who was tapped by the leaders of General American Life Insurance Company to create a separate business to work with the brokerage community in forty-one U.S. states. Way back then (in 1994), he felt that outsourcing and the Internet would give him a competitive edge. Conley knew that 80 percent of an insurance company's costs were typically tied up in buildings and labor. He felt he could lower this fixed overhead to 20 percent by challenging the notion that everyone but the insurance agents should be together in one building in order to communicate effectively.[8]

When GeneraLife's leaders went out to find service partners, they looked for people who were just as excited as they were about the challenge to reinvent the business model. They ended up outsourcing work to businesses in Texas, Pennsylvania, Indiana, and California in addition to their parent company across the river in St. Louis. The small staff in their Edwardsville, Illinois, headquarters includes the officers for the following divisions: Marketing, Operations and Compliance Monitoring, Technology, Underwriting, and Finance. These leaders set strategy and oversee the contracts of the outsource providers, which are held to very high service standards. According to Rodney Brown, chief financial officer, "This way of organizing helps us keep overhead low because we only incur expenses as transactions occur." One advantage, for example, is that GeneraLife does not have to deal with hiring or firing employees as the workload fluctuates. Another benefit of the virtual company structure is that the culture of the small headquarters office is very different from that of the parent company. Brown says it is more entrepreneurial and less formal. They occupy office space in a wooded business park that is part of the campus of Southern Illinois University. On any given day, roughly half of GeneraLife's seventeen employees may be off-site meeting with agents or service partners. Employees are trusted and equipped to do some of their work from home (the company paid for installation of an additional phone line).

The change didn't stop there. As GeneraLife and its strategic partners turned to the technology side, they didn't simply automate manual tasks. They took the opportunity to rethink the relationships among the insurance company, independent insurance agents, and policyholders. Then they custom-designed a computer system where data is only entered once and up-to-date information is constantly available to all who need it. One major difference was that they asked agents to communicate with the company through a Web site rather than through the mail or by fax. This involves having Internet access and a password, but does not require that agents buy any special software or hardware. After completing a short on-line enrollment application, agents are quickly certified to sell GeneraLife's insurance products.

Traditionally, agents would meet with prospective clients to complete a lengthy application and would handle arrangements for a medical review. Under the new system, the agent sends in a one-page application via the Web site; GeneraLife gathers the rest of the information from the client over the phone and then sets up the medical exam. It took some convincing for agents to accept this change (remember, these people are not employed by GeneraLife; they sell the products of many different insurance companies). They didn't particularly like the idea of losing control of the information or of GeneraLife talking directly to the customer. Conley and his staff explained that when these administrative burdens were lifted, agents would have more time to spend in face-to-face meetings selling insurance to clients. They also would have full access to the detailed information just by logging on to the Web site. The agent would receive the same fee for selling a policy, but would be doing less paperwork. GeneraLife also gave the policyholders direct access to the Web site so they could make changes such as address or designated beneficiaries (which saved time for the customer and the agent).

This process is faster and cheaper for GeneraLife staff to administer even though they have taken on more of the tasks in the policy-selling and servicing process. Policies are issued in less than thirty days on average (quicker than the competition). Savings are passed on to policyholders in the form of more innovative, affordable products that meet their needs. The first policies were issued in 1996; premium income for 1999 was about $20 million. GeneraLife plans to continue the growth trend by expanding existing channels and exploring new opportunities for direct selling to customers that would not infringe on the independent agents' territory.

GeneraLife examined the entire extended web of work, redesigned and redistributed activities, and improved productivity while lowering overhead costs. Have you considered changing the relationships among the players in your web by outsourcing some tasks and bringing some work in-house? By redrawing the lines in the traditional network so that some activities are handled over the phone or through a Web-based program, you may be able to improve the effectiveness of face-to-face meetings. By going to a virtual organization structure, your company may be able to save money on fixed overhead costs.

Managing the Effects of Distance

The key to success for American Express, the *Wall Street Journal*, Roper Starch Worldwide, Putnam Investments, OffSite Works, and GeneraLife is this: leverage good old-fashioned face-to-face interaction in combination with appropriate technology to create advantages for all the players in the system. These companies have optimized their connectivity and refused to view geographic separation as an insurmountable obstacle.

"Perceived distance is a stronger predictor of mobile workers' productivity and satisfaction than actual distance," says Sumita Raghuram of Fordham University. Along with two faculty colleagues from New York University, Raghu Garud and Batia Wiesenfeld, she has studied hundreds of mobile workers. "Actual distance is the distance that can be measured in terms of mileage or frequency of meetings with colleagues. In contrast, perceived distance is defined as the experience of distance regardless of how far the mobile worker lives from the central office or how frequently the mobile worker meets colleagues. The difference between the desired and the received contact equals distance," explains

Raghuram. As a result of their extensive surveying, the three have uncovered two other types of distance that affect perceptions among virtual workers: *informational* (concerning the information that individuals receive about organizational events or their jobs) and *social* (relating to the friendship and support they receive from their colleagues, supervisors, or subordinates).[9] According to Raghuram, "Informational distance may be perceived as high if the mobile worker wishes to access more information than is coming from a computer system or another human being. Similarly, social distance may be high if the mobile worker feels that there is a lack of understanding and trust with organizational counterparts."

All aspects of perceived distance must be addressed for business to thrive. While it is important to rethink the links in the network, it is just as essential to then support the new connections appropriately. This involves understanding workers' expectations about frequency of contact and the tools that are available to meet those expectations. Typically, we choose between two basic modes of communication: synchronous (face-to-face meetings, one-on-one phone conversations, audio and data conferencing, videoconferencing, and instant messaging and chat rooms where interaction is happening on a real-time basis) and asynchronous (e-mail, voicemail, fax, and Internet tools where information is exchanged at each participant's convenience).

According to Duarte and Snyder, "Synchronous methods are better for complex and ambiguous subjects, for brainstorming and reaching consensus, and for collaborative writing and authoring sessions. Asynchronous methods . . . can be used for updates and information exchanges and for collaborating on schedules."[10] Martha Haywood, author of *Managing Virtual Teams: Practical Techniques for High-Technology Project Managers,* trains virtual teams to use semi-synchronous communication techniques for many-to-many conversations as opposed to one-to-one discussions. These involve use of on-line bulletin boards where team members agree to post comments about a particular subject during a specified time period.

Haywood uses the example of an engineering design review, which is usually conducted by getting everyone in a room for a three-hour meeting to analyze a schematic design. Using Web-based tools, team members can look at the drawing when it is convenient for them and then post comments or questions on the bulletin board. The review can take place over several days with each day dedicated to a specific topic of the review. This technique helps overcome the time zone differences a virtual team experiences as a result of being dispersed around the world. One type of communication can be used to reinforce another. Using a combination of communication methods rather than relying solely on same-time, same-place interaction should be the goal in any system.

Use Face-to-Face Time Strategically

Corporate leaders should view face-to-face time as a valuable commodity, a scarce resource that needs to be managed wisely. Employees have a limited amount of time in a day to interact with others in person. If these conversations or meetings require travel, this absorbs additional time and greater expense. From a management perspective, ensure that your company is rewarding meaningful collaboration rather than visibility (being seen working late at the office) or frenetic travel that has little payback. Then think about when it makes sense to let employees make the tradeoff between face-to-face time with colleagues as opposed to families and friends, as the *Wall Street Journal* and Sue Shellenbarger have done.

In each of the examples discussed earlier in the chapter, face-to-face meetings were used to build or reinforce relationships and to discuss complicated or emotional issues. The highest need for this kind of interaction is typically in sales or other customer-facing activities. In all the cases, though, they did not require that everyone be co-located for the entire workweek. There are some situations, however, where co-location of work teams may still be sensible. Here are two examples.

Randy Haykin, managing partner of iMinds Ventures (a San Francisco–based venture catalyst firm), will not fund start-up businesses unless the key managers are in one location and that location is in close proximity to the iMinds office (most clients are within a one-hour drive). In the earliest phase, when the business plan is still being developed, Haykin may meet with the start-up team every day or every other day. After the plan and funding are set, he meets with them once or twice a week and may go out on client calls with them. As a venture catalyst who has helped launch more than twenty Internet-related companies, Haykin believes strongly that issues surface and get resolved faster when marketing (the people listening to the customers) and product development (the people who understand the technology) are in the same place during the development phase. Strong leadership and respect for colleagues are essential team qualities when nurturing a new venture; distance slows down the communication process, he feels. Once they are ready to go to market, it then makes sense to get more geographically dispersed.

At Jupiter Communications, when the company was young and jobs were not well-defined, employees needed to come to the office each day so everyone could pitch in and help others meet deadlines at the last minute. Amy Bromberg, vice president of human resources, observed that by the time the company had about fifty employees, roles and responsibilities were much clearer. At that point, it was able to extend to employees a great deal of freedom to work where and when they wanted.

Both iMinds Ventures and Jupiter Communications recognize certain phases when people spend more time together. This should not preclude use of remote work entirely. Some companies have tried setting core hours, say from 11 A.M. to 3 P.M., or core workdays (such as Monday to Thursday) as a way of meeting needs for collaborative time while allowing some flexibility in schedule.

Workers need to understand that during some stages of a project or start-up company, the percentage of work that requires face-to-face interaction is very high compared to the amount of solo work. But management should be very careful to monitor when the need for full-time co-location has passed.

Given that there may be a need for co-location of some employees, keep the following in mind: if you have even one remote or mobile worker, don't make the corporate office the center of the universe. According to Raghuram and her colleagues, "In our survey, teleworkers whose supervisors also worked away from a central office reported experiencing less distance from their managers than those whose supervisors did not telecommute."[11] If you make the office the default work location where employees should go if they are not at a client site, traveling, or have a good reason to be working from home, you will never get the full benefits of remote and mobile work.

Avoid categorizing team members as teleworkers and non-teleworkers or mobile workers and office-based workers. All workers are affected by dispersed work and need to learn how to deal with distance effectively. Many organizations have found that implementing mobile and remote work strategies encourages all employees to use each other's time more wisely. Meetings are typically shorter, more focused, and involve fewer people.

Optimizing use of face-to-face time should not lead to minimizing collaboration. As we saw in the examples in the first part of the chapter, technology can substitute very effectively for in-person interaction. When the proper tools are used correctly, teamwork can thrive.

Provide Good Technological Infrastructure

You may not need state-of-the-art, sophisticated technology tools, but your company must have access to information technology specialists with expertise in mobile and remote access applications, according to Glenn Lovelace, president of TManage, an Austin, Texas–based company that develops and manages the infrastructure for corporate telework programs. Lovelace has found that the technological infrastructure has been the downfall of many companies who have been unsuccessful in launching virtual office programs. Learning about mobile tools and systems is often too much of a burden for a corporate information technology department that is focused on maintaining office-based computer networks.

Since technology is its core business, it makes sense that IBM operates one of the most well-equipped mobility initiatives. From the start, IBM managers knew they'd have to go beyond simply handing out laptops and cell phones when they asked ten thousand salespeople to become a virtual workforce. Each worker is equipped with pager, cell phone, laptop, and extra phone line at home, but it is the systems that connect and support this equipment that make the real difference. The company phone system—called the "IBM Message Center"—provides single-number access to callers. Calls can be forwarded to any number (this is not obvious to the caller) or sent to voicemail. Every time voicemail or a fax is received, a message is sent to the employee's pager. The goal is for the IBM employees to get back to customers and other callers as quickly as possible. High customer satisfaction scores indicate that they are meeting this objective.

Bob Egan, managing principal for mobile and wireless competency at IBM, says the company has learned the importance of standardization of hardware and software. At any one time, there are only four different ThinkPad models being used by mobile employees. This makes it easier for the help desk to support them remotely and for tech support to provide a loaner laptop when repairs are necessary. All IBM ThinkPads that need repair are sent to Memphis, Tennessee, where the ThinkPad Repair Depot is located at the airport near the FedEx hub (this facilitates a three-day turnaround).

Initially, laptops come with software that is a standard client offering supported by the help desk personnel. A system called "Software Express" is used by employees to update software on-line.

Periodically, when employees log on to the IBM network, they receive a message indicating they should refresh the software on their laptop. A quick download process brings them up-to-date with the latest versions of all the standard software on their system.

Is it costly to maintain this high-service arrangement? Egan reports that the mobility infrastructure for the sales force costs about $18 million per year (not including the initial cost of the laptops). Since IBM saves $75 million annually on real estate costs, has improved customer satisfaction ratings, and broke even on the entire capital expenditure the first year, Egan describes this as "a tremendous investment."

Most companies have found that it makes sense to provide a computer, whether laptop or desktop, for remote workers. The majority have also determined that it is essential to install one or two extra phone lines or a high-speed data connection (such as ISDN or DSL) in the employee's home (if that is one of the off-site work locations). Employees need good remote access to the network. Beyond that basic setup, the specific configuration varies from company to company. Some have a policy that employees will be issued only one equipment setup, not a duplicate in the home and the office. Your company will have to determine what level of investment makes sense, just as IBM did. Remote and mobile workers don't necessarily need the latest, most technologically advanced cellular phones, hand-held computing devices, or desktop videoconferencing, for instance. The equipment must enable them to do their solo work and stay connected to others in their web of work. They also need good technical support twenty-four hours a day, seven days a week. This can be accomplished at a reasonable cost.

Use Technology Effectively

When your company has a good technological infrastructure, you need to help people use it effectively and responsibly. Paul Doherty, technology expert and adviser, reports that knowledge workers are saying, "I want to be connected, but in my own way." They want technology that gives them instant access to useful information and other people, but also enhances their ability to control interruptions.

Technology is often blamed for the increased speed and stressful pace of work life. Gil Gordon, author of *Turn It Off: How to Unplug From the Anytime-Anywhere Office Without Disconnecting Your Career*, points out that we should be careful not to confuse "speed of transmission with speed of review or decision-making." Just because a question can be sent almost instantaneously by e-mail doesn't mean the answer will or should come back just as fast. Some decisions require thoughtful discussion or time to mull over the facts. Gordon advises a "test of reasonableness," where teammates discuss, "what is the value of getting this done a day sooner? Is faster always better?"

In some cases, speed and accessibility are critical; in others, they are not. When we sort out the different levels of urgency and discuss the reason for the hurry, people's time can be used much more effectively and technology can be an advantage rather than an annoyance. Many workers have a love-hate relationship with their cellular phone, for instance. They like the convenience of making calls from anywhere, but often dislike the fact that they are reachable all the time. Gil Gordon's advice applies here: keep it turned off except when making a call. Technology can actually become a barrier to good communication, observes Will Pape, chairman of AgInfoLink. Some people hide behind their voicemail or check e-mail so often it becomes a distraction. At AgInfoLink, employees are asked to check their e-mail at least twice a day whether they are traveling, at an office, or at home.[12] Two times a day is frequent enough to stay informed without being consumed by e-mail correspondence.

These issues should be discussed by virtual team members at the start of a project. As Diane Crispell observed, people have different preferences about how they should be contacted; some workers prefer e-mail to the phone, others are overloaded with e-mail and can't seem to plow through their messages before the in-box fills up again. While an individual's preferences should be respected, each project team should come to a consensus about the meaning of "urgent communication," when to use asynchronous, synchronous, or semi-synchronous methods, how often to check e-mail or voicemail, and how to deal with breaches in these agreements. When a person's accessibility is routinely misused or abused, it creates unnecessary tension within the team. It is the team's responsibility to protect each member's ability to make an individual contribution—which requires solo time to think, write, and complete other tasks that call for concentration. There are no hard-and-fast rules about how technology is best employed in a virtual work environment, and technology will continue to change on an almost daily basis. Communication about communication is one of the most important activities of a virtual team leader.

Corporate leaders need to set a good example for how technology should be used to the best advantage. When Will Pape interviewed Hatim Tyabji in 1985, looking for a CEO for VeriFone, one of the questions was how fast Tyabji could type. Tyabji was taken aback by this and countered by asking why a CEO would need to type. Wouldn't he have at least one secretary? Pape explained that in their virtual organization it was important for every person, especially the leaders, to answer their e-mail quickly. Tyabji asked how fast he would need to be able to type to keep up. Within six months of getting the job, he surpassed Pape's recommended typing speed of thirty to forty words per minute and went on to lead the company well for thirteen years.[13]

Leaders and all employees need to use basic technology effectively before moving to more advanced tools. Two of the most fundamental tools for virtual workers are voicemail and e-mail, and many people are still struggling to use them in the best way. For instance, how many workers change their outgoing voicemail message often enough to give useful information to callers? Most systems permit easy, frequent changes to this recording; this function should be used to let callers know your general schedule and a rough idea of how quickly you might be able to return their call. Similarly, callers leaving messages often don't leave enough information about why they are calling so that a complete response can be given. E-mail is a great way to get straightforward questions answered quickly, but not if people refuse to read the message carefully (this is analogous to not listening attentively). It is frustrating to get a response to an e-mail message with the answer to only one of three questions, for instance. It is also annoying when people wait until the last minute to send a request or announcement believing that the speed of technology will make up for their lack of forethought.

Technology is most quickly adopted when it benefits all the users in some way. At Cisco Systems, exploiting Web-based technology is integral to the way people do business and the way they relate to everyone in their business network. Almost 85 percent of the nearly eight hundred thousand monthly customer queries are handled by the Cisco Connection On-Line and roughly 97 percent of customer orders are placed over the Internet.[14] Cisco distributes 90 percent of its software on-line to customers. Proficient users of these streamlined e-commerce applications have reported improved customer satisfaction and productivity and have reduced cycle time between requisition and delivery by three to seven days.[15]

At Cisco Systems, the on-line query system doesn't stop with the customers. Each employee accesses the intranet—the Cisco Employee Connection (CEC)—thirty times a day on average.[16] Use of the internal system effectively starts the first day an employee goes to work for Cisco and there are resources available to learn more on a continuing basis. New employees use the CEC to fill out forms, get passwords, and receive information on remote access to the computer system (sending a strong message that they are allowed to work off-site). According to John Hotchkiss, human resources manager, over 80 percent of the forty-two thousand workers have the ability to work from home or another location some of the time and 537 work almost full-time from home. This workstyle flexibility combined with the global distribution of the employee population drives a growing need for training on virtual teaming. Here, too, Cisco is leveraging the power of the intranet. Lisa Hall, senior manager of information technology, has been working closely with Human Resources to combine instructor-led training with self-paced, asynchronous education in a "blended e-learning program" on virtual work practices. For a few years, Cisco employees have been avid readers of the CEC-based "Virtual Team Guidebook" that covers topics such as communication tools, decision making at a distance, and rewarding remote workers. When Cisco managers saw the success of in-person courses based on the guidebook materials, they realized there was a need for more interactive training. Unfortunately, it is difficult for employees to attend classroom-based training and expensive from a travel and disruption standpoint. The solution is Web-based workshops that allow real-time interaction between instructors and students without having to be in the same classroom. Hall's goal is to make the e-learning fun, valuable, and cost-effective. There will always be new technology tools coming on-line for employees to use; ongoing learning opportunities that can be easily integrated into an employee's work schedule will be even more important in the future.

In addition to being used to facilitate collaboration among virtual team members, technology can be used to build informal communities outside of the formal communication network. At Viant, an e-commerce consulting firm, Chris Newell, chief knowledge officer, encourages formation of unstructured communities of interest. Any employee with passion for an idea can float the subject over the company network and encourage people to join the discussion via e-mail. As intensity for the subject grows, they may have conference calls or a summit meeting to get all the advocates from different offices together. These are natural communities that spring up outside of specific client-related projects and help to build relationships and new thinking.

These communities also exist outside the bounds of a single company or the web of traditional business relationships. Stacy Brice, founder and president of Assist University, has trained roughly 170 people to be certified professional virtual assistants. These virtual assistants are sole proprietors who work from home and handle a range of support activities for between two and ten clients who may not even be in the same time zone. Most virtual assistants worked in the corporate world for ten to twenty years as executive assistants, legal secretaries, or other highly skilled support roles before starting their own business. As much as they enjoy the freedom and flexibility they have now, the transition from being part of a large organization to being on your own could be isolating. Brice feels community building is an important part of her role as leader of AssistU: people shouldn't feel alone working at home. After trainees become certified through her program, they become part of the referral system she hosts on her Web site and have access to e-mail lists, instant messaging groups, and telebridges that facilitate communication with the other virtual assistants. This is a valuable resource where members can easily and quickly get answers to their questions about hardware, software, billing procedures, business development, or other issues where they need input.

These examples demonstrate that technology will be used effectively and extensively when it is simple to interact with and when there is value in it for all the participants. For some applications, training is an important part of being a sophisticated user. Discussing guidelines about appropriate use are valuable, but strict rules may be counterproductive.

Monitor and Refine Connectivity as Needed

Rethinking the links in the web of work is not a one-time activity. The nature of relationships and connections between players need to be reexamined as business and technology evolves. In addition to having a staff or outsource partner managing the help desk and daily equipment support, companies need a team examining equipment and applications that can improve connectivity in the future. They should be continuously evaluating the best tools for virtual workers to support their solo work and their collaborative work.

It is also helpful to monitor how well the system is being used. How many users are full participants? What are the benefits? What needs to be improved? What are the new barriers to communication? These questions should be asked on a regular basis and the answers should be used to improve the connectivity between customers, employees, suppliers, and other important members of your business network.

Chapter Summary: Connectivity

Remote and mobile work strategies can improve customer relationships and your ability to attract and retain talented workers if geographical and technological connectivity are optimized. By letting go of old ideas about co-location and rethinking how we use technology for communication, we can turn distance into an advantage for business performance.

WHAT CHANGE AGENTS NEED TO TAKE RESPONSIBILITY FOR:

- Assess the strengths and weaknesses of your company's current "World Wide Web of Work."

- Be open to rethinking the links in the web.

- Evaluate which geographic boundaries still make sense and which ones could be relaxed.

- Define when face-to-face interaction adds value and ensure that time spent this way is used effectively.

- Analyze whether technology is being used to best advantage currently.

- Be willing to equip mobile and remote workers with the proper technology tools and help desk support.

- Recognize that remote and mobile workstyles affect all workers in the process—even the ones whose jobs and work locations appear to be staying the same.

- Monitor the need for training on new tools and provide it on an ongoing basis.

WHAT ALL EMPLOYEES SHOULD ACCEPT RESPONSIBILITY FOR:

- Work with management to assess the strengths and weaknesses of your work relationships and the communication methods you currently use.

- Be open to using new tools and interacting with different players in new ways.

- Ask for training on new technology when you need it.

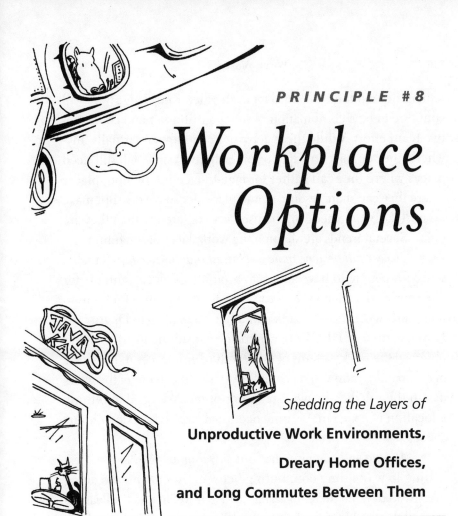

Workplace Options

Shedding the Layers of

Unproductive Work Environments,

Dreary Home Offices,

and Long Commutes Between Them

"The more you communicate electronically, the more you're going to need face-to-face meetings. And once you meet face-to-face, you're going to continue the conversation electronically," advises Paul Saffo, director of the Institute for the Future, based in Silicon Valley.[1]

The physical infrastructure of workplaces and the technological infrastructure of cyberspace are both critical elements of the new world of virtual work. One will not cause the demise of the other;

rather, they reinforce the need for each other. Knowledge work will continue to be a combination of solo contribution and collaborative team effort. While these activities can happen virtually anywhere, they do have to happen somewhere. People will still need places where they can gather for face-to-face interaction, places where they can share resources, and places for solo work. But make no mistake, workplaces will be used very differently than they are today. Several trends are shaping the workplaces of the future:

• *Access will become more important than ownership.* It makes sense for people to have access to a variety of places suitable for different work activities; it doesn't always make sense for them to maintain ownership of a particular office. According to Dr. Andrew Laing, partner of DEGW (a workplace consulting firm), who has observed the work patterns of thousands of employees in hundreds of companies, most workers only spend 30–40 percent of the workday in their dedicated workstation or office. We need to rethink allocation of space that is only occupied twelve to sixteen hours a week.

• *People will commute less but travel more.* Workers are less willing to waste time commuting between home and the office every workday, but there is greater need to travel to meet colleagues around the world. According to the 1999 Survey of Business Travelers conducted by OAG and the Travel Industry Association of America, between 1994 and 1998, the number of business travelers in the United States grew 14 percent to 43.9 million. The average business traveler took 5.4 trips in 1998 and spent 3.3 nights away per trip. The 6.2 million frequent business travelers (14 percent of all business travelers) took an average of twenty-three trips in the preceding year.[2]

• *Individual choice takes precedence over management control.* There isn't one "right answer" that management can dictate to staff about the most productive work environment for all knowledge workers. For instance, some people prefer a noisy, active environment for solo work while others need absolute quiet. Employees have been gaining more autonomy and flexibility regarding workstyles and they should be given the opportunity to match their work setting to their individual task and mood.

• *No more captive audience at "the office."* As more people have the mobility and connectivity to work anywhere, the traditional corporate office will have to be redesigned to attract occupants. The location and qualities of the workspace will have to draw people in, as it's no longer safe for management to assume employees will sit in boring cubicles forty hours a week. Business leaders will have to find out more about what brings people together if they want them to interact with each other in person.

• *More attention to workplaces in the home.* Tom Miller of Cyber Dialogue reports that 21.4 million workers used the Internet to conduct business from home in 1999. Full-time employees who worked from home during normal business hours totaled 9 million, a 30 percent increase from 1997. Increasingly, these people are not satisfied with working at the kitchen table or from a room they've cleared out in the basement. A comfortable, creative setting for work will be a more important feature of a home.

• *Blurring of leisure and work.* Roughly 20 percent of business travelers combined work-related trips with vacation in 1998.[3] Mike Jannini, executive vice president of brands at Marriott International, notes that until recently, resort hotels were not expected to accommodate work activities of vacationing businesspeople. Today, guests want access to business centers and the Internet while traveling for leisure—and business travelers are demanding more access to leisure and fitness services while they are away from home.

What Do These Trends Mean for Your Company?

Before you can fully understand the possible impact of these trends in the future, you need to understand how your company has already been affected by similar changes. Find out more about where your employees spend their work time by using this expanded version (pages 220–221) of Part 1 of the Job Activities Analysis Survey (a short form was discussed in the chapter on Principle #2: Trust), gain an understanding of the types of places workers are using, the kinds of activities they use these places for, and the amount of time they spend in each place. Have a discussion with employees about their favorite places and the reasons they like to work there. Find out what places are not working now and why. The output of the survey and the discussion that follows may surprise you. One client I worked with discovered that employees were only using their own workspace (office or workstation) for about 25 percent of the workweek. This led to a solution where individuals had a much smaller "home base" at the office with much more access to shared spaces for collaboration. Another client realized that employees were wasting so much time in airports that it was useful to arrange for memberships to airline clubs so people could work more effectively.

The World Wide Web of Workplaces

We need to move beyond thinking of remote work as a choice between a home office and a corporate office. The responses to the Job Activities Analysis Survey will probably demonstrate that your employees are already using a wide range of places to support their solo and face-to-face collaborative work, what I call the "World Wide Web of Workplaces." Their level of dissatisfaction with their current web of workplaces should indicate where improvements can be made in the future. Business leaders should strive to give their clients, employees, and suppliers access to a network of places that enhances productivity and well-being and offers variety to suit individual preferences. This does not mean that companies need to own and operate a broad range of places, but they do need to understand the value of enabling and encouraging workers to use a wide variety of spaces. The web of workplaces should definitely include corporate offices and home offices, but also embrace places such as restaurants, airplanes, hotels, incubators, telework centers, and more. Let's look at these workplace alternatives in more detail.

• *Public places with food* (or at least coffee). Cafés, restaurants, coffee shops, and diners have always been good places for formal and informal breakfast, lunch, and dinner business meetings. While these places will continue to provide good settings for face-to-face interaction, they are also very conducive to solo work. Providing power for laptops at the tabletop or counter makes these places even more popular with those workers who like to be surrounded by activity, other people, and good food and beverages while they are working on their own. (These are the people who studied in the student union, local coffee shop, or other public setting around campus when they were in school.)

• *Bookstores and libraries.* These public places offer quiet settings for solo work while also providing a chance to do some research. Working there may give a person a fresh perspective, stave off feelings of loneliness, or help keep work separate from home life. In some cases, there is the opportunity for social interaction, but there is generally not as much activity or noise as at a restaurant or coffee bar. (These settings appeal to people who preferred to study in the library as students.)

• *Natural settings and outdoor places.* The ability to take walks, write, and read in a park, at a beach, or in a backyard is a big advantage of having the freedom to choose your work setting. Employees should be encouraged to use mobile technology to work in pleasant, natural surroundings. These places provide a change of pace from other work settings and an opportunity for creative thinking.

• *Transportation links and nodes.* The number of business air travelers increased from 17.2 million in 1991 to 21.7 million in 1998.[4] Many people report that they get a lot of thinking and writing done when flying on a plane because there are very few distractions. (This may change as telephone technology makes it less

As part of the workplace project, we need to understand your current work patterns and how you use certain workspaces today. Please help us by completing the following matrix. We'd like to know approximately how much time is spent performing certain activities in the places listed below.

- The total number of hours in the matrix should be equivalent to the number of hours worked in an average week.
- Include all work hours, whether on-site or off-site and spent working from home.
- In a typical week, how many hours do you spend on each of the following activities in each type of place? (Fill in cells of matrix below with hours per week for each activity and place.)
- Please estimate time to the nearest half-hour.

Place \ Activity	Our Building or Site					Off-Site				Total Hours
	My Workspace	Someone Else's Workspace	Conference Room	Other On-Site Area (describe)	Client Site	Travel (Hotel, Airport, Plane, Train)	Home	Other Off-Site Area (describe)		
Face-to-Face Formal meetings (scheduled in advance)										
Informal collaboration with one colleague or client										
Informal collaboration with two or more colleagues or clients										

Phone calls (including teleconferences)								
Solo Independent work that requires a computer (including e-mail)								
Independent work without a computer (reading, filing, and so on)								
Other (please describe)								
Total # of hours								

(Please review chart and ensure that the number of hours for all activities in all locations equals the average number of hours worked per week.)

Job Activities Analysis Survey—Part 1 (Expanded Version)

expensive to send and receive phone calls while in the air.) Unfortunately, it has become more and more difficult to use a laptop when flying coach. Not only is it sometimes physically impossible to fully open a laptop given the row spacing, but, ergonomically, the relationship between the seat and the tray table creates an uncomfortable situation for extensive typing. For this reason, more companies are allowing employees to fly business class or first class on longer trips. This minimizes frustration and maximizes productivity.

Frequent travelers appreciate memberships in airline clubs and lounges where they can work productively or relax between flights. Some geographically dispersed teams use these lounges to conduct meetings; participants fly in from several different locations, meet for the day, and then fly back home.

In the Northeastern United States, Amtrak trains provide a comfortable, effective alternative to air travel. Business travelers can get more work done on a train trip from New York City to Washington, D.C., and arrive there at just about the same time as they would if they had gone by plane. On the train, riders can plug in a laptop as soon as they sit down (there is an outlet at each seat) and work straight through the trip (there is no need to turn off the computer for takeoff and landing).

Keep in mind, though, that only 36 percent of business trips involve air travel (and a very small percentage involve train travel); the majority of business trips still happen by car (61 percent), according to the 1999 Survey of Business Travelers.[5] This means that even if routine commuting is reduced, some workers will still be spending a lot of time in their cars. For safety reasons, though, should the automobile be viewed as a legitimate workplace? While use of cellular phones while driving can be dangerous, we can't overlook Csikszentmihalyi's research on creativity that showed that driving is a good activity for creative thinking.[6] Dan Pink, free agent, keeps a digital recording device clipped to the sun visor in his car so he can capture ideas that occur to him while he is driving. Some people who spend a lot of time in their cars report that listening to books on tape helps them feel productive on long car trips. In general, we need to make driving time less wasteful and frustrating while maintaining safety.

• *Home away from home.* Since business travel is primarily about building and maintaining relationships, hotels have changed to be more supportive of these activities. For example, presenting a great first impression used to be the primary purpose of the hotel lobby. After Marriott hired a consultant to observe how public spaces in its hotels were being used, it redesigned the lobbies to be more like a town center where people could gather and access services. Lobbies were reconfigured to support impromptu meetings and workers using laptops (cocktail tables were replaced with laptop-friendly ones). Marriott also improved the food and beverage options and expanded retail choices. Even the function of the guest rooms has changed. Mike Jannini of Marriott explains, "Hotel rooms used to be just a bedroom, a place to sleep away from home. Now, the guest room functions like a three- or four-room house with bedroom, den, office, and kitchen functions all housed in that one place." Pam Parsons, director of design and construction at Host Marriott, and her colleague Craig Mason, vice president of asset management, report significant changes in how guest rooms are furnished and equipped. High-speed connections to the Internet are desirable and many younger travelers appreciate having a CD player in the room so they can listen to their favorite music. Some rooms come with an ergonomic chair, good desk lamp, basic office supplies, and digital controls for the heating, ventilation, and air conditioning. Parsons and Mason also report that the properties they manage have more sophisticated spas and fitness centers and the overall level of service is higher. In some high-end hotels, a guest can order a "luxury bath" that includes having someone draw the bath (complete with rose petals) and deliver a glass of wine.

Business travel is no longer considered a special treat or perk. For many businesspeople, it is an annoying disruption. Frequent travelers usually find ways to make business trips more comfortable and enjoyable. Some prefer to stay at small bed and breakfasts. Others favor places with a good swimming pool or special recreational facility. Most company travel policies favor the business travelers who prefer to stay with the same hotel chain in each city they visit because good corporate rates can be negotiated. Corporate policies should allow for individual preferences within reason. Feeling comfortable when working away from home has a tremendous impact on productivity and attitude about business travel.

• *Special meeting places.* Many companies have found that there are advantages to hosting meetings in hotels, conference centers, and other special facilities that are somewhat removed from the corporate office. As Cornell University professor Frank Becker explains, "One of the great misunderstandings surrounding new ways of working and virtual work is that it means people never see or talk with another human being. Wrong! What's changing isn't the need for face-to-face interaction; it is the chunks of time and locations where it occurs. Like families who keep in touch by phone regularly and meet for days or a week at a time occasionally, mobile and virtual workers are more likely to interact with colleagues less frequently but for longer chunks of time, anywhere from a few hours to a few days. These meetings are important. They need to occur in environments that are pleasant, comfortable, and designed to support informal interaction as well as more formal exchange of information."[7]

Roughly half of the 43.9 million business travelers reported that the reason for their last business trip was to attend a meeting, trade show, or convention.[8] Larger meetings and conferences are held in hotels and convention centers. Smaller, more intimate business retreats are often held in conference centers. These conference centers are usually in more secluded locations and offer a variety of recreational diversions such as golf, tennis, and hiking. Universities and colleges are also filling this niche, hosting business education and strategy sessions on campus.

Some businesspeople are using meeting places where there is a staff to facilitate dialogue between participants. "Most meetings are not about thinking. They are about messaging, getting everyone on the same page. People arrive late, engage in formalities, discuss a little content, and then the attendees start thinking about where they need to be next," says Gail Taylor. That's why she and her husband, Matt, founded MGTaylor Corporation and developed places like the Knowhere Stores (in Palo Alto and Hilton Head) to host facilitated workshops that would bring out the genius in organizations. These "DesignShops" help diverse groups of thirty to eighty people compress six months of work into three days, Gail explains. MGTaylor offers clients a neutral workspace where participants are encouraged to take risks and explore new ideas. The environments are flexible, homey, full of books and toys, and nothing at all like the typical conference room or office setting, which the Taylors regard as likely to block creativity. There are no clocks, but there are lots of large boards to draw or write on ("think big, work big") creating an "information-rich environment." The tables fold up and move out of the way because sometimes standing encourages different thinking than sitting. The groups are made up of all the key stakeholders including customers, suppliers, decision makers, and implementers; people often come from around the world to spend these three intense days together discussing new products, mergers, or other complex business problems.

Globally dispersed, virtual teams need these specialized types of gathering places, but not on a full-time basis. It makes sense for companies to rent spaces and services only when needed rather than own and operate these meeting places themselves.

• *Places for shared equipment or services.* One of the functions of the corporate office has been to provide access to shared equipment (such as special printers and copy machines) and support services (such as mail and courier services). Many mobile and remote workers now look to companies such as FedEx, Mail Boxes Etc., and Staples for these services. Some employers have set up corporate accounts and negotiated national discounts with these vendors. Mobile workers then have access to consistent service throughout the United States and in some foreign countries.

- *Client sites.* While it is very important to spend time interacting with customers, the traditional accounting and management consulting model where consultants spend four days a week working at a distant client site can be a real obstacle to attracting and retaining staff.

Viant, an e-commerce consulting firm started in 1995, has been successful at turning the typical consulting model around. Its offices (nine and growing) are located near clients and the Viant employees that work in those locations live nearby. Viant management is committed to minimizing business travel. In an industry where it is typical for 50 percent of consultants in a company to be traveling at any one time, Viant's rate is a low 15 percent, says Bob Gett, president and CEO.[9] Viant's low turnover rate, below 9 percent,[10] is proof that employees favor this arrangement. Viant staffers have also persuaded clients to spend time working with their project team at the Viant site. Clients like the open, collaborative, energetic atmosphere of Viant's offices, says Chris Newell, chief knowledge officer; they look forward to getting away from the interruptions in their own workplace and working collaboratively with their consultants. Some are so impressed with the culture of Viant that they try to recreate it within their own companies.

Clients are happily accommodated at Cisco's sites, too. According to Denise Ng, a planning and design manager, 22 percent of the New York City field office is dedicated to client spaces such as sophisticated training rooms and equipment testing and demonstration areas.

These relationships will continue to evolve as clients start working remotely, too. More of this interaction may happen at independent locations in the future.

- *Home offices.* The practice of working from home will continue to increase as more full-time employees are given the flexibility to work from there and as more free agents and small business owners set up shop at home. Having a workplace in the home, even if it is just for after-hours work, will become increasingly more important.

To what extent, then, should employers be involved in equipping and furnishing the home offices of their employees? Most companies who have formal telework policies provide computer equipment for the home office. In many cases, a laptop is provided for mobility or to avoid having to equip an employee in two places (home and office). Typically, management has been less willing to provide furniture for the home office.

Diane Phelps, who directs telecommuting sales for Herman Miller for the Home (a division of furniture manufacturer Herman Miller, Inc.), reports that companies are more willing to furnish the home office if they can outsource the entire operation, which can be a logistical nightmare for a company that isn't in the furniture business. Herman Miller has been handling the entire process, from ordering through installation in the home, for several large clients including Nortel Networks. Typically, remote and mobile workers at these companies are given a furniture allowance of between $500 and $2,500. Herman Miller can set up a Web site where employees can view several options for worksurfaces, ergonomic chairs, and storage units and order the pieces that fit within the allowance and match the décor of their home. Once the order is fulfilled, Herman Miller arranges for delivery, installation, and removal of the shipping boxes.

According to Mary O'Neill, workplace alternatives program manager for Herman Miller, the company's own employees have access to the same furniture provision program that their clients use. More than 5 percent of Herman Miller's 2,500 Michigan-based office workers participate in the company's Homesite program and work from home two to three days a week. When they sign up, each remote worker gets a laptop, a second phone line, and a $1,500 furniture allowance in return for agreeing to give up their on-site workstation or office. Herman Miller has decided not to inspect home offices, but remote workers do receive education on safety and ergonomics so they can set up a productive work environment at home. O'Neill, trained in design, works one-on-one with Homesite participants to review the proposed floor plan for the home office, select furniture that will work in that space, and ensure that the teleworker's ergonomic needs are met and access to utilities is safe.

As more companies realize that it is less expensive to set up an employee in a safe, comfortable office at home than in a corporate office (because they are not paying for walls or partitions and sophisticated cable management), they will be willing to invest in furniture for home offices. A good quality, adjustable chair and work-surface can significantly affect the performance of knowledge workers, and when used properly, can stave off wrist, neck, and back injuries associated with repetitive motion tasks.

- *Workplaces close to home but not at home.* When the U.S. government initiated its Flexiplace program in 1990, 750 people volunteered to work from home one or two days a week. Through an extensive, year-long pilot study, program leaders learned that although telework offered many benefits, home would not be the best alternative work site for everyone. Some government workers faced too many security hurdles to permit access to computer systems from home. Others reported being distracted by small children or just didn't want to be at home alone all day. Still, these employees wanted to reduce the long commute required to get to a downtown office. Their managers agreed that remote work, away from their colleagues and bosses, would be permissible. Telework centers, small worksites located in suburban areas, seemed to be a good alternative to working from home.

According to Dr. Wendell Joice, Flexiplace team leader for the Office of Governmentwide Policy, twenty-five thousand federal workers are considered teleworkers. Of that group, more than one thousand use one of the more than forty telework centers around the country.

The greatest concentration of federally funded telework centers is in the Washington, D.C., area where there are a total of seventeen sites: seven in Maryland, eight in Northern Virginia, one in the District of Columbia, and one in West Virginia. According to Darryl Dobberfuhl, executive director of the Washington Metropolitan Telework Centers, an organization that promotes use of these centers, there are approximately 660 users of the telework centers, which range in size from fourteen to thirty-four seats each. While still used primarily by public sector employees, the centers are gradually attracting private sector workers. One center, located in Fairfax, Virginia, is open on weekday evenings and weekends to residents of the community who can use the computer equipment at no charge. Based on the average utilization rate of 55 percent, Dobberfuhl estimates that between 500 and 600 more users could be accommodated within the existing network of seventeen centers.

The centers are funded by the General Services Administration but are operated by community colleges, a university, economic development commissions, and private companies. The typical user works from the telework center one to two days a week and commutes to their downtown Washington office for the remainder of the workweek. Most are drivers, not mass transit users; going to the telework center allows them to avoid a fifty- to seventy-minute commute (one-way), on average. The Jefferson County TeleCenter, in Ranson, West Virginia, offers users a way to reduce the hour-and-a-half to two-hour drive between their home and downtown Washington.

Dobberfuhl advises that telework centers play an important role in the virtual workplace. He's observed that some people start working from home and then come to the center while others make the transition to working from home by using the telework center for a while first. "These centers provide an efficient, productive work environment for employees who want to reduce their commuting time, but either cannot or choose not to work from home," says Darryl Dobberfuhl, adding, "Telework centers provide a valuable way for reluctant managers to test the waters and become comfortable with supervising remote workers." Joice's surveys of federal government teleworkers show that 90 percent report higher job satisfaction and 70 to 80 percent report performance improvements as a result of participating in the Flexiplace program (regardless of whether they are working from home or a telework center).

Throughout the 1990s, telework centers were hailed as the ideal solution for people who did not want to work from home but also did not want to commute a long distance to the office. Employers liked them too because they could protect data security and seemed to be a more professional setting for work than a home office. There have been several different initiatives to bring telework centers to nongovernmental employees in various parts of the country. Private sector, multiple-employer telework centers, though, have never really flourished. There are some signs that single-employer sites may be a useful alternative, and some progress has been made in the San Francisco area.

"Sun Microsystems is building an infrastructure of campus-hubs, work from home, and drop-in centers to allow work to happen anytime, anyplace," reports Brent Daniel of Sun's Workplace Effectiveness Group. Drop-in centers are located in Campbell, Pleasanton, and San Francisco, where there are concentrations of employees living nearby who commute more than twenty-five miles to the nearest campus in Palo Alto, Menlo Park, or one of Sun's other Silicon Valley locations. Each center can accommodate forty to sixty people at a time and any Sun employee can use any site for any reason; they do not have to live nearby. These three locations are also in close proximity to customer and partner sites so they are often used by sales representatives. Ann Bamesberger, director of Sun's Workplace Effectiveness Group, says they've found that employees work off-site 35 percent of the time on average.

Knowing that home is not always the best workplace for everyone, Sun wants to provide other options so workers can use their time effectively and avoid sitting in traffic jams.

The Workplace Effectiveness Group has monitored the usage patterns of these drop-in centers and found that they are heavily utilized, especially on Fridays. When surveyed, employees who work from these sites when they don't commute to their regular office say they save an average of two hours' driving time and can concentrate better. They and their managers report that this arrangement does not detract from teamwork. According to Brent Daniel, people choose the drop-in center rather than work from home because the technology is better. He adds, "Many people find too many distractions awaiting them at home, but a drop-in center still says 'office' and hence 'work.'"

One of the reasons some experiments with single-employer telework centers have failed in the past is that a network of small centers can be expensive to lease and operate. Charles Schwab Corporation has taken an approach that should head off this problem. It has partnered with HQ Global Workplaces, providers of full-service, multitenant work environments, to offer the benefits of telework centers to employees.

Schwab views telework centers as "another important way we can achieve our goal of being a responsible employer and a responsible corporate citizen," according to Parkash Ahuja, Schwab's executive vice president for corporate services. Offering employees viable ways to cut commute times lets workers spend more quality time with their families and helps communities by reducing traffic and air pollution. Because roughly 60 percent of Schwab's nine thousand San Francisco–based employees live in the East Bay area, Schwab teamed with HQ Global Workplaces to provide an alternative workplace (nicknamed "Hotel Schwab") in Walnut Creek, California. Eligible employees can reserve space at this site for a few hours or a few days and reduce their commuting time by at least an hour. HQ Global Workplaces operates twenty-two thousand square feet at the Walnut Creek site; half of that space is dedicated solely to Schwab's drop-in center. HQ Global Workplaces provides the space, furniture, and administrative services as well as managing the reservation system for Schwab. Based on the popularity of the Walnut Creek telework center (80 percent occupancy on a weekly basis), Schwab will be opening two more sites in different regions near San Francisco by the end of 2001.

Deloitte & Touche has not set up separate telework centers, but through the SmartSpace program in the New York region, employees can reserve space in any of the Deloitte & Touche offices in Manhattan and the surrounding areas. This system has the same effect of helping employees avoid a long commute while giving them access to high-speed lines and special equipment in the office.

Telework centers are not just a big city phenomenon. Herman Miller, headquartered in Zeeland, Michigan, operates its own telework center at a point midway between the headquarters and Grand Rapids, Michigan. (The two cities are about thirty miles apart.) A full 20 percent of the employees live in Grand Rapids, but any employee can reserve one of the fifteen workstations or large and small meeting rooms. Some employees stop there on the way to or from the Grand Rapids Airport to get high-speed access to the company network. Some people use it for solo work and some project teams work there on a short-term basis to get away from interruptions in the main office. According to Mary O'Neill, workplace alternatives program manager, the center is 75–85 percent occupied most of the time with heaviest use on Mondays and Fridays.

According to the Telework America 2000 study, 7 percent of the 16.5 million regularly employed teleworkers in the United States are solely telework-center-based, and another 4 percent work from both home and a center when they are not working from their assigned office location.[11] More of these types of remote workers will emerge as business leaders recognize the need for some employees to work in an office environment (rather than at home) and reduce time wasted in heavy traffic or on long commutes. Traffic conditions can discourage employers from locating in certain areas, according to a 1999 Telework Study conducted by Washington State University's Cooperative Extension Energy Program in partnership with US West. Interviews were conducted with 450 businesses in the state of Washington to determine the most important business-related issues faced by Washington companies and the extent of use of telework programs. The two most important business issues, meeting customer needs and attracting qualified employees, were both negatively affected by traffic conditions. The major traffic concerns include customers who are less willing to travel to a company's site and employees who are late to work.[12] These problems could be resolved if there were more telework centers that decrease commute time and distance.

• *Workplaces for new business ventures.* Some people call them incubators, but Chris Wittman, executive vice president of TechSpace, prefers to think of his company's workplaces as "pollinators." Unlike a landlord, who only provides space, or a venture capitalist, who only provides money, TechSpace provides the infrastructure to help technology and new media companies grow. Started by three frustrated commercial real estate brokers in New York City who couldn't find "short-term, wired, cool space" for their clients, TechSpace's flagship site is two floors in an old loft building located in the heart of Manhattan's Silicon Alley. This forty-thousand-square-foot space holds roughly two hundred people, which translates into about thirty-five companies at any given time. These companies are considered members, not tenants, and they sign service agreements, not leases.

Members include newly formed ventures as well as Internet spin-offs from established enterprises and large companies who want to build a presence in the New York market. "TechSpace is meant for hypergrowth businesses," says Wittman. "We want young, growing companies with big ideas." And TechSpace wants high turnover. The start-ups are only expected to be there for three to twelve months. Most members move in with two to four people—and when they grow to thirty-five employees, it's usually time to move on. When that happens, TechSpace helps them find, fit out, and move into their own office space. At that point, former members officially become alumni. Wittman says that most stay in touch and come back to TechSpace for events.

Since opening in June 1998, Wittman and his colleagues have been successful at tapping into the high demand for the kind of community that TechSpace creates. As part of the application process, they review the companies' business plans to ensure that new members complement the companies that are already there. They would turn away a major competitor of an existing member. Through the design of the space and organized events, interaction between companies is encouraged. Some of the members have even collaborated on business ideas as a result of working side by side at TechSpace.

The location combined with the funky yet functional interior design makes TechSpace a great employee-attraction tool for these rapidly expanding ventures. It also gives potential financiers, vendors, and customers a sense of stability and credibility about the companies when they come to visit. Unlike some incubators, TechSpace does not take an equity stake in lieu of rent. Members pay reasonable rates for workspaces (team rooms of varying sizes), conference space, and any of the services they use such as Web site design and hosting, technical support, human resources advisers, and more traditional administrative services. TechSpace provides virtually everything except the computers; members can move in, plug in their equipment, and be ready to get to work. In this high-activity, twenty-four-hour environment, start-ups don't have to feel that they are "going it alone."

Wittman says the demand is high for this kind of infrastructure. By 2001, TechSpace will have two locations in Manhattan and offices in Toronto, Boston, and San Francisco.

TechSpace and other companies that fulfill some of these "incubator" functions recognize that start-ups and spin-offs need this strong sense of community in the early stages of development. Access to these types of spaces will be an important part of the web of workplaces in the future.

- *Office suites and business centers.* Some companies are coming to the conclusion that they're devoting a lot of time and attention to facilities management even though they're not in the facilities management business—and there are other companies that would be delighted to take it on for them. Outsourcing the management of office space and services to specialized suppliers makes sense for companies who need access to a network of work sites, but don't need to occupy them on a full-time basis. These places are an excellent alternative for virtual teams who occasionally need meeting facilities and remote and mobile workers who aren't comfortable working from home (the former library-studier, for instance) but can't afford to lease and furnish their own offices. In the same way that hotels have been taking on the role of providing meeting space for medium to large groups on an as-needed basis, these outsourced office companies will provide workspaces for more of the mobile and remote workforce.

Regus Instant Offices Worldwide and HQ Global Workplaces are both in the business of providing a network of fully serviced office spaces for short-term and long-term agreements. Regus promotional materials say, "You run your business. We run your office." HQ Global Workplaces describes itself as, "Empowering your business virtually anywhere." These types of shared office centers used to be occupied primarily by entrepreneurs and small businesses that needed a high-profile address and someone to answer their phones. In 2000, 70 percent of HQ's space inventory is occupied by global or national companies who are entering new markets, want a place for their mobile and remote workers to hold meetings or work in between client calls, or simply need additional workspace on short notice. In both Regus and HQ Global Workplaces centers, users can obtain a private office, team workspace, conference room, videoconference room, or other facilities for one hour, one year, or any length of time they desire. The facilities also provide mail, phone, and fax service to people who are working from home.

As of midyear 2000, Regus operated 270 office locations in forty-seven countries and HQ Global Workplaces had 250 centers in seventeen countries; both predicted further expansion. Bob Gaudreau, leader of Regus's U.S. operation, says the company targets areas with low unemployment and a high percentage of knowledge workers when deciding on new locations. In some cases these are urban areas and in others suburban. Regus goes wherever business is booming and clients are looking for flexibility in how they use office space. Most of the centers are in top-quality buildings, in high-profile locations, and offer a very professional image. Gaudreau says the company is developing a new brand to appeal to high-tech and new media clients, but will not get involved in funding these ventures as some incubators do.

Gaudreau reports that 30–40 percent of clients are mobile workers who use multiple sites. They know what to expect when they arrive at a new location and the rate structure has been predetermined. They can get right to work in a place that they have selected. Gaudreau notes, "Users will go where they want so we work hard to win their hearts."

Where Does That Leave What We Think of as the Traditional Corporate Office?

Consider for a moment the role that traditional corporate offices have played in the past. The functions of these workplaces include providing

- A place for employees to work productively in teams and alone
- A place that expresses the values of the company

- A place for sharing equipment and resources
- A place that impresses visiting customers and the public

What has happened to each of these functions? Has the need for them diminished? No, there is still a need for shared workspaces. Fritz Steele, expert on organizational and environmental change, notes that "going to the office" gives colleagues a way to reconnect with each other and catch up on things they wouldn't communicate by phone or e-mail. "People are more willing to share their personal side when they are in-person. That's part of what builds glue among team members," according to Steele. These company-provided workplaces do need to be reinvented to serve the mobile and remote workforce.

When we compare traditional corporate offices to the other workplace options now available to knowledge workers, they often don't measure up. Many office environments have become somewhat unsuitable for either collaborative or contemplative work. Workers complain about noise, interruptions, inadequate lighting, and poor air quality. Scott Adams, creator of the *Dilbert* cartoon, has made millions poking fun at the endless rows of identical cubicles housing many of corporate America's workers and tapping into readers' frustrations with these dehumanizing settings. Some people prefer working at home solely because there are fewer distractions. How did we get to this point?

Many business leaders view office buildings as pure overhead, a cost to be minimized. Partially in an effort to cut costs, some companies have pushed the limits of the "open office" and reduced the overall space per person. The dollar savings may look good on paper, but the impact of this higher density can be devastating. "The darling of design magazines—the really groovy, wide open office, with folks shown interacting informally all day—is a visually seductive myth. Research shows it doesn't support work very well and, in fact, can incur significant losses in individual and team performance and job satisfaction," according to Mike Brill, president of BOSTI Associates, and his colleagues, Ellen Keable and Judy Fabiniak.[13] Vivian Loftness, professor and head of the School of Architecture at Carnegie Mellon University, adds, "There is some evidence that health care costs may go up. Increased density and low partitions have been linked to greater stress in employees as well as to a higher number of cold and flu cases."[14] In some extreme cases, cost cutting in operations and maintenance and basic design flaws have resulted in "sick building syndrome" where contaminants and poor air quality actually cause illness.

From a symbolic standpoint, many work settings can be judged unsuccessful. There is a terrible mismatch between espoused organizational values and the office environment in many companies today. When a business leader speaks repeatedly about flattening the hierarchy and improving communication yet stays cloistered away in a large private office, there is a glaring inconsistency of messages. When management claims "employees are our most valuable asset" while making the cubicles smaller and allowing the work environment to become crowded and noisy, what should employees believe? "Broadcasting the wrong message through design damages business," warns Francis Duffy, chairman of DEGW, an international architectural firm. "Misleading, and especially untruthful, messages are quickly picked up by employees—leading to cynical and sub-optimal behavior—and eventually by outsiders, customers, and suppliers, eroding trust, interest, and commitment."[15] So where do we go from here? What will company-provided workspaces look like as more people gain the freedom to choose where and when they work?

The U.S. government, which occupies approximately 636 million square feet of office space,[16] has been addressing the question of the workplace of the future by developing and monitoring work environment experiments. In one case, the General Services Administration worked with the National Partnership for Reinventing Government (NPR) in 1998 to develop a workplace that would set an example for the rest of the government. NPR is an inter-agency task force started by former Vice President Al Gore to improve the performance of government and consists of sixty to eighty team members who are "on loan" from various departments and agencies of the federal government.

Given that NPR's role is to be a think tank for innovation and change, Morley Winograd, director and senior policy adviser to the vice president, wanted an open, interactive environment where high performance and creative teamwork would flourish. It was also important that people be able to work whenever and wherever they wanted, says Susan Valaskovic, deputy director of NPR, in support of the government's goal to be more family-friendly. These two goals may seem to be at odds with each other, but as Winograd explains, "We need communication to creatively connect previously unconnected ideas, but new insights don't happen unless people have quiet time to concentrate."

The environment was created with the notion that people would do their solo, contemplative work at home or another setting of their choosing and would come to the NPR office for collaborative work. Lois Bennett, GSA's project manager for the NPR space, describes the environment the group created as very flexible and adaptable to its changing organizational structure. The 7,200-square-foot workspace originally housed forty workstations, eight team areas, three small enclosed rooms, and a kitchen and lounge area. All workstations are roughly the same size (there are small differences because the group tested products of three different furniture manufacturers), there are no private offices, and team areas are located by the windows. Initially, team members were supposed to take a nonterritorial approach to the workspaces with each team deciding who would have a dedicated workstation and who would share. But Valaskovic explains that taking the time to set up in a new workstation each day was a glitch and the goal was to create a "glitch-free workplace." The group subsequently turned some of the team spaces into individual workspaces.

Over time, NPR realized that some employees were coming to the office for both individual work and teamwork. (This makes sense since any group is bound to have a mix of former "library-studiers" and "dorm room–studiers" as described in the chapter on Principle #4: Individuality.) In general, people spent more time there than they thought they would. Unfortunately, because most of the meeting areas and the workstations were very open, employees became frustrated with the level of noise and distraction in the environment when they tried to concentrate. Bennett says that the group learned an important lesson: open team areas and open workstations generally don't mix. At the Federal Technology Services offices and the Adaptable Workplace Laboratory, two GSA projects designed after the NPR offices, Bennett says most of the team areas have been enclosed to address this problem.

NPR has been very successful at creating and maintaining an environment that is consistent with its corporate culture. Winograd explains that the group has changed the organizational structure at least three times since moving in, and members have been able to easily reconfigure the furniture themselves to support new team structures. Rank has no meaning in the organization or in the physical setting. Valaskovic says, "Morley Winograd has created a culture where people can talk about mistakes and where it is safe to make changes." The environment reflects this philosophy. When the members realized that one of the furniture systems didn't work well, they admitted the mistake and replaced it.

The NPR office space has been visited by thousands of people from both the public and private sectors, and from other countries. Some love it and some hate it. It offers an alternative to the traditional office, but is not the final word on workplaces for the future. Mike Atkinson and Lois Bennett created and now oversee the GSA's Adaptable Workplace Laboratory (developed and monitored in partnership with Carnegie Mellon University's Center for Building Performance and Diagnostics), where they are studying the benefits of raised flooring, plug and play technology, and modular workstations. The key to success is continued experimentation and recognizing that one solution will not work for all types of workers.

Just because nonterritorial officing did not work for NPR doesn't mean it can't work in other settings where people are out of the office more consistently. Hoteling works at Deloitte & Touche, for instance, because people spend a significant amount of time off-site at client offices. Each work environment needs to respond to the particular work patterns of the potential occupants—this is where the data from the Job Activities Analysis Survey can be used to provide insight into preferences and behaviors.

What Do We Know About What Will Attract Knowledge Workers to a Particular Place?

Whether they are employer-owned and operated or not, the places that attract knowledge workers have several features in common. For collaborative work, the most important quality of a place is the opportunity to interact with smart people. For solo work, it is critical that users have control over interruptions and the environment (lighting, temperature, air quality, and noise); they need a comfortable place where they can concentrate. In both cases, free food and beverages seem to go a long way toward attracting and retaining occupants.

A high level of service is also desirable. State-of-the-art technology and high-speed connections to the Internet are critical. Users are attracted to places where they simply plug in their laptop and can get to work. In some cases this means they would like to leave work in progress out on worksurfaces or pinned up on display boards as visual reminders of what they need to work on next. Hoteling environments such as Deloitte & Touche's SmartSpace have recognized this need to set up a work area for more than a day by allowing longer-term reservations.

Research and experience have shown that when users participate in the planning and design of places (even if they are not the eventual occupants), the settings are much more suitable for the activities housed there. The most successful environments are the ones that offer a variety of options to suit individual work, one-on-one collaboration, small team interaction, and large group meetings. Robert Luchetti, architect and leader of Robert Luchetti Associates, Inc., calls for an "activity settings" approach to workplace design where we admit that "the all purpose workstation cannot do it all." He designs multisetting environments that support both concentration and discussion by giving each person access to multiple settings.

In some cases, people are attracted by amenities such as a fitness center or day care center, but this may not appeal to all age groups. Prospective and recent college graduates rated flextime and telecommuting as more important job benefits than on-site fitness or day care centers in the 2000 Graduating Student and Alumni Survey conducted by the National Association of Colleges and Employers.[17]

What Should a Business Leader Look For in a Workspace?

Like many users of places, those paying for office spaces now recognize the advantages of high-service buildings and building owners and operators are accommodating these needs. John Gilbert, chief operating officer of Rudin Management Co., responded to the changing needs in the real estate market by developing 55 Broad Street into the New York Information Technology Center. This 1967 building had been unoccupied for six years and deemed obsolete when Gilbert decided to invest in an extensive upgrade in 1995. Rudin attracted tenants by providing four things that companies wanted: low cost, flexible space; an advanced telecommunications infrastructure; a facility that is operational twenty-four hours a day, seven days a week; and a sense of community. The carrier-neutral technology backbone makes it possible for each tenant to use the service providers they choose. Rudin rents office spaces as small as nine hundred square feet and as large as fifty thousand square feet to more than seventy companies through short-term and long-term leases. (Typically, a building this size would house five major tenants on average.) According to Gilbert, the company has selected a combination of occupants who will "create a dynamic community where little tenants mix with big tenants." It has provided a "Digital Sandbox"—a high-tech conference center that is used by 55 Broad tenants and other new media enterprises. The building also has a Digital Clubhouse and Hearth where people can hold classes, parties, or just play pool.

Alan Traugott, principal of Flack & Kurtz Consulting Engineers LLP, has seen growing interest in sustainable design among business leaders since the early 1990s, when he was one of the founding members of the U.S. Green Building Council. He defines high-performance, green buildings as, "energy and resource efficient, non-wasteful and non-polluting, highly flexible and adaptable for long-term functionality; they are easy to operate and maintain, and are supportive of the productivity and well-being of the occupants."[18] These high-performance buildings may cost more initially, but over the life span of the building that investment pays off, especially in terms of employee productivity. In 1992, VeriFone decided to invest an extra $900,000 in natural building materials and electricity-saving devices for its new Costa Mesa, California, office and warehouse facility. By adopting these measures, it saved $110,000 a year in energy costs and delivered a healthier work environment for employees. The absentee rate was 40 percent lower and productivity 5 percent higher than at comparable VeriFone buildings.[19] "U.S. companies could save as much as $58 billion annually by preventing sick building illnesses and an additional $200 billion in worker performance improvements by creating offices with better indoor air," report William J. Fisk and Arthur H. Rosenfeld, researchers at the Lawrence Berkeley National Laboratory.[20]

When making investments in workplaces, remember the old adage, "You get what you pay for." Vivian Loftness, professor of architecture, points out that many people understand the difference in quality between a $10,000 car and a $30,000 car yet far fewer understand the differences in quality level when it comes to ergonomic chairs, worksurfaces, lighting, and heating, ventilation, and air conditioning systems in office buildings. She and her colleagues at Carnegie Mellon University are developing and testing a Web-based tool that allows users to understand the trade-offs between initial investment and life-cycle costs. There is significant room for improvement here and these types of tools will help solve this problem.

Business leaders need to evaluate the cost for providing a network of places and infrastructure for technology. In some cases, choices need to be made about access as opposed to ownership (membership in a place like HQ Global Workplaces versus leasing your own office). In other cases, choices have to be made about how much space or equipment is dedicated versus shared. These decisions have to be made in a context where employers are competing for the best employees. Some workers may select a company that offers private offices to every employee while others may prefer being equipped to work from anywhere and set up to work from home. These choices should be made with the input of all stakeholders and with an understanding of how, when, and where they work most effectively.

What Are the Advantages of Having a Network of Workplaces?

The right combination of places should position workers to use their time effectively in surroundings that are well-suited to their activities and are healthy and inspiring. As mobility increases and people use their autonomy to work only in places where they enjoy spending time and can be productive, the nature of workplaces will change. Francis Duffy, architect and author of *The New Office*, believes that with more imaginative thinking on the part of those who design and build environments, "It is possible to invent cities, buildings, and places that increase options rather than diminish options."

This web of workplaces with many options has significant benefits for those who are seemingly outside the network of knowledge work. If commuting were reduced, for instance, everyone would benefit from less pollution and energy consumption. If more adults spent time working from home or near home, there would be fewer "latchkey kids" and less criminal behavior between 3 P.M. and 6 P.M.—a period when many children and teenagers are left unsupervised. As security and safety improved in residential areas, a greater sense of community would build.

As mobile and remote work strategies flourish, people will have more control over where they live, which will in turn affect cities, suburbs, resort towns, and even rural communities. Dee Christensen, telework program manager for Washington State University's Cooperative Extension Energy Program, has been working with private and public sector entities to bring work to isolated rural communities that have been negatively affected by declining timber and fishing industries. By improving the telecommunications infrastructure and providing training for residents, the effort will link the local workforce with large employers that can use the talents of remote workers. This provides an expanded labor pool for employers and avoids the costs and crowding associated with workers relocating to urban areas for jobs. Urban renewal efforts may have new life too as remote and mobile work increases, says Jack Nilles, author of *Managing Telework*, adding, "Older cities may lose their anemia and have fully functioning downtowns again. Bedroom communities may become entire communities, where people live, work and play in the same general location."[21]

Freeing employees to work where and when they are most effective is a simple, straightforward concept with profound implications for the future.

Chapter Summary—Workplace Options

Technology has given us the ability to work anywhere, anytime. To use this capability most effectively, we need to have access to an array of workplaces that support teamwork and individual work, and give us access to the resources we need to work effectively.

WHAT CHANGE AGENTS NEED TO TAKE RESPONSIBILITY FOR:

- Understand the full range of potential workplaces: The World Wide Web of Workplaces.

- Find out how employees, customers, and suppliers are currently using that network of places.

- Evaluate how well your company's work environments accommodate the needs of employees, clients, and suppliers.

- Involve users in the selection and design of workplaces.

- Provide flexible, healthy settings that respond to the needs of all the stakeholders in your web of work.

- Equip and encourage your employees to use a wide range of places to accomplish their work.

- Understand the impact your company's work habits have on traffic, the environment, and the community—and make decisions accordingly.

WHAT ALL EMPLOYEES SHOULD ACCEPT RESPONSIBILITY FOR:

- Discover new places that enhance your creativity and productivity.

- Let your employer know what you like and dislike about current work settings.

- Participate in generating new alternatives to traditional workplaces.

- Choose work settings that are healthy and promote high performance.

Summary and Resources

If you are not willing to free employees to "work naked," you are constraining the performance of your company.
If you are willing to let employees work where and when they are most effective, you will reveal the full potential of your organization.

To recap, here are the eight principles to bear in mind:

- If you take the *initiative* to explore remote and mobile work strategies, you can accelerate your company's move into the knowledge economy.

- If you *trust* your employees to work out of your sight, they will be more committed, more productive, and more satisfied.

- If you encourage *joy* in the workplace, you can reap the true rewards of technology and mobility while avoiding overwork and burnout.

- If you celebrate the value of *individuality*, you will encourage creativity, self-management, and stronger solo contributions.

- If you emphasize *equality* more than hierarchy and status symbols, you will remove barriers to communication and avoid wasting money on outdated trappings.

- If you are willing to engage in open, honest *dialogue*, your global workforce will be better informed and more collaborative.

- If you optimize *connectivity* between all the stakeholders in your business, you will strengthen business relationships and improve your ability to attract and keep valuable workers.

- If you provide access to a wide range of *workplace options*, your employees will use their time more effectively and be well-supported for both solo and collaborative work.

Having the freedom to work where and when we are most effective should be as integral to knowledge work as mandated work hours and centralized workplaces were to the industrial era. The full potential of remote and mobile work will not be realized until all eight principles discussed in this book are embraced and embedded in a company's corporate culture.

The relationships among the principles are strong. We can't have true dialogue if we are still holding on to traditional status symbols. Good communication is needed before distance can be added to the equation. Individuality is more valuable with connectivity (just as a computer is more powerful with an Internet connection). Connectivity is useless unless people have access to a wide range of workplace options. Trust is not as powerful without the expectation of joy. None of these qualities can be revealed unless we take the initiative to change.

The profiles of companies such as Cisco Systems, Autodesk, VeriFone, AgInfoLink, GeneraLife, The Promar Group, Just Ask A Woman, and SAS Institute show us that it makes a big difference to start out with a different vision of how work should be structured. The founders of these organizations challenged the traditional ideas about work and the workplace from the very beginning of their venture. The other profiles in this book demonstrate that a traditional company can be transformed into one that is supportive of new ways of working. These companies that are making or have made a successful transformation have several qualities in common with those that built their companies on nontraditional ideas: strong leadership, active participation, and commitment to ongoing refinement.

Change leaders need to be passionate about the value of remote and mobile work strategies. Being a champion is not enough, though—being a good role model is essential.

Getting people involved in defining the existing problems and creating solutions is an important part of the transformation process. Not only are better solutions developed, the level of commitment among all the players is much higher than in a nonparticipative company.

Culture, workstyles, and technology are constantly changing. A good system needs to be monitored and allowed to evolve over time.

Trends in the virtual workplace will continue to change after the publication of this book. The resources listed in the following section will help you stay up-to-date and provide a more detailed discussion of some of the subjects addressed in this book.

Resources

Please join the on-line conversation about how and why corporate leaders should free employees to work where and when they are most effective at http://www.worknakedbook.com and by e-mailing the author at ccf8@cornell.edu.

For the most up-to-date information on telework and alternative officing go to http://www.gilgordon.com, a comprehensive Web site sponsored by Gil Gordon Associates. Gil Gordon updates this site monthly with news about technological innovations, relevant publications, and links to other sites. Another good site with excellent links to other telework resources on the Web is hosted by David Fleming at http://www.mother.com/dfleming/index.htm.

You can learn more by joining the International Telework Association & Council (ITAC), which describes itself as "a non-profit organization dedicated to promoting the economic, social and environmental benefits of teleworking." The group's Web site can be found at http://www.telecommute.org.

The book *Managing Telework: Strategies for Managing the Virtual Workforce* by Jack Nilles (Wiley, 1998) is the best reference guide for implementing a program, complete with sample policies and agreements. For Web-based insight on the implementation process, go to http://www.inteleworks.com.

If you want to study the effects of remote and mobile work within your company, contact Sumita Raghuram at Fordham University (raghuram@fordham.edu) and Raghu Garud (rgarud@stern.nyu.edu) and Batia Wiesenfeld (bwiesenf@stern.nyu.edu) at New York University. They have worked together as a research team conducting excellent studies on telework.

To keep up with the latest thoughts on the integration of work and personal life, read Sue Shellenbarger's weekly "Work & Family" column in Wednesday's *Wall Street Journal* and Lisa Belkin's column, "Life's Work," which appears every other Wednesday in the *New York Times*.

The Families and Work Institute does good research in this area; descriptions of its studies and findings can be found at http://www.familiesandwork.org. The Society for Human Resource Management (SHRM) provides valuable resources on family-friendly benefits and the trends in human resources. See http://www.shrm.org. LifeCare.com maintains a good library section on its Web site, summarizing work and life research (http://www.lifecare.com).

For an in-depth analysis of why employees were not taking advantage of "family-friendly policies" in one company, read *The Time Bind: When Work Becomes Home and Home Becomes Work* by Arlie Russell Hochschild (Henry Holt, 1997).

To stay current on collaborative technology and knowledge sharing, check out the Web site for Collaborative Strategies—http://www.collaborate.com—and the knowledge sharing resource maintained by Buckman Laboratories at http://www.knowledge-nurture.com. The Institute for the Future is another good resource on technology trends; see http://www.iftf.org. To experience one of the best Web-based collaboration tools, sign up for a PlaceWare Web Seminar at http://www.placeware.com.

If you are interested in a detailed discussion of the integration of people, technology, and facilities, check out Ken Robertson's book, *Work Transformation: Planning and Implementing the New Workplace* (HNB Publishing, 1999).

Resources that cater to the individual remote and mobile worker include June Langhoff's book, *The Telecommuter's Advisor: Real World Solutions for Remote Workers* (Aegis, 1999), and *Home Office* magazine, which covers workstyles, technologies, and resources (http://www.hocmag.net). If you are interested specifically in the home office, read Marilyn Zelinsky's *Practical Home Office Solutions* (McGraw-Hill, 1998).

For more information on the federal government's efforts, read *The Integrated Workplace: A Comprehensive Approach to Developing Workspace* (published by the U.S. General Services Administration, Office of Governmentwide Policy, May 1999) or go to the General Service Administration's Office of Real Property Web site at http://policyworks.gov/org/main/mp/library/policydocs/agiwp.htm. Go to the Web site for the Washington Metropolitan Telework Centers at http://www.wmtc.org to learn more about federally funded telework centers.

There are several good resources if you want to focus on the physical work environment. To see good case studies with photos and drawings of work setting options, look at Frank Duffy's book

The New Office (Conran Octopus, 1997) and Marilyn Zelinsky's book *New Workplaces for New Workstyles* (McGraw-Hill, 1998). A good discussion of alternative workspace strategies can be found in *Workplace by Design: Mapping the High-Performance Workscape* by Frank Becker and Fritz Steele (Jossey-Bass, 1995), and for the latest research in this area check out the Web site of the International Workplace Studies Program under the direction of Franklin Becker and William Sims at Cornell University, http://iwsp.human.cornell.edu/.

To keep up with the latest on building and workplace technology, see the Web site for Carnegie Mellon University's Center for Building Performance and Diagnostics at http://www.arc.cmu.edu/cbpd/.

Two professional organizations address issues of the workplace: the International Development Research Council (IDRC) at http://www.idrc.org and the International Facility Management Association (IFMA) at http://www.ifma.org.

Notes

Introduction

1. Shellenbarger, S. "Madison Avenue May Need to Alter Image of '90s Telecommuter." *Wall Street Journal*, Aug. 20, 1997, p. B1.

2. Shellenbarger, S. "These Telecommuters Just Barely Maintain Their Office Decorum." *Wall Street Journal*, Sept. 24, 1997, p. B1.

Why Work Naked?

1. Nilles, J. M. "Telework in the US: Telework America Survey 2000." Oct. 2000. This study was a project of The International Telework Association & Council (ITAC) and was sponsored by AT&T. Contact ITAC to get a copy of the findings: http://www.telecommute.org.

2. Chambers, E. G., Foulon, M., Handfield-Jones, H., Hankin, S. M., and Michaels, E. G. "The War for Talent." *McKinsey Quarterly*, 1998, 3, 44–57.

3. "People Issues a Top Challenge for Companies Trying to Compete in Today's e-World." Hewitt Associates press release dated

June 1, 2000. Available on-line: http://was.hewitt.com/hewitt/
resource/newsroom/pressrel/2000/06–01–00.htm.

4. "This Labor Day, Keeping and Attracting Workers Is Cause to
   Celebrate." Broadcast e-mail message sent by the Society for
   Human Resources Management (SHRM) on Aug. 31, 2000,
   reporting the results of a June 2000 survey of members.

5. "Work Trends: America's Attitudes About Work, Employers, and
   Government." Survey conducted by the John J. Heldrich Center
   for Workforce Development at Rutgers University and the Center
   for Survey Research and Analysis at University of Connecticut
   from Feb. 5 through 22, 1999, with 1,000 adult members of the
   United States workforce. See http://heldrich.rutgers.edu.

6. Nilles, "Telework in the US."

7. Pratt, J. "Cost/Benefits of Teleworking to Manage Work/Life
   Responsibilities." 1999 Telework America National Telework
   Survey, Oct. 1999. This study was a project of The International
   Telework Association & Council (ITAC) and was sponsored by
   AT&T.

Principle #1: Initiative

1. Comments associated with this Fast Company Community Poll
   can be found at http://www.fastcompany.com/cgi-
   bin/votato/in.cgi?toxic_r. (Note that the vote tallies change over
   time; the tallies in Jan. 1999 were 48 percent for toxic environment, 52 percent for workplace values people.)

2. Johnson, B. *Polarity Management: Identifying and Managing
   Unsolvable Problems.* Amherst, Mass.: HRD Press, 1992.

3. Froggatt, C. C. "Telework: Whose Choice Is It Anyway?" *alt.office
   Journal,* Spring 1998, pp. 18–21. Quote is from pp. 19–20. Note:
   some portions of the NCR case study, the Nortel Networks case
   study, and the discussion of the pros and cons of mandatory versus
   voluntary initiatives were published previously in the article cited
   in this note.

Principle #2: Trust

1. Duarte, D. L., and Snyder, N. T. *Mastering Virtual Teams.* San Francisco: Jossey-Bass, 1999, p. 140.

2. "WorkUSA 2000 Survey Finds Only Half of U.S. Workers Are Committed to Employers: But Companies with Highly Committed Workers Deliver Much Higher Returns to Shareholders." Study conducted by Watson Wyatt Worldwide, reported in a press release dated Jan. 11, 2000. Available on-line: http://www.watsonwyatt.com/homepage/us/new/pres_rel/Jan00/work_usa2000.htm.

3. "1999 Employee Relationship Benchmark." Results of a survey conducted between mid-Apr. and May 1999. Study sponsored by Walker Information and Hudson Institute, http://www.walkerinfo.com/products/err/ee_study.cfm.

4. Handy, C. "Trust and the Virtual Organization." *Harvard Business Review,* May/June 1995, pp. 40–50.

5. This text has been adapted from material that was previously published in Froggatt, C., "New Work Directions: Creative Environments for the Future Can Improve Productivity, Maximize Space Efficiency, and Reduce Real Estate and Operations Costs," *Canadian Interiors Magazine,* Oct./Nov. 1995, pp. 24–25; and Froggatt, C. C., "Telecommuting Offers Viable Option for Workplace," *Facility Management Journal,* Nov./Dec. 1997, pp. 4–9.

6. Pratt, J. "Cost/Benefits of Teleworking to Manage Work/Life Responsibilities." 1999 Telework America National Telework Survey, Oct. 1999. This study was a project of The International Telework Association & Council (ITAC) and was sponsored by AT&T. Contact ITAC to get a copy of the findings: http://www.telecommute.org.

7. This version of the Job Activities Analysis Survey and all subsequent versions included in this book have been adapted from surveys previously published in Froggatt, C. C., "The Changing Face of Interaction: Implications for Workplace Planning," *Facility Management Journal,* May/June 1997, pp. 8–13; and Froggatt,

C. C., "Time for a Change?" *Stern Business*, Summer 1998, pp. 22–25.

Principle #3: Joy

1. Bond, J. T., Galinsky, E., and Swanberg, J. S. *The 1997 National Study of the Changing Workforce.* New York: Families and Work Institute, 1998.

2. "Great Expectations?" *Fast Company*, Nov. 1999, pp. 212–224. The full results of *the Fast Company*–Roper Starch Worldwide Survey can be found at http://www.fastcompany.com/online/29/survey.html.

3. Saad, L. "American Workers Generally Satisfied, but Indicate Their Jobs Leave Much to Be Desired." Gallup Poll Release, The Gallup Organization, Sept. 3, 1999. Available on-line: http://www.gallup.com/poll/releases/pr990903.asp.

4. Sharkey, J. "Try to Relax. At Least Two Psychologists Are Paying Attention to Stress from Life on the Road." *New York Times*, Jan. 12, 2000, p. C8.

5. Schnall, P. "A Brief Introduction to Job Strain." May 1998. Available on-line: http://www.workhealth.org/strain/briefintro.html.

6. "1999 Omnibus Sleep in America Poll." Conducted by the National Sleep Foundation in 1999. Available on-line: http://www.sleepfoundation.org/publications/1999poll.html.

7. Maas, J. B., Wherry, M. L., Axelrod, D. J., and Hogan, B. R. *Power Sleep: The Revolutionary Program That Prepares Your Mind for Peak Performance.* New York: HarperCollins, 1999, p. 51.

8. Maas, Wherry, Axelrod, and Hogan, *Power Sleep*, p. 52.

9. Bond, Galinsky, and Swanberg, *The 1997 National Study of the Changing Workforce.*

10. Galinsky, E. *Ask the Children: What America's Children Really Think About Working Parents.* New York: Morrow, 1999.

11. Bond, Galinsky, and Swanberg, *The 1997 National Study of the Changing Workforce.*

12. From the SAS Institute Web site, http://www.sas.com/corporate/worklife/.

13. Society for Human Resource Management (SHRM) 2000 Benefits Survey, 2000. Available on-line: http://www.shrm.org.

14. Bond, Galinsky, and Swanberg, *The 1997 National Study of the Changing Workforce.*

15. "Getting Things Done: 1999 Annual Review of Retention Initiatives." Ernst & Young LLP, 1999.

16. McIlvaine, A. R. "Hearing Them Roar." *Human Resource Executive*, June 4, 1999.

17. "Weaving a Richer Culture: 1998 Office for Retention Annual Report." Ernst & Young LLP, 1998.

18. Chambers, E. G., Foulon, M., Handfield-Jones, H., Hankin, S. M., and Michaels, E. G. "The War for Talent." *McKinsey Quarterly*, 1998, 3, 44–57.

19. "New Nationwide Survey on 'American Dream' at Millennium Reveals Surprising Ambivalence About Work and Technology." Roper Starch Worldwide Inc. survey commissioned by Hearst Magazines, summarized in press release dated Jan. 4, 2000. Available on-line: http://www.roper.com/news/content/news169.htm.

20. Pink, D. H. "Free Agent Nation." *Fast Company*, Dec./Jan. 1998, pp. 131–147.

21. "AT&T Survey Reveals Boomers Taking Control of Their Lives Through Telework." News release issued by AT&T on Oct. 20, 1997, reporting the findings of the 1997 AT&T National Survey of Teleworker Attitudes and Work Styles, conducted by FIND/SVP and Joanne H. Pratt Associates.

22. "When Technology Works at Home, So Will I." Report on AT&T's 1999 Employee Telework Survey, 1999. Available on-line: http://www.att.com/ehs/telework_survey.html.

23. *The Radcliffe-Fleet Project: Creating Work and Life Integration Solutions.* Cambridge, Mass.: Radcliffe Public Policy Institute, 1998.

24. Pratt, J. "Cost/Benefits of Teleworking to Manage Work/Life Responsibilities." 1999 Telework America National Telework Survey, Oct. 1999. This study was a project of The International Telework Association & Council (ITAC) and was sponsored by AT&T. Contact ITAC to get a copy of the findings: http://www.telecommute.org.

25. Rucci, A. J., Kirn, S. P., and Quinn, R. T. "The Employee-Customer-Profit Chain at Sears." *Harvard Business Review,* Jan./Feb. 1998, pp. 82–97.

26. Morgan, B. S., and Schiemann, W. A. "Measuring People and Performance: Closing the Gaps." *Quality Progress,* Jan. 1999, p. 48.

27. Morgan and Schiemann, "Measuring People and Performance."

28. Hochschild, A. R. *The Time Bind: When Work Becomes Home and Home Becomes Work.* New York: Henry Holt, 1997.

Principle #4: Individuality

1. Bartlett, C. A., and Ghoshal, S. "Changing the Role of Top Management: Beyond Systems to People." *Harvard Business Review,* May/June 1995, pp. 132–142, quote on pp. 132–133.

2. From the Autodesk Web site, http://www3.autodesk.com/adsk/item/0,,304914-123112,00.html.

3. Amabile, T. M. "How to Kill Creativity." *Harvard Business Review,* Sept.-Oct. 1998, pp. 77–87, quote on p. 77.

4. Amabile, "How to Kill Creativity," p. 82.

5. Amabile, "How to Kill Creativity," p. 82.

6. Mauzy, J. H. "Managing Personal Creativity." In *Innovationsforschung und Technologiemanagement,* Berlin and Heidelberg: Springer-Verlag, 1999, pp. 19–31, quote on p. 21.

7. Csikszentmihalyi, M. *Creativity.* New York: HarperCollins, 1996, p. 138.

8. Smolensky, M., and Lamberg, L. *The Body Clock Guide to Better Health: How to Use Your Body's Natural Clock to Fight Illness and Achieve Maximum Health.* New York: Henry Holt, 2000.

9. Drucker, P. F. *Management Challenges for the Twenty-First Century.* New York: HarperCollins, 1999, pp. 163–164.

10. Davenport, T. O. *Human Capital: What It Is and Why People Invest It.* San Francisco: Jossey-Bass, 1999, p. 122.

11. Croghan, L. "Jupiter Signs 15-year Lease; First to Pick Astor Place." *Crain's New York Business,* Mar. 20, 2000, p. 20.

Principle #5: Equality

1. Bunnell, D. *Making the Cisco Connection: The Story Behind the Real Internet Superpower.* New York: Wiley, 2000, p. 58.

2. Bunnell, *Making the Cisco Connection.*

3. Bunnell, *Making the Cisco Connection,* p. 25.

4. From the Cisco Systems Web site: http://www.cisco.com/warp/public/750/corpfact.html.

5. From Cisco Systems Web site: http://www.cisco.com/warp/public/779/largeent/issues/ecomm/cisco_best.html.

6. From Cisco Systems Web site: http://investor.cisco.com/media_files/nsd/csco/faq.html.

7. Lewandowski, J., and O'Toole, J. "Forming the Future: The Marriage of People and Technology at Saturn." Presentation given at Stanford University, Mar. 29, 1990, p. 4.

8. Chase Manhattan Casual Dress Policy, dated Mar. 13, 2000.

9. Froggatt, C. C. "The Effect of Corporate Space and Furnishings Policies on Employee Workspace and Policy Satisfaction." Unpublished master's thesis, Cornell University, 1985.

10. Froggatt, "The Effect of Corporate Space and Furnishings Policies on Employee Workspace and Policy Satisfaction."

11. Hall, T. "Place: And the Walls Came Tumbling Down." *New York Times Magazine,* Dec. 13, 1998, pp. 82–86.

12. "Alcoa Corporate Center." The Design Alliance Architects brochure for the Alcoa building in Pittsburgh, Pennsylvania, 1998.

13. Hall, "Place."

14. Becker, F., Sims, W., and Davis, B. "Managing Space Efficiently." Cornell University, International Facility Management Program, 1991.

15. Becker, Sims, and Davis, "Managing Space Efficiently."

16. Bell, M. A. "From Space to Cyberspace: Transforming Business Infrastructure." *Business Technology Journal,* Spring 1999, p. 5. This journal is published by GartnerGroup.

17. "Practices and Techniques: The Accounting Classification of Workpoint Costs." Institute of Management Accountants, Montvale, New Jersey, July 1, 1997, p. 11. To order this document call 800-638-4427 extension 278 and ask for Statement on Management Accounting number 4BB.

18. "Practices and Techniques: The Accounting Classification of Workpoint Costs."

Principle #6: Dialogue

1. Pape, W. R. "Size Matters." *Inc. Technology,* 1999, 3, 31–32, quote on p. 32.

2. Pape, "Size Matters."

3. Pape, "Size Matters."

4. "VeriFone: The Transaction Automation Company." Harvard Business School Case Study #9-195-088, revised July 12, 1995.

5. Pape, W. R. "Relative Merits." *Inc.,* Mar. 15, 1998.

6. Pape, "Size Matters."

7. Anderson, K. "By the (Open) Book." *Inc. Technology*, 1999, 3, 33–34.

8. Sieloff, C. G. "The Sorcerer's Apprentice." *Knowledge Management*, July/Aug. 1999, 2(10), 9–14.

9. Sieloff, "The Sorcerer's Apprentice."

10. Meyers, P. "Sun's Customized Intranet: Smoothed Sale-ing." The Next Big Thing (http://www.tnbt.com/jsp/), posted Aug. 4, 2000.

11. "Buckman Laboratories." Harvard Business School case study number N9-899-175, Rev. Sept. 17, 1999.

12. Buckman, R. H. "Knowledge Sharing and Innovation." PowerPoint slides for speech given in Mar. 2000.

13. Buckman, "Knowledge Sharing and Innovation."

14. Buckman, R. H. "Lions and Tigers and Bears: Following the Road from Command and Control to Knowledge Sharing." 1997, available on Buckman Laboratories Web site: http://www. knowledge-nurture.com.

15. Meek, T. "The Evolution of Information Technology at Buckman Laboratories." *Knowledge Management Review*, Nov./Dec. 1999, p. 11.

16. Meek, "The Evolution of Information Technology at Buckman Laboratories."

17. "Buckman Laboratories."

Principle #7: Connectivity

1. Gordon, G. "American Express Takes Long, Slow, and Successful Road to the Virtual Office." *Telecommuting Review*, 1994, 11(10), 1–4.

2. Sims, W., Joroff, M., and Becker, F. *Managing the Reinvented Workplace*. Norcross, Ga.: International Development Research Foundation, 1996.

3. Sims, Joroff, and Becker, *Managing the Reinvented Workplace*.

4. Zelinsky, M. *New Workplaces for New Workstyles.* New York: McGraw-Hill, 1998.

5. Gordon, "American Express Takes Long, Slow, and Successful Road to the Virtual Office."

6. Pape, W. R. "Far Out: The Village Outpost Can Be Good for Living. Thanks to Technology, It Can Be Good for Business, Too." *Inc. Technology,* 1995, p. 2.

7. "Virtual Integration: Putnam Investments Creating 100 New Virtual Jobs in Rural Maine, 100 More on College Campus." From Blockbuster Deal of the Week, July 31, 2000, http://www.conway.com/ssinsider/bbdeal/.

8. Pape, W. "The Fewer the Merrier." *Inc.,* Dec. 1, 1998.

9. Raghuram, S., Garud, R., and Wiesenfeld, B. M. "Telework: Managing Distances in a Connected World." *Strategy & Business,* First Quarter, 1998.

10. Duarte, D. L., and Snyder, N. T. *Mastering Virtual Teams.* San Francisco: Jossey-Bass, 1999, p. 78.

11. Raghuram, Garud, and Wiesenfeld, "Telework."

12. Pape, W. R. "Size Matters." *Inc. Technology,* 1999, 3, 31–32, quote from p. 32.

13. Pape, W. R. "Chairman of the Keyboard." *Inc. Technology,* 1998, 3, 23–24.

14. Thurm, S. "Eating Their Own Dog Food." *Wall Street Journal,* Apr. 19, 2000, pp. B1, B4.

15. From Cisco Systems Web site: http://www.cisco.com/warp/public/779/largeent/issues/ecomm/cisco_best.html.

16. Thurm, "Eating Their Own Dog Food."

Principle #8: Workplace Options

1. Lawrence, P. "Futurist Paul Saffo on Design." *@issue: The Journal of Business and Design,* n.d., 5(2), 5.

2. "Business Travel in 1999." Fast Facts reporting the results of the Survey of Business Travelers, 1999 Edition sponsored by OAG and conducted by the Travel Industry Association of America. Available on-line: http://www.tia.org/press/fastfacts91.stm.

3. "Business Travel in 1999."

4. "Business Travel in 1999."

5. "Business Travel in 1999."

6. Csikszentmihalyi, M. *Creativity*. New York: HarperCollins, 1996, p. 138.

7. Froggatt, C. "The Changing Face of Interaction." *FM Journal*, May/June 1997, pp. 8–13, quote from p. 12.

8. "Business Travel in 1999."

9. Welles, E. O. "Mind Games." *Inc.*, Dec. 1, 1999. Available on-line: http://www.inc.com/incmagazine/article/printable/1,6988,ART15700,00.html.

10. Welles, "Mind Games."

11. Nilles, J. M. "Telework in the US: Telework America Survey 2000." Oct. 2000. This study was a project of The International Telework Association & Council (ITAC) and was sponsored by AT&T. Contact ITAC to get a copy of the findings: http://www.telecommute.org.

12. "Washington Telework Study: Study Results." Sponsored by Washington State University Cooperative Extension Energy Program and US West, 1999. Available on-line: http://www.energy.wsu.edu/telework/survey-results.htm.

13. Brill, M., Keable, E., and Fabiniak, J. "The Myth of Open Plan." *Facilities Design & Management*, Feb. 2000, pp. 36–38, quote on p. 36.

14. Vischer, J. "Will This Open Space Work?" *Harvard Business Review*, May/June 1999, pp. 28–40, quote on p. 39.

15. Duffy, F. *The New Office*. London: Conran Octopus, 1997, p. 238.

16. "Real Property Performance Results 1999." U.S. General Services

Administration, Office of Governmentwide Policy, Dec. 1999. Available on-line: http://policyworks.gov/realproperty.

17. "'Room for Advancement' Holds Greatest Appeal for College Job Seekers." Press release on the 2000 Graduating Student and Alumni Survey conducted by the National Association of Colleges and Employers (NACE), Apr. 18, 2000. Available on-line: http://www.naceweb.org/press/display.cfm/2000/pr041800.htm.

18. Traugott, A. "Green Building Design = High Performance Building Design." *Consulting Specifying Engineer*, Jan. 1999, pp. 68–74, quote on p. 69.

19. Pape, W. R. "Healthy, Wealthy, and Wise." *Inc. Technology*, 1998, 2, 25–26.

20. Conlin, M. "Is Your Office Killing You?" *Business Week*, June 5, 2000, pp. 114–130, quote on p. 118.

21. Chonin, N. "Living at the Office: Workplaces Will Double as Housing—But Poor Will Commute Longer." *San Francisco Chronicle*, Nov. 16, 1999, p. D13.

Index

Companies Profiled in the Book

The Author

Cynthia C. Froggatt, principal of Froggatt Consulting, has spent the last fifteen years advising Fortune 500 companies on aligning their workplace strategies with their business plans. She studied environmental psychology and organizational behavior, earned a bachelor's degree from Penn State University in 1982 and a master's degree from Cornell University in 1985, and started her own consulting practice in 1994.

In 1993, as director of consulting for HOK's New York office, Cynthia worked with AT&T on their telework program and has been a vocal advocate for remote and mobile work strategies ever since. Froggatt enjoys teaching seminars and leading workshops on new ways of working, strategic workplace planning, communication strategies, and change leadership. She has been an instructor at Cornell University's College of Human Ecology.

Froggatt has authored a number of articles on remote and mobile work strategies, overcoming resistance to change, and the virtual workplace. Her comments have appeared in the *Wall Street Journal, Fortune, Home Office Computing, Telecommuting Review,* the *San Jose Mercury News,* and *Stern Business Journal,* among others. She is the Chair of the Student Life Committee for the President's Council of Cornell Women (PCCW) and an active member of the International Telework Association & Council (ITAC), International Development Research Council (IDRC), New York

Women in Communications, Inc. (NYWICI), and International Facility Management Association (IFMA). Froggatt serves on the Advisory Boards for the Outdoor Computing Network, an Internet start-up, and Work[place]2010, a working lab about new workplace concepts in Denver, Colorado.

Cynthia works from her home office in a brownstone on Manhattan's Upper West Side. She gets her best ideas while lying in bed in the morning, walking in Central Park, or taking a shower.

For more information on the author, send e-mail to her at ccf8@cornell.edu or visit http://www.worknakedbook.com.